Change and Continuity in
Spatial Planning

Change and Continuity in Spatial Planning addresses a question of enduring inter-est to planners: can planning really bring about significant and positive change? In South Africa the process of political transition appeared to create the pre-conditions for planners to demonstrate how their traditional humanitarian and environmental concerns could find concrete expression in the reshaping of the built environment.

The requirement that the segregrated apartheid cities be restructured, reinte-grated and made accessible to the poor was high on the agenda of the new post-apartheid government, even prior to their election. The story of how planners in the metropolitan area of Cape Town attempted over the last decade to address this agenda is the subject of this book. Integral to this story is how plan-ning practices were shaped by the past, in a rapidly changing context character-ized by a globalizing economy, new systems of governance, a changing political ideology, and a culture of intensifying poverty and diversity.

More broadly the book addresses the issue of how planners use power, in situ-ations which themselves represent networks of power relations, where both planners and those they engage with operate through frames of reference fundamentally shaped by place and history.

Vanessa Watson is Associate Professor of City and Regional Planning at the University of Cape Town, South Africa.

Cities and Regions: Planning, Policy and Management
A series edited by Seymour J. Mandelbaum
University of Pennsylvania, Philadelphia

Cities and Regions: Planning, Policy and Management is an international series of case studies addressed to students in programs leading to professional careers in urban and regional affairs and to established practitioners of the complex crafts of planning, policy analysis and public management. The series will focus on the work-worlds of the practitioners and the ways in which the construction of narratives shapes the course of events and our understanding of them. The international character of the series is intended to help both novice and experienced professionals extend their terms of reference, learning from 'strangers' in unfamiliar settings.

Battery Part City
Politics and planning on the New York waterfront
David L.A. Gordon

Constructing Suburbs
Competing voices in a debate over urban growth
Ann Forsyth

A City Reframed
Managing Warsaw in the 1990s
Barbara Czarniawska

Planning in the Face of Crisis
Land Use, Housing and Mass Immigration in Israel
Rachelle Alterman

Change and Continuity in Spatial Planning

Metropolitan planning in Cape Town
under political transition

Vanessa Watson

London and New York

First Published 2002
by Routledge
11 New Fetter Lane, London EC4P 4EE

Simultaneously published in the USA and Canada
by Routledge
29 West 35th Street, New York, NY 10001

Routledge is an imprint of the Taylor & Francis Group

© 2002 Vanessa Watson

Typeset in Goudy by Wearset Ltd, Boldon, Tyne and Wear
Printed and bound in Great Britain by TJ International Ltd, Padstow,
Cornwall

British Library Cataloguing in Publication Data
A catalogue record for this book is available from the British Library

Library of Congress Cataloging in Publication Data
A catalog record for this book has been requested

ISBN 0-415-27058-8 (HB)
ISBN 0-415-27059-6 (PB)

Contents

List of figures   vi
Preface   vii
Acknowledgements   x
Abbreviations   xi

Introduction   1

1 'What's needed is a metropolitan plan'   13

2 Cape Town as a 'compact, integrated' city?   27

3 Legitimating the plan: the Western Cape Economic
   Development Forum   42

4 'No-one disputed that there should be a physical plan . . .':
   the participation process in practice   56

5 South Africa post-1994: new systems of government and
   planning   71

6 Dusting off the old planning legislation: can we make the
   metropolitan plan legal?   88

7 Practices of representation: the Metropolitan Spatial
   Development Framework (1996 Technical Report)   98

8 New discourse coalitions and the marginalization of spatial
   planning   117

9 Beyond the MSDF: issues for planning   141

   Chronology   155
   Notes   157
   References   164
   Index   173

List of Figures

1.1   Locality map of Cape Town   14
1.2   Aerial photograph of Metropolitan Cape Town   15
1.3   An informal settlement (KTC) burns   17
1.4   Guide Plan provision for the deconcentration of Cape Town   21
1.5   Proposed locations for new housing for African and coloured
      people   24
2.1   Contrast between an older (pre-apartheid) working-class area of
      Cape Town and a newer, planned apartheid township   33
4.1   The structure of the Western Cape Economic Development
      Forum and the Urban Development Commission   58
4.2   The Cape Town City Council vision for the future of
      Cape Town   63
5.1   South Africa's changing macro-economic policy   73
5.2   Perceptions of the South African bureaucracy   77
5.3   New municipal boundaries created in 1996   82
6.1   The public launch of the MSDF Technical Report, 1996   95
7.1   The Metropolitan Spatial Development Framework   99
7.2   The MSDF process   101
7.3   Spatial problems and opportunities in Cape Town   104
7.4   The divided city   106
7.5   Three possible scenarios for Cape Town   109
8.1   Some of the main role-players in the MSDF process   123
8.2   An existing 'activity corridor' in Cape Town   127
8.3   A conceptual diagram of a corridor   129
8.4   Little has changed on the bleak Cape Flats   137
9.1   Major developments completed and proposed, June 1998–1999   146
9.2   Two responses to growing poverty   147

Preface

I returned home to South Africa from London in 1980, giving up the struggle between the desire to escape the horrors of apartheid and the desire to contribute in some way towards its demise. These were tumultuous times in Cape Town. Organizations of resistance were beginning to find their feet. Civic groups, squatter movements, trade unions and women's organizations were beginning to meet and campaign openly, and in return were attracting the wrath of the government.

As an urban planner, located within a university research institute, the scope for my involvement was wide. Planning and spatial intervention, at both urban and regional scales, were key tools of the apartheid government in their attempts to manage racial segregation. Access to the city and issues of settlement within it became prime areas of contestation between government and opposition movements. For those planners who aligned themselves with the opposition movement there was work to be done. Civic organizations demanded information: was a proposal to upgrade an informal settlement likely to benefit them, or was it a forced removal in disguise? Was it true that land for new low-income settlement was not available close to work opportunities? Was a move to increase public housing rents really justified, or were fund surpluses being hidden within the municipality? Was a reorganization of local government simply another attempt to legitimize racially defined organs of government and disenfranchisement? Endless meetings with community organizations in back rooms of township houses or in dilapidated community centres formed the night-life of those of us who chose to use our skills in this way.

And so a politics of resistance to particular urban interventions became a central plank of grassroots organizing. There was less concern here, understandably, with the form which an alternative to the apartheid city may take. For most community activists, involved in day-to-day evasion of security police, running street battles, or hastily organized meetings, thoughts of what they might do should they be in a position to control the shape of the city were remote indeed. But for planning academics within the University of Cape Town, removed from the immediate heat of battle but nonetheless deeply concerned about the future of the city, this was a central issue.

Through the late 1970s and the 1980s a position on an alternative city form emerged through publications of the Urban Problems Research Unit of the University of Cape Town. It was a position which embodied principles of spatial equity, access and integration. It drew on the international (and particularly European) exposure of its main protagonists to urban forms which appeared to work well in other contexts. It was essentially a spatial vision, strongly informed by the design philosophy of the architects and planners involved. But its rhetoric, which posed integration and equity in opposition to separation and exclusion, was inevitably ignored by most government decision-makers involved in shaping the city.

This was to change dramatically at the end of the 1980s. Cape Town was in crisis, large township areas had been successfully 'rendered ungovernable' and Nelson Mandela walked to freedom. For the first time I and my colleagues were able to put the case for an alternative city form in official circles, and be heard. As the new ANC government came into power in 1994, it appeared, moreover, that the need to restructure the apartheid cities had been recognized at the highest level. The central ANC policy document, the Reconstruction and Development Programme, supported far-reaching public intervention in the urban realm. Ideas about creating equitable, integrated cities had found their way into this document and into new planning initiatives in the other major cities of South Africa. This was surely the time, many of us felt, that positive planning ideals could find concrete expression and demonstrate their ability directly to improve the lives of those previously marginalized and excluded.

It was not to be. Six years have passed, and Cape Town has certainly changed, but not in the direction that we perhaps naively hoped for. Today I can visit the vast new malls and theme parks (reachable only by car) in the north of the city and well away from the poverty and squalor of the townships and informal settlements. I can walk through the city centre, now clean, policed and under camera surveillance, courtesy of the new Business Improvement District initiative. I am far more reluctant to penetrate the townships and informal settlements than I was in the 1980s. Crime has spiralled out of control. In coloured townships such as Manenberg, gangs (linked to international syndicates) vie with local authority structures, controlling the allocation of public housing and collecting the rents. The sea of tin and plastic shacks in the metropolitan south-east, once seen as evidence of the apartheid government's failed attempt to control migration to the city, is still there and has grown. Recent workshops for councillors and officials to debate a metropolitan vision placed tourism promotion and global positioning as their top priorities. The metropolitan spatial planning process, born in the euphoria of the early days of transition, is now on hold.

The choice for me seemed to be either to give in to disillusionment, or to regard this as a potential learning experience. This book, which traces the rise and fall of metropolitan spatial planning in Cape Town during the 1990s, represents the latter. I remain convinced that the ideals which began this journey are right. There has been much to learn about the problems of simplistic spatial thinking and the dangers of imposing abstract ideas on a context not properly understood. But as many planners before me have undoubtedly discovered, understanding the inextricable linking of planning and power has to form the foundation for anyone wishing to take this journey further.

Vanessa Watson
December 2000

Acknowledgements

I am deeply grateful to the informants who gave of their time and energy to participate in this research process. I am particularly grateful as well to Alan Mabin, adviser to the dissertation version of this work, and to Bent Flyvbjerg for an inspiring workshop on case study research, held in Tanzania in 1999. Tumsifu Nnkya and Fred Lerise (of the University College of Lands and Architectural Studies, Dar es Salaam) showed, by example, the tremendous value of case study research and narrative writing, and I thank Jorgen Andreasen (Department of Human Settlement, Royal Danish Academy of Fine Art) for making these connections for me. Series editor Seymour Mandelbaum gave valuable support and encouragement, as well as useful comment on the final draft.

I am very grateful to Kathy Forbes (University of Cape Town) for her remarkably thorough proof-reading and editing, and to Philip Burns for the graphics.

The financial assistance of the National Research Foundation towards this research is hereby acknowledged. Opinions expressed in this publication, and the conclusions arrived at, are those of the author and are not necessarily attributed to the NRF.

Abbreviations

ANC	African National Congress
CAHAC	Cape Areas Housing Action Committee
CBD	Central Business District
CMC	Cape Metropolitan Council
CODESA	Convention for a Democratic South Africa
COSATU	Congress of South African Trade Unions
GEAR	Growth, Employment and Redistribution
IDASA	Institute for a Democratic Alternative in South Africa
IDP	Integrated Development Plan
LDO	Land Development Objective
LUPO	Land Use Planning Ordinance
MDF	Metropolitan Development Framework
MDF-CWG	Metropolitan Development Framework Co-ordinating Working Group
METPLAN	Metropolitan Planning Agency
MOSS	Metropolitan Open Space System
MSDF	Metropolitan Spatial Development Framework
MSDF-CWG	Metropolitan Spatial Development Framework Co-ordinating Working Group
MSDF-SWG	Metropolitan Spatial Development Framework Statutory Working Group
NGO	Non-governmental Organization
NSMS	National Security Management System
PDF	Progressive Development Forum
RDP	Reconstruction and Development Programme
RSC	Regional Services Council
SACP	South African Communist Party
SANCO	South African National Civics Organization
SWOT	Strengths, Weaknesses, Opportunities, Threats
TMS	Transitional Municipal Structures
UDC	Urban Development Commission
UPRU	Urban Problems Research Unit
WCCA	Western Cape Civics Association

WCEDF	Western Cape Economic Development Forum
WCHDA	Western Cape Hostel Dwellers Association
WCRSC	Western Cape Regional Services Council
WECUSA	Western Cape United Squatters Association

Introduction

South Africa in 1994 was a place of great promise, for many. A relatively peaceful transformation from authoritarian rule, based on the ideology of apartheid, to a liberal democracy had been achieved, and the ruling majority party, the African National Congress (ANC), espoused a policy of equality and democracy. For those spatial planners both within and outside government structures who had supported these ideals, it appeared as if planning could at last shake off the shackles of apartheid and begin to play an important role in building a new and better society. New ideas about spatial planning (not too different from what is now known as 'new urbanism' and the 'compact city') were gaining increasing acceptance in professional planning circles, coinciding with a demand that the towns and cities divided by racial and spatial segregation now be restructured, reintegrated and made accessible to the poor (RDP 1994). If ever the time was ripe for spatial planners to demonstrate that their traditional humanitarian and environmental concerns could find concrete expression in the shaping of the built environment to these new ends, it was during South Africa's political transition.

This book is about how one of these efforts,[1] the production of the Metropolitan Spatial Development Framework (MSDF) for metropolitan Cape Town, came into being. The story of the MSDF is a lengthy one, spanning ten years of the political transition, and is one which reflects, in the various stages of its unfolding, many of the dynamics occurring both in national political negotiating chambers and on the streets of Cape Town itself. The book is also about change and continuity in efforts to promote spatial planning at the city scale. One of the most remarkable aspects of the MSDF story is that while so many facets of both the planning process and the product represent a significant break with the past, many other facets demonstrate the constraints to change in the realms of ideas and forms of practice. The period is marked by a shift from the enforcement of racial and spatial segregation through 'blueprint' planning, to an approach to planning aimed at urban integration and redistribution, and thereafter to a view of planning as integral to 'global positioning' and 'entrepreneurial' government. However, the persistence of a modernist planning philosophy provides continuity to these planning efforts. At the same time as change appears to be the defining aspiration of present planning, it also appears to be extremely difficult to achieve.

Planning is about change: either through its attempts to prevent change and preserve the status quo, or through efforts to induce change and bring about improvements, however these may be defined. A process of political or economic transition offers a unique opportunity to understand more closely the role of planning in change. This is because a transition process involves rapid and far-reaching societal change in which all kinds of fluidities are brought into being, and in which a great deal, particularly in the realm of government policy, must be reinvented to suit the new and emerging society. It is a time in which planners, the forward thinking professionals, can potentially make their mark. The extent to which the spatial planners of Cape Town's metropolitan authority were able to seize this opportunity, and the ways in which they were trapped in continuities both of their own making and those inherent in society and economy more generally, forms the fabric of this book.

South Africa's political transition

A prime factor propelling change in South Africa in the last decade has been the political transition to a liberal democracy. This was coupled with the increasing insertion of the South African economy into a globalizing international economy, giving rise to what may be considered a 'double transition'. The magnitude of these transitions may not equate with those experienced by countries undergoing a shift from communist and totalitarian regimes (such as many of the countries of Central and Eastern Europe), but nonetheless, compared to the relatively stable political economies of most developed and even many developing countries, change in South Africa in the 1990s was indeed dramatic.

Political transition theorists have identified three stages which appear to characterize events in countries shifting from authoritarianism to a liberal democracy. Stepan (1986) describes these as Reforma, in which limited reforms are undertaken by the ruling authoritarian government; Reforma-pactada, in which reform is worked out with the democratic opposition; and Ruptura-pactada, in which there is a rupture with the past, negotiated with the opposition. South Africa in many respects represents a unique case of political transition (in no other context has the authoritarianism of the outgoing government been racially differentiated in quite the same way as it has been in this country), but various writings on the political transition have used Stepan's three phases as a framework within which to examine the sequence of events experienced in this country.

In South Africa, the beginnings of Reforma have to be sought in the mid-1970s, when a resurgence of conflict between government and opposition forces prompted the government to mount a large scale militarization of white society, as well as new initiatives aimed at co-opting sections of the African and coloured population. By the mid-1980s, growing economic recession and international censure of apartheid, together with local protests and violent confrontations with the police, prompted limited political reforms, a softening of the laws which controlled the free movement of African people, and improvements in material living conditions for those considered essential to the 'white' economy. The growing strength of the opposition movements in the late 1980s within a context of increasing economic stress and political division, and the apparent inability of tactics of either reform of repression to quell the upsurge of violence, paved the way for a negotiated political settlement, or Reformapactada. Significantly, however, the government of the day entered these negotiations from a political position which was seriously challenged, but not defeated. The ruling National Party had been able to maintain an effective system of administration, security and defence (although these had been successfully challenged in many urban African townships), a highly developed, if regionally uneven, system of infrastructure and communication, and an operational system of tax collection and welfare for at least part of the population. The Party also retained cautious support from elements of capital and, in the first democratic elections of 1994, showed that it had the support of 20.4 per cent of the total electorate. It retained the ability, therefore, to be a powerful player in the negotiation process and to influence the path of reform significantly.

The opposition movement, in the form of the African National Congress (ANC) and its alliance partners, the powerful labour movement (COSATU) and the South African Communist Party (SACP), historically had strongly socialist leanings. However, negotiations were occurring at a time when the collapse of the Soviet Union and the east bloc discredited left economic policy, and ensured that the prime international players in the transition were the United States and its allies. Inevitably, 'the price these powers demanded for disciplining the apartheid government and extending promises of material aid to the ANC was a commitment by the ANC to embrace western-style free-market principles' (Webster and Adler 1999, 369).

Analysts of the South African political transition debate the extent to which the process was shaped by elite negotiators, or by the extensive mass action which was occurring outside the negotiating chambers (Saul 1991). Przeworski (1991) has suggested that peaceful political transitions are usually negotiated by reformers from the authoritarian bloc and moderates from the prodemocracy opposition, who rein in more radical opposition groupings.[2] They seek a suboptimal solution that nonetheless allows themselves and society to survive (Adler and Webster 1995), and as such, Przeworski argues, the ensuing pact is 'inevitably conservative, socially and economically' (1991, 98). In the context of South Africa, the negotiations were highly conflictual and repeatedly threatened to derail, but in the end compromises were made on both sides. The ANC's original draft economic policy was revised to the extent that when it finally emerged, in the form of the Reconstruction and Development Programme, it was eagerly adopted by all political parties and by business. And in the negotiation process, the ANC conceded to the important 'sunset clause' which safeguarded the positions of existing civil servants. The possibility of both economic and administrative continuity was thereby greatly strengthened.

The extent, therefore, to which the first democratic elections of April 1994 represented Ruptura-pactada, or a break with the past, has been questioned. Clearly a break of some significance had been made, and the obtaining of full political rights by people of colour was not without importance. It is also possible to point to a new constitution regarded as progressive in world terms, new policies in almost every field of government, major institutional reorganization and important new legislation, particularly in the realm of labour. But the continuities (particularly in terms of the economy) are there as well. In fact in the years following the 1994 election, macro-economic policy has shifted closer to a neo-liberal position, and an emphasis on economic growth has replaced the previous concern with redistribution.

Part of the problem with political transition theory is that it is able to offer limited insight as to the nature and causes of the dialectic of change and continuity in times of transition. With its focus on events at the national level and on elite pact-forming processes, there is little concern for how change is, or is not, taking place at the level of lower order institutions and bureaucracies or within civil society more generally. While significant decisions may be taken by pacting national elites, which indeed impact on the course of history and on people's everyday lives, it is not possible simply to 'read off', or predict from these events, what the dynamics will be beyond the negotiating chambers. The impacts and implications of these decisions depend heavily on how they are received, used, interpreted, or ignored within the multiple and complex networks which make up society. In turn, the path taken by a transition process is fundamentally shaped by broader local and international political and economic milieu, and by collective actors outside the process, all of which provide a constraining set of possibilities for the individual actors within it (see Howarth and Norval 1998).

The Cape Town metropolitan planning process, which forms the subject of this book, was taking place concurrently with political transition in South Africa, and it is clearly evident that these events impacted on the planning process. However, understanding such a planning process requires an unpacking of how these events articulated with the dynamics of existing and long-standing local institutions (which in turn had shaped and been shaped by a wide range of regional – Western Cape – specificities) and with the particular philosophies, personalities and ambitions of the planners involved in the process. In this sense, the book aims to provide a view of transition from below, rather than above. This in turn requires the drawing on of alternative theoretical frameworks to help explain processes of change and continuity.

No account can be simple description. The values and perspectives of the writer are critical determinants of what questions are asked, what material is chosen for presentation, and what interpretations are made of events. The relationship works in the other direction as well: the empirical material throws new light on theory and concepts and renders them more or less useful. I now turn to the conceptual informants which helped my telling of this story.

Concepts of power and the role of discourse

As I began discussions with the planners involved in the MSDF process, as I pieced together the events from the minutes and memos and sat through meetings, it seemed that the best way to understand the unfolding of the process was through paying attention to power. The manoeuvres, tactics and strategies, exercised consciously or unconsciously by individuals (singly or jointly) and which impacted on the planning process, resonated with the particular conception of power used by Foucault, and it is on certain of his ideas that I have drawn to understand and explain the events that follow.

More specifically, Foucault's concept of power[3] has value in terms of its diffuse form, operating in a capillary fashion from below. The idea of a 'microphysics of power' suggests its location in everyday practices and as part and parcel of all other relationships. It is not a property or possession, held by some and not others, nor is it imposed from the apex of a hierarchy. Power is exercised as the effect of one action on another action, rather than one individual over another, but not deterministically so: the exercise of power on the part of an individual may lead to a certain kind of action on the part of another, but this is not inevitable. This in turn leaves room for opposition and potential change. Also important is the insistence that power can be both positive and productive as well as negative and repressive.

Important as well, for a concern with planning, is the particular form of power which Foucault terms 'government', through which the exercise of power is extended to the populations of political units. His analysis of the changing form of government led him to distinguish between, on the one hand, its sovereign role (the preservation of territory and the submission of its population to the rule of law), and on the other, its increasingly dominant 'pastoral' concern with the welfare of this population. With population as both subject and object of government, new tactics and techniques of power have arisen, dependent on new forms of knowledge – the disciplines. The twinned notion of the exercise of the rule of law with enhancing of productivity and capacity of the population through the disciplines is therefore central to understanding the role of government. A number of authors (see Boyer 1983; Escobar 1993; Flyvbjerg 1998) have cast planning, and the science of development more generally, as one of these disciplines. Escobar draws on Foucault's ideas of the emergence of 'governmentality' to explain how the city and space came to be conceived of as an object, able to be analysed scientifically, and manipulated in the interests of both management and the addressing of 'social problems'. Both pastoral and disciplinary concerns are evident in planning: 'One cannot look on the bright side of planning', he argues, 'without looking at the same time on its dark side of domination' (Escobar 1993, 133).

The particular trajectory taken by the MSDF planning process involved the exercise of power relations in a number of forms and originating from a number of sources. Beyond the power relations exercised in the immediate 'vicinity' of the planning process, events at a national level, and related to the processes of political and economic transition, also had particular effects. Rather than casting the emerging political and economic transformations as all-determining 'structures', as is the tendency in political transition literature, I follow Foucault's notion of power relations which are stabilized and stratified by integrating factors which align and homogenize particular features. These integrating factors make up the institutions, which may be political, economic, etc. (Deleuze 1986, 75). This conception allows for the possibility that individuals or groups involved in the political transition process in South Africa were able to formulate policies, rules and resourcing strategies which had effects in a range of arenas, including the local bureaucracies. However, these effects could not be predetermined. The power exerted through these new institutions was relational, and its effects depended as much on the tactics and strategies of individuals in the local bureaucracies as on the nature of the policies and rules themselves. Moreover, this conception allows for the possibility that such policies, rules and resourcing strategies may not form a coherent, non-contradictory position: 'different rationalities meet in a determinate historical landscape and establish coalitions for the pursuit of aims that, for a time at least, complement one another' (Ransom 1997, 70).

A final issue here has to do with the way I understand the process of change to have taken place in the ideas and actions of Cape Town's metropolitan spatial planners. It has been argued that Foucault does not present a clear conception of how change occurs in society (Hajer 1995). His notion of change is highly circumstantial, even accidental: 'many things [that] can be changed, fragile as they are, bound up more with circumstances than necessities, more arbitrary than self-evident, more a matter of complex, but temporary, historical circumstances than with inevitable anthropological constraints' (Kritzman 1988, 156). I draw here on writers who have attempted to develop Foucault's ideas on the role of discourse, to explain change and continuity in the 'middle-order' arena[4] of policy formulation. In particular, Hajer (1995) has built on Foucault's later ideas about the role of discourse. Using Harre's (1993) notion of 'story-lines' to understand how distinct but related discourses influence one another, he puts forward the concept of 'discourse-coalitions' which posits ongoing struggles for discursive hegemony in which actors try to secure support for their definition of reality.

Foucault viewed discourse as a body of statements and practices whose organization is regular and systematic and whose production is governed by certain rules which delimit (although not entirely) what is acceptable or 'true'. These rules have a constraining effect which lends continuity to a discourse: they imply prohibitions which make it difficult to raise certain questions or argue certain cases, or they may only authorize certain people to participate in a discourse (Hajer 1995, 49). However, unrelated discourses can come together and, in doing so, create new discursive space. Hajer develops the idea of how new discursive spaces are created by introducing the role of the discoursing subject or agent, interacting with other agents. Drawing on the writings of Rom Harre, he sees human interaction as based on the exchange of arguments, or contradictory suggestions as to how one makes sense of reality. Such arguments derive from broader 'positions' or understandings of what constitutes the truth, and in the process of argumentative interaction, concepts and practices can mutate and change, or alternatively be reinforced.

Harre uses the concept of the 'story-line' as a mechanism for creating and maintaining discursive order. Story-lines allow actors to draw on various discursive categories to give meaning to specific physical or social phenomena. They facilitate the reduction of the discursive complexity of a problem and allow for the formulation of a coherent and acceptable explanation, understanding or strategy. As certain story-lines are accepted and used, they take on a ritual character and gain permanence and status. Story-lines also play a role in creating a social and moral order in a particular domain. Through such story-lines particular ideas of 'blame', 'responsibility' or 'urgency' can be attributed, and actors (or groups of actors) can be positioned as victims, perpetrators, etc.

Hajer takes the idea of story-lines further to suggest that coalitions occur amongst actors operating with similar or related story-lines, allowing what can become struggles for 'discursive hegemony' between differing coalitions, in attempts to secure support for a particular definition of reality. It is such struggles, he argues, that become prime vehicles of change. New story-lines and coalitions emerge which re-order understandings of reality. However, such struggles cannot be grounded entirely in the actors who participate in them, or in the particular strategic choices they make. Foucault's idea of the 'tactical polyvalence of discourses' refers to the way in which a number of discursive elements can come together to create a new discursive space within which problems can be discussed, or, presumably, strategies can be pursued. Story-lines thus operate in the middle ground between epistemes and individual construction.

Case studies and narrative writing

The focus in this book on a single case of planning, and the way in which the case material has been presented, needs some explanation. There is a growing recognition amongst planning theorists that a distinct and identifiable approach to the theorizing of planning has been emerging. Broadly termed the 'practice movement' (Liggett 1996), this new approach is characterized by the study of individual planners and planning practice. There is a strong focus on agency. Mandelbaum (1996, xviii) describes 'a pervasive interest in the behaviour, values, character and experiences of professional planners at work', and in the practices of these planners which encompass 'ways of talking, rituals, implicit protocols, routines, relational strategies, character traits and virtues'. Innes (1995) argues that such specific and context-bound accounts of planning activity are better able to bridge the gap between planning theory and practice, and are able to give better insight into the nature and possibilities of planning practice than previous planning theories were able to do. This new thrust has turned the attention of planning theorists to the documenting of cases of planning practice. This writing has sometimes taken the form of analysing extracts of planners' conversations or daily routines (see, for example, Forester 1989, 1997, 1999; Healey 1992) and sometimes that of fully contextualized case studies of planning initiatives (see, for example, Flyvbjerg 1998; Throgmorton 1996; Forsyth 1999).

There is a strongly pedagogical intent underlying this position in planning theory (Watson 2000). Most practice movement writers, some more, some less explicitly, see the purpose of their focus on the doings of planners to be the building of some kind of understanding, which can in turn be of help, or guidance, to practising planners and, presumably, to students of planning as well. The notion of learning from practice, in order to assist practice, is therefore a central one. Schon and Rein (1994, 196) are very clear on this point. They argue for collaborative research between academics and practitioners, which benefits the academic – first, through the satisfaction gained from helping practitioners generate usable knowledge, and second, through giving the academic better insights into practice than could otherwise be gained. If policy academics disregard what practitioners already know or are trying to know, then they will neither grasp what is going on nor succeed in getting practitioners to listen to them.

The 'learning from practice in order to improve practice' theme is evident in other writings as well. Yiftachel (1999, 268) notes that 'communicative scholars analyze planning with a clear normative task of reforming and improving planning from within', and communicative action theorist Innes (1995, 185) believes that 'the planning theorist's goal should be to help planners develop a new type of critical, reflective practice which is both ethical and creative'. Flyvbjerg (1998), as well, has been clear that he sees the analysing of relations of power in planning processes as a precursor to the development of strategies that can counter the negative exercise of power.

These theorists commonly assume that learning takes place on the basis of experience, and further, that experience can yield a more useful learning process than, for example, learning from general theories or rules. There is a growing body of writing that supports this position. From within the planning field, Schon and Rein (1994, 193) argue that the purpose of understanding policy practice is 'not to draw from it rules of effective policy making'. Policy designers, or planners, they suggest, do generalize from particular situations that they have been in, but not in order to produce 'covering laws'. They build up a mental 'usable repertoire of unique cases' (p. 205). When confronted with a new situation, they scan their repertoire of cases looking for points of similarity, and from past experience construct an understanding appropriate to the new situation. In this process of 'reflective transfer', both the pattern carried over from the previous situation and the understanding formed in the new one are transformed. Rather than applying abstract and decontextualized rules, they are using judgement based on experience.

My intentions in writing this book are in line with this thinking. I believe that, by reflecting on the specific experience of planning in Cape Town, particularly at this time of rapid transition, planners here will be better placed to move forward. This conviction has in turn demanded that this experience be documented in a particular way. First, if it is to fulfil a learning function, then it has to be presented as a fully contextualized case study, recognizing that it offers a window on one particular planning process. I cannot generalize from this case to others in South Africa, although I have drawn parallels with planning in other cities at certain points in the book. Case studies are about particularization, not generalization: generalization happens in the mind of the reader to the extent that it is useful in understanding a new situation.

Second, if the aim is to produce mediated accounts of experience, that can be interpreted, incorporated and mobilized in the practitioner's mental repertoire of cases, then 'process' or 'history'[5] is a crucial dimension of these experiences. As Fischler (1998) has suggested, history is a source of good case studies of planners-in-action, as it provides instructive precedent, and it is of great value to explanatory planning theory when we want to understand why planners act in particular ways, as well as understanding what they do. In Foucaultian terms such inquiry takes the form of documenting sequences of actual events, rather than focusing on the history of discourse or theories. It addresses the question: how did the practices which we can observe come about? It also addresses the development of professional modes of thinking and acting, or practices of analysis and action that have been developed to address particular problems, and how particular planners operate within and against these practices. For Fischler (1998, 27) there is, further, a need to take into account the evolution of the institutional and legislative context within which planners operate, bringing together 'the ethnographic analysis of planners' behaviour, the geneological analysis of planning practices and the political-economic analysis of planning institutions'.

Third, accounts of planning practices which are rich in contextual detail also allow readers to add to their mental repertoire of unique instances of planning, and judge the extent to which there are sufficient points of similarity with a current problem for it to be useful. Perhaps one of the most difficult problems which has to be faced when trying to draw on understandings or ideas developed in a different context, is that of how transferable they are – what is unique to a particular time and place, and what is more general? It is only depth of contextualizing detail (thick description) that will allow this kind of judgement to be made. 'Deep situational understanding' is essential input to new problems and circumstances, as is the need to show the full complexity of the world, and how outcomes may have been other than they were.

Fourth, and linked to the above, actors or practitioners need to be portrayed in text as richly and transparently as possible. Baum (1996, 378) has argued that we need to 'discard reassuring but simplistic notions of what planners do'. Rarely are they neutral, technical, rational beings. They think and feel about their work, experience pleasure and anxiety, have 'irrational' feelings, operate on the basis of particular values or ethics, and, importantly, function in a context in which they try to exert power and are impacted on by power.

Beauregard (1999, 93) has demanded that planning theorists report on more than just the activities that comprise practice, but also 'write the planner who will carry out these actions'. They must 'address the identity of their planners' and hence the often implicit assumptions which underlie what they do and say. The tactic of allowing actors and practitioners to speak, through the use of direct quotes, has been effectively used by most practice movement writers. But it is also necessary to understand this discourse in its context of a sequence of events, if the reader is to move beyond a partial and simplistic view of who is doing the talking.

In the same vein, writers of planning texts, documenters of planning experience, are also rarely, if ever, neutral, technical and rational beings. Being as transparent as is possible, in terms of who is doing the writing, why, under what circumstances, and with what conceptual baggage, can allow the reader greater scope for interpreting the meaning and usefulness of the material. This requires a degree of self-reflection and the writing of the author into the text. Beauregard (1998, 195) urges us to adopt a form of writing which involves 'surfacing the author, confessing to fallibility and bounded rationality and writing history with humility . . . one should write in the active voice, and make use of conditional sentences, stylistic elements that reinforce a sense of possibilities'.

Fifth, I have adopted an approach to the presentation of the case material which is now being termed 'narratology'.[6] Hoch (1996, 43) has suggested that planners become 'storytellers of practice', and several recent examples of planning case study writing (Flyvbjerg 1998; Forsyth 1999; Throgmorton 1996) have indeed adopted the narrative approach. Bruner (1986; 1996, 130) has argued that 'ordinary people go about making sense of their experiences' by construing their reality through the narrative mode. Relating planning experiences through narrative can thus be the most effective way of communicating and transferring this experience to others. This is particularly the case since the aim of relating experience is less to provide the reader with universal truths or generalizations about plans or planning (the usefulness of which in any event is questionable, in the highly particular and context-bound situations in which much planning occurs), but more to give insight into how messy problems involving values, judgement, multiple interpretations, planners' particular identities, and personal and group agendas, have unfolded in particular contexts. Each narrative on its own cannot provide the definitive guidance which planners seek in their daily work. But, as the literature on learning referred to above suggests, the building of a 'mental repertoire' of many such narratives and cases can provide the basis for the kind of 'expert' judgement required in the day-to-day work of planners.

Finally, my interest in the documentation of planning cases, in order to provide a learning experience, has led me to follow a particular method in the preparation of this book. My sources of information lay largely in the archives of the Cape Town metropolitan authority, but I also drew extensively on interviews with those people who had been involved in the planning process.

Chapter drafts, based on documentation and interviews, were then fed back to those I had interviewed and they were then re-interviewed, both to correct my interpretations and to record their response to the unfolding story. The narrative style was particularly useful as I started to feed back drafts of the work to individuals. It seemed that busy professionals, who spent much of their working time processing formal reports, found it easy and interesting to read a story, particularly since it often featured themselves. My drafts were read quickly and people were keen to spend long periods in follow-up interviews, embellishing and explaining their view of events. Most importantly, it soon became clear to me that a learning process was starting to take place. Individual planners, involved in the issues and crises of the moment, tend to forget the bigger picture within which they have been working and the longer-term shifts and trends which they have been part of. Reasons for continuity rather than change began to become clearer. At the point where one senior planning official told me that he was raising issues in my drafts with his staff, I felt that the learning potential of the process was beginning to be revealed.

Structure of the book

The chapters tell the story of the metropolitan planning process from 1989 to the end of the year 2000. The planning process has not yet come to an end, but it reached a particular watershed in 2000, making this a convenient break point. Chapters 1 and 2 describe the origins of the planning process and how it emerged in response to the loss of confidence in the ability of the apartheid government to manage racially segregated cities Chapters 3 and 4 cover the establishment of a new discourse coalition around an approach to planning based on ideas of urban integration and redistribution. This was the 'heyday' of spatial planners in Cape Town, when they could claim that their ideas had been subject to a fully democratic and inclusive consensus-seeking process, and had been strongly supported. Chapter 5 breaks from the story sequence to discuss the magnitude of the institutional and policy changes which were happening in South Africa at the time, and which were significantly changing the context within which planners were operating. Chapter 6 picks up the thread of the story again to show how the planners initially responded to these changes, primarily through a retreat into familiar bureaucratic procedures and practices. Chapter 7 again breaks from the story sequence to examine in detail the main text which sets out the metropolitan plan: it is a text which, like any other, selectively organizes the readers' attention, conceptually frames problems and issues in certain ways, and present facts, strategies and drawings in a way which exercises persuasive power over the reader. Chapter 8 explores the way in which metropolitan spatial planners find themselves gradually marginalized in the face of an emerging new discourse coalition, within local institutions, grounded in a philosophy of neo-liberalism and 'entrepreneurial local government'. In each of these chapters the conclusion draws out the implications of the events for understanding processes of change and continuity. Last, Chapter 9 raises the question of what future there may be for planning in Cape Town. It looks at the changing space-economy of the city as an informant for future action, and considers the kinds of actions which might help to overcome the growing problems of segregation and marginalization.

1 'What's needed is a metropolitan plan'

June 16 is now a public holiday in South Africa. It commemorates a day in 1976 when police opened fire on a protest march of African schoolchildren in Soweto, Johannesburg, and it represents a turning point in the long history of resistance to the apartheid government. It was this resistance which, gathering force during the 1980s, was to culminate in a process of political transition to a liberal democratic government, officially marked by general elections in April of 1994.

But 16 June 1989 was still a normal working day for some sections of the South African population.[1] It was certainly a normal working day for the officials of the metropolitan and local authorities in Cape Town, although there was no doubt that the wind of political change was making itself felt in the modern, well-guarded buildings which housed these institutions. Significantly, however, 16 June 1989 was to become an important date in the history of metropolitan planning in Cape Town. Although unaware of it at the time, the small group of planning officials who came together on that winter's morning to discuss the idea of a 'regional development strategy' were embarking on a metropolitan planning process which was to become the longest and most extensive yet undertaken in the city. As a planning process which was born in the early days of the political transition, and which has continued through ten years of this transition, it was to mirror in a number of ways the struggles and strategies affecting the country as a whole.

Certain of the planners at this meeting were destined to play an influential role in the subsequent planning process, and they need an introduction. Peter de Tolly, articulate, persuasive and authoritative, was a South African born, English-speaking planner in his forties. He had trained at the University of Toronto and worked extensively there and in the United States. In both his training and subsequent work he had become convinced that process was the key to successful planning and that the ideas of 'growth management' were particularly appropriate to the kinds of problems facing Cape Town. At the time of the meeting he was Deputy City Planner of the Cape Town City Council, the largest and most powerful of the various Cape Town municipalities, and generally acknowledged as the 'core' municipality of metropolitan Cape Town. A second important role-player was Francois Theunissen. An

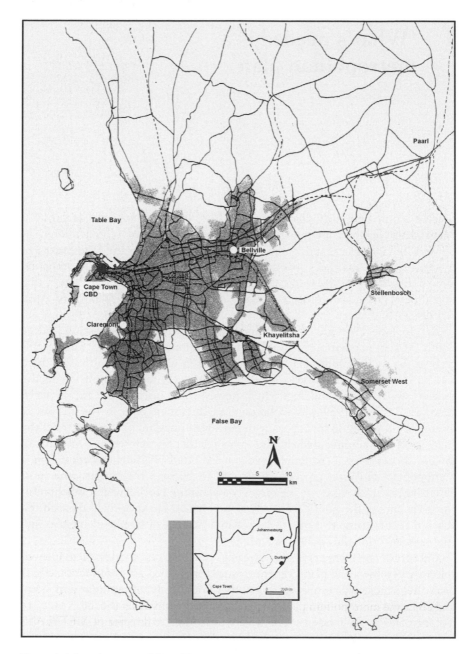

Figure 1.1 Locality map of Cape Town.

Figure 1.2 Aerial photograph of Metropolitan Cape Town.
Source: MLH Architects & Planners (2000).

Afrikaans-speaking South African, he had graduated as a planner from the University of Stellenbosch (one of the three universities in the region and alma mater to many Afrikaner bureaucrats and professionals) and for most of his career had worked in government. Polite, deferential, but very determined, he was most at home with the procedures and regulations which made up the day-to-day work of planning officials of the time. He was at the meeting as a representative of the Provincial government, where his experience had been in statutory planning and development control, but was soon to join the Western Cape Regional Services Council[2] (the newly created metropolitan authority) and chair the metropolitan planning process for the following decade.

Chairing the meeting on 16 June was the outgoing director of METPLAN, the Joint Town Planning Committee which had previously been tasked with the function of metropolitan planning. With the metropolitan planning function about to be transferred to the Regional Services Council, this man would have been aware that his power base was under threat. As a career bureaucrat who had taken care not to challenge official thinking on urban planning, he was soon to move on to positions in the Provincial and central government administrations. There were five others at the meeting as well, representing various local and Provincial departments: all were white, all were male, all mid-career planning bureaucrats. This was not particularly unusual at the time.

What was somewhat unusual was that a group of local authority planners should be meeting in 1989 to consider the need for a metropolitan plan. There were, after all, existing statutory 'Guide Plans' controlling the development of the Cape Town metropolitan area. These were typical, comprehensive, 'blue-print' land-use plans drawn up in the 1980s by a central government Guide Planning Committee and were mainly concerned with the designation of parcels of land for settlement by different racial groupings.[3] It had not, previously, been within the powers of the metropolitan or local authorities to deviate from these plans. It was also significant that the meeting was convened by the new metropolitan authority: the Regional Services Council. This system of supra-local government, which covered both urban and rural areas of South Africa, had been brought into existence by the government in 1985 in an attempt to secure the legitimacy of the crumbling system of racially separate local authorities. The Regional Services Council,[4] which formed the second tier of government in metropolitan Cape Town, was ostensibly under the firm political control of the ruling National Party and, in a political system which was highly centralized, there would appear to be little room for questioning a fundamental cornerstone of apartheid – the nature and growth of urban areas.[5]

However, 1989 was a time of crisis for South Africa and for Cape Town, and as is often the case, planning was viewed as one way of responding to crisis. While our prospective metropolitan planners were setting their agendas for the next phase of their work, on the other side of the city, in the squalid townships and squatter settlements which held the majority of Cape Town's African and coloured population, a low-intensity civil war was underway. Before following further the efforts of the metropolitan planners, it is necessary to consider some aspects of this crisis.

The 'tinderbox' of Cape Town

At the time this story opens, in 1989, an upsurge of resistance to the particular system of racial capitalism in South Africa had made itself felt for nearly two decades. Worker strikes, school stayaways and marches, and civic, women and squatter protests had been met with combinations of state reform and repression. But increasingly, an ailing economy, international pressure, divisions within the ruling party, and the violent nature of internal struggles, made the abandonment of the apartheid project and an acceptance of some form of power-sharing seem possible.

In Cape Town, as in other cities, the issue of physical access to the city became a highly conflictual one. Fierce battles raged between police and squatters (Figure 1.3) throughout the late 1970s and 1980s, as African people without legal rights to remain in the city, as well as those without access to state-approved urban housing, attempted to secure a living space. In what was becoming a familiar pattern of twinned reform and repression, concessions were on occasion granted to those who had the legal right to remain in Cape Town (that is, those with recognized employment), while efforts to prevent further migration from the rural 'homelands' were intensified. The residents of the Crossroads squatter camp gained international fame in their efforts to resist removal and demolition. In an apparent exercise of divide and rule, those Crossroads residents with legal urban 'rights' or with means of economic support, were allowed to remain in Cape Town and were promised formal housing. At the same time 'illegal' migrants were subject to intensified pass raids, arrest and forcible removal back to the rural 'homelands' (Cole 1986). However, the emergence of numerous new informal settlements, the estimate that a thousand additional people per day were migrating to the city,[6] and the growing strength of squatter resistance organizations, made it clear that the system of influx control was breaking down. In an attempt to cope with the crisis, and in a clear reversal of previous policy, the government announced in 1983 that a large new tract of land for African people would be opened up in Cape Town: Khayelitsha was planned to house some 450,000 people and was located on the remote fringe of the city, some 40 km from the centre.

The government had not abandoned the hope that the delivery of improved urban living conditions would dampen demands for political rights. A series of reforms in the 1980s demonstrated not only a continuation of the twinning of reform and repression, but also the increasing divisions within the ruling

Figure 1.3 An informal settlement (KTC) burns.

Source: Cole (1987).

National Party and different approaches adopted by the various government departments. Most important was the official end to influx control, announced in 1986, and a new White Paper on urbanization (Republic of South Africa 1986). The latter accepted that African people could move freely to the cities, but that separate living areas for the various 'population groups' in towns and cities should be observed. In particular the White Paper advised local officials to identify new areas of land for African settlement well in advance, bearing in mind national spatial policies which promoted the idea of 'deconcentration points' around the major centres. This advice had been taken seriously by officials in Cape Town's metropolitan planning agency, as we shall see below.

By the late 1980s the government was under increasing pressure both from beyond its borders (the ANC had called for the intensification of the armed struggle at its consultative conference in 1985, delegations of South Africans had been meeting with ANC heads outside the country, and in 1986 the US Congress passed the Comprehensive Anti-Apartheid Act) and from within, where the resistance forces began to regroup in 1989. It was during this period that the government significantly altered the mechanisms through which control and reform were channelled. The National Security Management System (NSMS) had been set up in 1979 as part of the 'total strategy', but was only fully activated in the latter part of the 1980s. It represented a 'parallel system of state power which vested massive repressive and administrative powers in the hands of the military and police' (Marais 1998, 55). Committees were set up which shadowed each level of regional and local authority, and which essentially shifted the balance of power from the official organs of government to the president and the security forces. The role of these committees was to identify 'trouble spots' and to focus on them investment in social facilities and infrastructure, while at the same time collecting information on oppositional movements and attempting to destabilize them.

The NSMS was able to undermine the opposition, but was not able ultimately to contain it. In the first months of 1989 the Minister of Law and Order was able to say that unrest in Cape Town's townships had abated to such an extent that the government could now press ahead with reform (*Cape Times* 14/2/89). However, only six months later the streets of Cape Town had 'been turned into a battleground' (*South Newspaper* 24/8/89). The national elections for the Tricameral Parliament, set for September 1989, became the focal point for a revitalized resistance movement. Protest action was initially centred in the schools of the coloured townships of Cape Town, where rallies were held, roads blocked off with burning barricades, and vehicles stoned. From the schools, the unrest spread to the universities and eventually into the centre of the city, where running battles between demonstrators and the police became a daily event. Two weeks before the election Cape Town was recorded as the country's worst trouble spot (*Star* 24/8/89) and there was speculation that it would become the 'tinderbox' which would set the rest of the country alight (*Star* 29/8/89). The security forces responded with a full range of repressive measures, and the wave of shootings and detentions which accompanied the protests were ultimately to provide a major setback to efforts of the new president, F.W. de Klerk, to present himself as an enlightened leader. In a surprising about-face, de Klerk sanctioned a planned march in central Cape Town to protest against police action. On 13 September 1989, 30,000 people of all races marched peacefully through the streets of central Cape Town behind the ANC flag, in the first legal demonstration of its kind (*Cape Times* 13/9/89). The Cape Town City Council mayor and most of the councillors led the march. Similar large-scale, government-sanctioned marches followed in the other major cities and smaller towns: the country had taken a decisive step towards political transition.

By late 1989 therefore, the government was challenged but not fundamentally threatened. Marais (1998) points out that the security apparatus and the military remained relatively intact, and that the ruling party had the support of large sections of business. It was very evident, however, that the situation was not a stable one. The onset of severe recession in early 1989 made urban infrastructural reform efforts more and more difficult, and fuelled the discontent of both workers and business. The rent and services payment boycott in the townships had proved particularly successful and services and administration in many townships were in a state of collapse. Occupants of the rapidly growing informal settlements of Cape Town had been concerned primarily with internal conflicts during 1989. This, largely, had taken the form of battles between Comrades – those aligned to the ANC – and warlords, traditional and politically conservative, sometimes self-appointed leaders, ruling often with tacit government support. But these areas too were showing signs of increasing political cohesion, as well as a tendency to voice their grievances outside government offices in central Cape Town: a march on the Provincial Administration days before the general election had presented demands for an end to forced removals, and the delivery of housing and services 'on our present land' (*Cape Times* 1/9/89). It was in these uncertain times, and in the context of growing pressure for the accommodation of African people within the metropolitan area, that the metropolitan planning authority of Cape Town turned its attention to the future of the city.

The battle of the spatial models: Cape Town as the 'multi-nodal' city

The group of planners who met on 16 June 1989 saw themselves as continuing the work of an earlier, 1988, committee which had met under the auspices of METPLAN at the offices of the Cape Town City Council. This earlier committee (the METPLAN Sub-committee Investigating Land for Future Housing for the Low-Income Group) had been set up in response to the 1986 government White Paper on urbanization, which had advised local authorities to think ahead on the issue of low income settlement. This issue had been a pressing one. The idea that racial groups should be spatially separated within urban areas was certainly being challenged on the ground, but was nonetheless still officially enshrined in the legislation of the government of the day. With influx control having been scrapped in 1986, and an expected rapid rise in the rate of African urbanization, it would need forward planning to ensure that new African urban-ites were accommodated on land in a way which conformed with the principles of 'separate development'.

By initiating an investigation into future land for settlement in Cape Town, METPLAN had opened up an important opportunity, and that was to challenge the official statutory Guide Plans for Cape Town – the planning instrument through which central government controlled urban settlement. There had been widespread recognition at this stage that the Guide Plan was outdated. Drawn up as a draft in 1984 (prior to the scrapping of influx control) the Guide Plan committee had simply not met since, and the approval of the draft plan in 1988 was probably no more than an attempt to keep up the appearance of central government planning control. As Theunissen, then a member of the METPLAN sub-committee, explained: 'We were in injury time. Things were changing very fast and we had to fill the gap' (Interview 1 1998).

The Guide Plan for the Cape Peninsula (Department of Development Plan-ning 1988) had put forward a particular spatial model for the future develop-ment of the Cape Town metropolitan area. The 1975 National Physical Development Plan had first set out the concept of deconcentration and decen-tralization points around the larger metropolitan areas as a way of avoiding the growing concentration of (African) people in the cities. These ideas had their roots in the internationally influential British Barlow Commission Report of 1940 which had argued for constraining large city growth (that of London in particular) and the directing of population 'overspill' to new towns beyond the urban fringe. In the Western Cape this concept had also been applied to the coloured population (which in Cape Town has long formed the numerical majority), and the deconcentration point of Atlantis had been created as a 'coloured city' some 45 km north of the metropolitan area. The 1988 Guide Plan held with the 1975 multi-nodal concept and stipulated that future urban growth should be accommodated outside the boundaries of Cape Town, in a series of deconcentration points (Figure 1.4). Atlantis had been pinpointed as an area of future settlement, as had the small existing towns of Somerset West, Paarl, Wellington and Stellenbosch, just beyond the metropolitan periphery. By the late 1980s, however, it had become clear that the deconcentration strategy had serious failings. Atlantis had failed to grow, either in terms of jobs or housing, at anything like the rate anticipated. It had become a peripheral slum and a pool of unemployment, with many of its residents making the long trip back to Cape Town each day for work and services. And the demand from the civic and squatter organizations was for land close to sources of employment.

With the provisions of the 1988 Guide Plan clearly inadequate to cope with the reality of urban growth, METPLAN had appointed a consultant to under-take the task of identifying future land for low-income housing. The particular consultant chosen had long associations with government authorities in Cape Town and would have been well known to the METPLAN committee. The search for land had been designed to cover a very large area: the entire area of

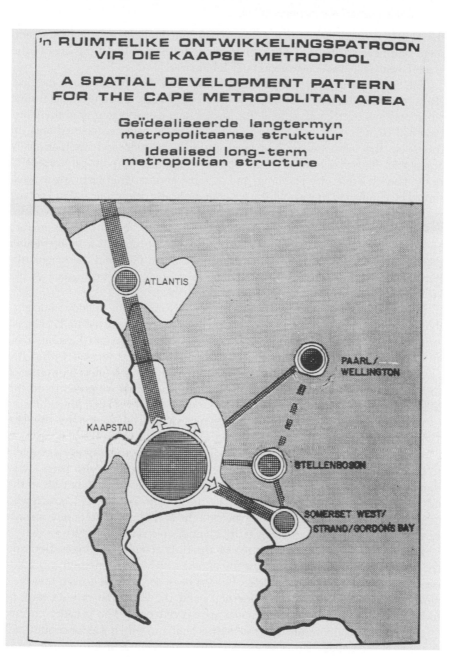

Figure 1.4 Guide Plan provision for the deconcentration of Cape Town.

Source: Department of Development Planning (1988).

the Regional Services Council (Cape, Paarl and Stellenbosch branches) and some land beyond this. The distance from the furthest point of this area to the Cape Town CBD was approximately 75 kilometres!

The approach used by the consultant had been that of the 'sieve method' (Report to METPLAN 1988). A set of criteria had been drawn up to determine what land was deemed acceptable for low-income development, and these criteria had been applied evenly to the entire Regional Services Council area. In this sense the methodology had been entirely scientific and internationally acceptable, and therefore, it would appear, untainted by political considerations. The idea that city planning, and regional and national planning as well, should be conducted in ways which were scientifically defensible and in keeping with trends in other parts of the world was not new. Planners of the townships which were created in terms of pre-apartheid notions of 'separate development', and those later created to hold the victims of forced removal from previously racially mixed areas, drew on the ideas of the Garden City and the neighbourhood unit, and the design of Milton Keynes strongly influenced some of the later coloured township planning (Dewar *et al.* 1990).

For a METPLAN consultant it was particularly important to adopt a defensible planning approach. While METPLAN was funded largely by the Provincial Administration (the tier of government above Regional Services Council level, and an appointed administrative body after 1988), it was located within the offices of the Cape Town City Council, the largest and most powerful of the Cape Town municipalities, and the latter had a significant presence on the METPLAN board. The Cape Town City Council had long been known for its (sometimes contradictory) liberal stance against apartheid, and by the late 1980s most of its councillors were aligned with the national political opposition party, or were local businessmen for whom apartheid was sometimes an obstacle to profit-making (Cameron 1986). The consultant may have also been aware that the 1988 Guide Plan, with its proposal to deflect new growth outside of the city, had been strongly rejected by officials of the Cape Town City Council who argued for the scrapping of Group Areas and the accommodation of new growth inside the existing city boundaries (City Planner's Department 1989).

How this particular consultant felt at the time about racial segregation and the proposals of the Guide Plan, or the extent to which his method was influenced by the METPLAN committee, has not been determined. It was, however, almost inevitable that his 'sieve method', and the particular criteria used to identify land, would have a particular spatial outcome. The primary criteria chosen related to environmental constraints and land which was 'uncommitted' in terms of the Guide Plan. The secondary criteria related, first, to Group Areas policy, and second to the availability of employment and transport routes. The tertiary criteria related to 'political considerations' (undefined), existing zoning schemes and availability of recreational facilities.

The amount of land which had to be found was large: between 28,000 and 55,000 hectares would be needed by the year 2000, assuming that the low-density form of development, which had come to characterize township development in South Africa, would continue. This implied that large sites had to be found, and there were few of these left in those parts of metropolitan Cape Town which were designated by the Guide Plan for African and coloured settlement. Large pieces of empty land certainly existed within the built-up part of the metropolitan area, and most of them were very well located with regard to employment and transport routes, but these were within defined 'white' areas. This land would have been excluded in the 'sieving' process by the criteria of 'Group Areas', and, presumably, 'political considerations'.

The outcome of the 'sieve' process had been the identification of five potential sites (Figure 1.5), all very far removed from the existing built-up area of Cape Town, and with no indication of how poor people living there would gain access to work or services. The conclusion of the report also stated that it supported the idea of accommodating growth within Cape Town and the creation of a more 'compact urban structure', but in the next paragraph this idea is de-emphasized by the warning that higher densities can give rise to 'adverse socio-economic conditions, particularly amongst the low-income group' (Report to METPLAN 1988, 30). The thrust of the recommendations was clearly in favour of the five deconcentration points and was in line with the multi-nodal spatial model put forward by the Guide Plan.

Theunissen describes the response of the METPLAN sub-committee to this report as 'not comfortable' (Interview 1 1998), but this may disguise what could have been major differences of opinion amongst the members of the committee. The brief minutes of the meeting held to discuss the report indicate that it had some support, particularly from a representative of the national Department of Local Government, Housing and Agriculture (which dealt with 'coloured' housing), and from a Regional Services Council official. It is unlikely that it would have been supported by the Cape Town City Council planner, given the previous condemnation of the Guide Plan by the municipal councillors, and given the fact that this particular planner had long aligned herself with the oppositional political movements in the city. Perhaps more important in making the meeting 'not comfortable' had been the reality beyond the doors of the civic centre: the resurgence of political opposition to apartheid, the apparent shifts at central government level towards the accommodating political demands, and the growing critique from some local planners of the existing city spatial structure (City Planner's Department 1989; Dewar et al. 1990).

What was most significant about this uncomfortableness, however, was that it was indicating a shift in support away from the prevailing spatial paradigm of multi-nodalism, and the racial ideology which it implied. Quite what was to replace it was not clear at this point. The suggestion had been made in a letter from de Tolly to the METPLAN chair, dated July 1988, that a 'regional development strategy' should be drawn up 'to determine how future development can best be integrated with the potential of the region' (Report to METPLAN 1988, 31). This statement in itself represents a major conceptual shift from a reactive search for leftover land, racially assigned, to the idea that planners should engage with ideas of development and integration. This was an

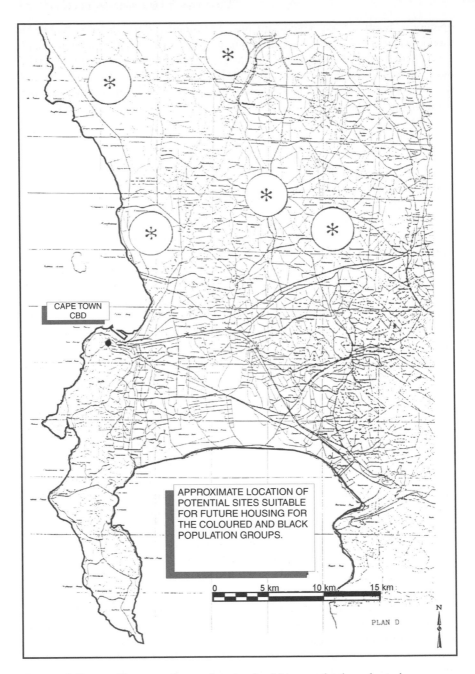

Figure 1.5 Proposed locations for new housing for African and coloured people.
Source: Report to METPLAN (1988).

argument that had been made within certain planning and academic circles for some years, but politically the space was only now opening up for it to be heard. It offered, at least, a way out for the METPLAN sub-committee, which could argue that a further round of work was necessary if it was to address the issue of urbanization and city growth. But it was not until 16 June 1989 that the group reconvened to address once again the issue of the spatial future of Cape Town.

Conclusion

Spatial planning, as a function of government, has long been used in South Africa to play both a managing role in relation to the spatial separation of racial groups[7] and a welfare (and modernizing) role in relation to the planning of housing and facilities for those of the African and coloured population deemed necessary for the urban economy. Planning's former role, that of racial segregation, manifested itself in an ad hoc manner prior to the election of the apartheid government in 1948, and was an outcome, primarily, of efforts to remove slum and 'unsanitary' areas, and to provide public housing for those so displaced. In the post-1948 years, however, urban racial segregation became an explicit policy of government, and town planning was viewed as the primary tool through which the new urban landscape could be fashioned (see Mabin and Smit 1997). The latter role, that of providing healthier and more 'modern' environments, had been promoted by particular individuals (particularly architects) in the early part of the century, and was formally proposed as a role for planning by a non-statutory, advisory body to government in 1944.[8] The terms of reference of the Social and Economic Planning Council required it to 'suggest plans which are objectively well thought out on their merits, apart from purely political considerations ... following as much as possible scientific lines' (in Wilkinson 1996, 154). The proposals of the Council included introducing a planning function at the level of national government, the adoption of a broader regional view on settlement patterns, and, in relation to the urbanized 'non-European population', the following of international planning principles of planned neighbourhoods separated by green belts (Wilkinson 1996).

Throughout the apartheid years these two planning discourses co-existed in ways which at times appeared to be mutually reinforcing. In particular, planners involved in the layout of new, racially segregated townships were able to justify the design of discrete residential 'neighbourhoods', surrounded by green belts (or buffer zones, as they were locally known) and with few access routes (which in turn allowed more effective policing and control), by citing their compatibility with international practice and contemporary scientific principles of planning. The 'sieve approach' adopted by METPLAN's planning consultant was likewise justified as being a scientific approach to land identification. The fact that certain of the criteria informing the 'sieve method' were ideologically informed did not appear to detract from the status which the approach held as scientific, and therefore unassailable, at least for the consultant and certain of the Committee members. The 'planning as tool of racial segregation' story-line was able to gain legitimacy from its association with the 'planning as improving welfare and modernization' story-line.

What occurs in the late 1980s, however, is that events in the poorer areas of Cape Town begin to demonstrate that planning, as a tool for the management of African and coloured settlement, and racial segregation, is becoming less effective. The power exercised by growing numbers of shack dwellers, in their efforts to lay claim to urban land, and by the squatter organizations in visible and disruptive protest demonstrations in the 'white' centre of Cape Town, increasingly provides a challenge to the apparent rationality of spatial planning as a disciplinary (racially segregating) mechanism. But the challenge is only a partial one. When Cape Town City Council planner, de Tolly, argues that the Committee should be considering the long-term integration of the region and the optimization of its potential, he is re-emphasizing the 'planning as improving welfare and modernization' story-line which had long been present in South African planning discourse. It is an argument that the Committee formally accepts in its minutes (seemingly without great difficulty) and agrees to pursue at its following meeting, perhaps because it is a shift of emphasis which is being proposed here rather than a fundamental challenge to the legitimacy of planning as an arena of population management.

What these events also indicate is the importance of the local and the contingent in the unfolding of South Africa's history. An interpretation of political transition which focuses on the actions of national pacting elites, by-passes micro-processes such as these which were occurring, in highly varied form, in any locale one might care to examine.

2 Cape Town as a 'compact, integrated' city?

It was to be six months before METPLAN took the next step towards a 'regional development strategy'. Part of the delay was due to the transfer of the METPLAN function into the Regional Services Council and the resignation of the METPLAN director. Before he left, however, the director of METPLAN chaired the first meeting of the new committee tasked with formulating a regional development strategy, on 16 June 1989.

Immediately clear at this meeting were the very different perceptions held by the planners as to what constituted a regional development strategy. The chairman was concerned about limiting both the scope and nature of the exercise to a product which would conform to the provisions of existing legislation. He argued that it should be a sub-regional structure plan which could comply with the minimum requirements of the Land Use Planning Ordinance of 1985, including the provisions for public participation (undefined in the legislation, other than it should be carried out to the satisfaction of the Provincial Administrator). Following this route would have produced a conceptual spatial plan for the metropolitan area with possibly minimal public input. De Tolly (the Cape Town City Council planner) strongly opposed this. He argued that what was needed was a development strategy which was both spatial and non-spatial, which contained a vision of a rather different future Cape Town and which had been subject to extensive public participation (RSC file 1989a). Both positions were noted in the minutes and the committee adopted no resolutions. A date was set for a following meeting a month later, but it was cancelled. Two weeks thereafter the METPLAN chair left to take up an appointment with a national government department, and the new metropolitan planning function of the Regional Services Council was left in some disarray. At the same time Cape Town was plunged into violent turmoil in the lead-up to the September general election, and the launch of a regional development strategy was sidelined by other considerations.

The idea of a regional development strategy may have died at this point had de Tolly not kept up a degree of pressure on the Regional Services Council. In a lengthy letter written after the 16 June meeting (RSC file 1989b) he emphasized the need for 'a process rather than a fixed-state master plan' which 'changes the emphasis of planning from finished drawings to establishing procedures, design and decision criteria, and development strategies to meet agreed-on goals'. He argued for the use of a 'strategic planning process' to address both spatial and non-spatial issues in the development of a growth management strategy. There was no response from the Regional Services Council, although an internal mission statement by the Metropolitan Planning Branch in January of 1990 (RSC file 1990a) announced that the first task of the branch was to produce a regional planning strategy, through a strategic planning process. De Tolly's arguments, it would seem, were starting to influence the planning rhetoric, if not yet the practice.

In April of 1990 Theunissen took up the job as Head of Regional Planning at the Regional Services Council. With the inadequacies of the official Guide Plan still in his mind, he immediately set about a process of commissioning a set of sub-metropolitan structure plans which would cover the entire Regional Services Council area. The question of a regional development strategy was not one of his considerations. He believed that fitting together a whole set of sub-regional plans, like a jigsaw puzzle, would produce an overall metropolitan plan. But de Tolly began to phone Theunissen regularly to raise the issue of a regional development strategy and at the same time discussed the issue with Cape Town City Councillor Clive Keegan who was also chair of the Regional Services Council Planning Committee.

De Tolly explained (Interview 2 1998) that he was reflecting a more general worry amongst some of the planners in the Cape Town City Council that the metropolitan planning function had been transferred to 'a bunch of rural managers': the Regional Services Council established in 1985 had been fashioned out of the previously existing Cape Divisional Council which had carried out local administration only for the more peripheral and rural parts of the metropolitan area. The new Regional Services Council had a very small planning staff, mostly experienced in local development control. The Cape Town City Council, on the other hand, had a planning staff of over fifty, with a range of skills and with local and international experience. Moreover, these planners had, in the previous few years, undertaken a number of large-scale planning exercises aimed at addressing the problems of the metropolitan area as a whole. For example, a 1990 Cape Town City Council report entitled 'Economic Development Planning for Cape Town' was well-developed and sophisticated, and had been debated with the local trade unions. A copy of this report was forwarded to the chief planner at the Regional Services Council for information, and attracted the following response in a letter: 'Any plan which has the effect of expanding the economy of Cape Town is supported, but strategic planning is a function of *this* regional planning branch and we need to ensure that this is appreciated' (RSC files 1990b). These exchanges reflect an institutional 'jealousy' over the metropolitan planning function which was to continue to influence the metropolitan planning process for years afterwards.

Challenging 'apartheid' planning

While the revival of the Regional Development Strategy Committee was not in de Tolly's hands, the possibility of initiating a broader discussion forum to discuss the need for metropolitan planning, was. The idea of a workshop on larger-scale planning was agreed to, with Theunissen now enthusiastic as well.

The workshop was held in July 1990. De Tolly delivered a paper arguing that metropolitan planning must be made an integral part of metropolitan management. Drawing on the work of Stren and White (1989) and the documentation of growth management strategies in American cities, he suggested that growth management should be natural systems performance-based, strategic, comprehensive, integrative and participative. Theunissen remembers this workshop well. Years later he recalled: 'there were three things that stuck in my mind after this workshop – all planning must be tested against the environment, there is a need for a vision, and this thing of growth management' (Interview 1 1998).

The workshop succeeded in reviving interest amongst Regional Services Council staff for metropolitan planning, and at the conclusion of the workshop a commitment was made, now a year later, to reconvene the committee of 16 June.

However, the battle of the spatial models was not yet over. The old METPLAN staff who had come over to the Regional Services Council were possibly reluctant to give up what they saw as one of their primary roles: that of collecting data on land availability and use (Interview 1 1998). Whatever their motivation, they succeeded in persuading the Council to appoint a consultant to continue the work of a land search for low-income housing which had been left off by METPLAN late in 1988. The continuity between these two pieces of work is clear. In the letter of invitation to the new members of the reconstituted Regional Development Strategy Steering Committee, meeting for the first time in October 1990, reference was made to 'the first phase of work' which had resulted in the identification of various sites for low-income housing, and this 'new second phase' which involved a more detailed land availability study (RSC file 1990c). The choice of consultants was also important: a firm of planning consultants, who had worked on these issues before for the Provincial and local government, was proposed to Council. The Planning Committee accepted the recommendation, with no more than a mild rebuke to the planning officials for violating protocol and putting forward only one possible consultant rather than the usual choice of three (RSC files 1990d)! The work needed to fall under a steering committee, as was the practice at the time, and it was decided to place it under the Regional Development Strategy Committee of the Regional Services Council.

It is no wonder then that the group which gathered on 22 October 1990 in the Regional Services Council offices were a little confused as to their exact role. On the one hand they were present because they had agreed to join the already named Regional Development Strategy Steering Committee. On the other, the first and most important item on the agenda was the land identification study, and it appeared as though their prime task was to guide this work (RSC files 1990e). Here, for the first time, the two approaches to metropolitan planning were brought into direct juxtaposition with each other. Which approach won was clearly going to be a major issue affecting future events.

Some influence certainly lay with the new committee members. The decision had been taken[1] to open up the Steering Committee to representatives of certain non-governmental bodies because of 'parallel' work which some of them had been doing. In the context of a rapidly growing city experiencing economic and political crisis, and in the absence of an effective and legitimate metropolitan planning and administrative system, these bodies had started their own planning initiatives. WESGRO, an organization set up to promote economic investment and the interests of business in the Western Cape, had earlier that year launched 'Growing the Cape'. This initiative was intended to provide an economic vision and strategy for the city through a participatory and inclusive process. The Urban Foundation, a national body established by the private sector some years before to strategize on housing and urbanization issues, had been promoting urban development policies aimed at establishing a stable African and coloured middle class and accommodating free market principles. Finally, the Urban Problems Research Unit, attached to the School of Architecture and Planning at the University of Cape Town, had long been promoting a particular framing of the problems of Cape Town and a spatial planning strategy aimed at addressing these problems. The spatial form promoted by this strategy was, in many respects, the direct opposite of the multi-nodal strategy promoted by the Guide Plan and the earlier METPLAN work.

Also on the new Steering Committee were planning officials from the three levels of sub-national government: the Cape Town City Council, the Regional Services Council and the Provincial Administration. De Tolly was there unofficially, having fallen prey to an effort, within the City Council, to marginalize him (Interview 2 1998). A councillor with extensive local property interests had managed to insert a man who would be sympathetic to his ambitions into one of the top planning positions. De Tolly, being too vocal a critic of these ambitions, had to be curbed, and another planning official was directed to attend the Steering Committee meetings in his place.[2] De Tolly's response: 'What the hell, I went anyway' (Interview 2 1998).

It is very likely as well, though, that rapidly shifting events in the rest of the country affected the thinking of the new Steering Committee members. In January of 1990 the African National Congress and the South African Communist Party had been unbanned, and Nelson Mandela had been set free in February. Talks had begun, if shakily, between the government and the ANC, and it was clear to all that some kind of important political change was on the way. Resistance organizations could no longer be dismissed as a 'security threat' which could be dealt with through increased oppression, and civic and labour organizations were presenting themselves as bodies which had to be taken into account. It was also clear that the existing system of local government was seen to be ineffective and illegitimate, and that major changes were on the cards. An important precedent had been set in Johannesburg, the largest urban centre of South Africa, where the establishment of the Witwatersrand Metropolitan Forum, consisting of opposition organizations and local authorities, had been agreed to in August 1990, to consider an alternative vision of the city based on the slogan 'one city – one tax base'. Officials at the 22 October 1990 Steering Committee meeting could not have been confident that either their institutions or their jobs would last long into the future.

Furthermore, those planners who, in the past, had uncomplainingly implemented the spatial manifestations of the apartheid project were being made to feel more and more self-conscious. Only a month before the October 1990 meeting, the local branch of the South African Institute of Town and Regional Planners (traditionally a conservative and uncritical body) had held a conference on the campus of the University of Cape Town entitled 'Post-apartheid Planning in South Africa'. The title itself was significant, as it would still be almost four years before the first democratic elections and the real beginning of the post-apartheid era. In an uncharacteristically enlightened speech at the conference, the Provincial Administrator, Kobus Meiring, announced that South Africa had 'irrevocably embarked on the road to a new society', and that the planners' role should be seen as planning for a post-apartheid society. If this surprised some of the planners attending the conference, they must have felt even more concerned by the speech of Trevor Manuel, then ANC Interim Convenor and later Minister of Finance. Pulling no punches, Manuel basically accused the planning profession of siding with the evil of apartheid. In a talk entitled 'Community Perceptions of Planning', he said that not only apartheid but also planning had come to be a euphemism for the misery of the people. Forced removals were seen as a result of planning and planning was seen by many as an ideological tool for the implementation of apartheid policies. For those planners who had used their skills against the apartheid system (and there had been many of these in Cape Town in the 1980s) this must have been pleasantly vindicating. Those who had been part of planning the township wastelands and isolated 'deconcentration points' may not have felt confident about their future.

Hence, on 22 October, the forces in favour of a retreat to the old METPLAN style of land identification as metropolitan planning were not strong. Almost immediately after welcomes and introductions, the question was raised, both by outside organizations and the Cape Town City Council planners, as to how a land identification study could be conducted in the absence of a broader metropolitan strategy which indicated where and how future growth and development was to occur. Member after member made the point that energies should first go into a broader strategy and then into examining parcels of land. Those who had promoted land search as one of the major tasks of the committee did not challenge this (perhaps they did not have to: the consultants who were tasked with undertaking this work had already been appointed), and Theunissen in the chair did not disagree with those calling for a broader strategy:

'In my mind the purpose of the committee was to take forward the ideas from the earlier regional planning workshop, which I liked. The land identification exercise was no more than technical data gathering' (Interview 1 1998).

The land search approach was, however, being supported from a different quarter. It was reported at the October meeting, under the heading 'Other Parallel Planning Processes', that the Provincial Administration had appointed a consultant (the same one responsible for the 1989 METPLAN report which had identified five new sites for coloured and African settlement) to quantify the need for low-income housing and to evaluate certain sites in metropolitan Cape Town. The overlap with the work of the Regional Services Council land search consultant was clear to everyone, and over the next couple of years many attempts were made to meet with the Provincial Administration and discuss the duplication, and to rationalize it. Theunissen later agreed with the hypothesis that the Province no longer trusted the Regional Services Council, child of the National Party as it was, to toe the party line and identify land which furthered the aims of separate development (Interview 1 1998).

Two important decisions, which were to influence the process for some time to come, were taken on 22 October by the new Steering Committee. The first was that a small group should be formed to set out a 'framework for a growth management strategy for Cape Town'. De Tolly and the Urban Problems Research Unit representative were to work with Theunissen on this one, and as I, the author, was acting as the UPRU representative at the time, I have to enter the story for a brief period here. The second decision was that the UPRU representative should make a presentation on the particular spatial ideas which it had been promoting. As these ideas were, in various ways, to shape the product of the planning process, it is necessary to examine their roots in more detail.

The alternative spatial model: the compact city

In 1970 the City and Regional Planning Programme at the University of Cape Town had been turned into a full-time Master's course with a new head and new staff. Roelof Uytenbogaardt, who had studied architecture, urban design and planning under Louis Kahn at Pennsylvania, took over as head of the programme and, together with a close-knit group of colleagues from both architectural and non-architectural backgrounds, they began to fashion their own approach to spatial planning. The upsurge of violence in Cape Town townships in the mid-1970s convinced the group that a central factor underlying dissatisfaction was the poor quality of living environments – in particular the lack of good public spaces, the unifunctional and monotonous nature of these environments, and a physical urban structure which located the poorest people on the far edge of the city, well removed from the jobs, services and facilities which were concentrated in the historic core of Cape Town (Figure 2.1). The conceptualization of these factors as the key problems with which spatial planners should be concerned, emerged from an independent and professional assessment

Figure 2.1 Contrast between an older (pre-apartheid) working-class area of Cape Town and a newer, planned apartheid township.

Source: Urban Problems Research Unit, University of Cape Town.

of the city by the planners involved. The blame for the physical problems of Cape Town was not specifically laid at the door of apartheid or the Group Areas Act, but rather in the thoughtless and inappropriate application of First World and modernist spatial planning concepts to the local context. In 1975 the group established the Urban Problems Research Unit, with funding from the Anglo-American Company, and began to publish a series of books (Dewar *et al.* 1976; Dewar and Uytenbogaardt 1991) and working papers expounding an alternative.

The particular approach to planning adopted by these planning academics was compatible with what Healey (1997, 17) terms the 'physical development planning' tradition of planning thought. Physical space was objectified and regarded as an element capable of independent manipulation. The approach drew on writers such as Mumford, Jane Jacobs, Lynch, Crane, Alexander, and others, and supported the belief that good spatial principles were to be found in an understanding of 'precedent'; that is, successful urban environments elsewhere. The precedent which was considered to be most useful was to be found particularly in those settlements which had developed prior to the impact of the motor car, and which in terms of their structure and scale accommodated 'man on foot' – the pedestrian. Uytenbogaardt's training under Kahn, and his two years spent as a Rome Scholar at the British School, influenced his interest in the qualities of older European (and particularly Italian) settlements with their public spaces, their 'clarity of spatial structure', their high densities and human scale, and their 'respectful' relationship to the countryside in which they were placed.

In the latter half of the 1980s the Urban Problems Research Unit produced a number of publications which framed the planning problem of metropolitan Cape Town as lying in its inequitable and inefficient spatial structure. This, they argued, not only exacerbated problems such as poverty and unemployment, but also impacted negatively on the use of valuable natural resources, particularly agricultural land on the urban edge. In a final document in the series, South African Cities: A Manifesto for Change (Dewar and Uytenbogaardt 1991), the authors argued for a vision of Cape Town as

> a compact, intensive and convenient city which operates as an integrated system, which works well at the level of the lowest common denominator (people on foot), which makes maximum use of limited resources, and which is respectful of its beautiful natural setting.
>
> (Dewar and Uytenbogaardt 1991, 79)

The specific measures recommended to achieve this included reserving land where (because of its environmental value or character) development should not go, planting a regional grid of trees as a site-making action, compacting and densifying development, promoting the emergence of 'a network of interlocking linear activity systems' accommodating an intensive mix of development and public transport systems, and introducing an 'ethos of space-making into all urban projects' (Dewar and Uytenbogaardt 1991, 79–84). These ideas had much in common with what was becoming known in the international literature as the 'compact city' approach (see Breheny 1992).

The approach to spatial planning advocated by this group ran counter to much mainstream planning of the time, and particularly mainstream planning in South Africa, where the concept of neighbourhood units, separated from each other by freeways, had dovetailed conveniently with the spatial project of apartheid. However, their beliefs about the role of the planner were entirely modernist. The planner, through his or her creative expertise, can see beyond the parochial and immediate needs of the people being planned for. The planner is accountable to future generations as well as to the people of today and should therefore be given the freedom to imagine a future which may not always meet with full agreement or understanding by citizenry in the shorter term (Dewar and Uytenbogaardt 1991). The dominatory potential of this position was intended to be constrained by the idea of 'minimalism': that is, the planner is responsible for determining primarily those minimal and essential elements of physical structure which impart an enduring quality to living environments. These are the physical 'clues' to which both economic interests and private individuals are presumed to respond.

Throughout the late 1970s and 1980s, batches of graduate planning students were dispatched into the government authorities and private consultancies of Cape Town (and other South African cities), many of them filled with reformist fervour and a particular vision of the 'well-performing' city. Cecil Madell was one of the few black planners to graduate from the course in the late 1980s. One of his first jobs was with the planning consultancy which was subsequently engaged by the Regional Services Council to work on the new metropolitan plan, and as a result he soon found himself in the midst of the tussle between the Regional Services Council and Cape Town City Council planners. His planning education, he believed, gave him a particular confidence in such debates:

> the course does give certain people the perspective, not that you know it all, but that everything out there is wrong, that the planning approach taught at UCT is better, and I am better equipped to do it ... being very critical, very assertive and that UCT graduates are far better equipped [than planners from elsewhere] to deal with the development challenges facing Cape Town.
>
> (Interview 3 1999)

At the same time the University of Cape Town position on urban planning was disseminated through large numbers of publications and conference papers. What is interesting, then, is how little impact it had on the thinking of established government planners and consultants until the late 1980s. It can be assumed that the origins of these ideas in a liberal English-speaking university, the highly critical and often disparaging stance taken against local planning practitioners, and the clear incompatibility between this vision of the city and that promoted both by the ideology of separate racial development and the private developers of suburbs and shopping malls,[3] meant that the University of Cape Town position was found to be unacceptable. However, as the activity of planning became more highly politicized in the late 1980s, and as issues such as the location of lower-income communities were increasingly challenged, many establishment planners found it opportune to consider alternatives. The University of Cape Town position on city form, well-honed and based on a fully argued critique of existing city form, represented a politically acceptable alternative.

The emergence of the 'Metropolitan Development Framework'

The suggestion made at the 22 October meeting of the Regional Development Strategy Steering Committee, that the proposals of the Urban Problems Research Unit of the University of Cape Town should be presented at the next meeting, was taken up. I presented the particular framing of the physical problems of Cape Town which had been developed in the Unit, emphasizing the point that the planning problems of Cape Town were not a result of its size and growth (as previously argued in the official Guide Plan), but of its physical structure. I then put forward a set of spatial principles to guide the growth, reconstruction and reintegration of the metropolitan area. While the earlier work of the Unit had been cautious about portraying this alternative as a means of 'normalizing' the apartheid city, it was now clearly strategic to do so, and I placed some emphasis on the fact that it offered a way to redress the spatial distortions caused by the apartheid system. In doing so I probably helped to fuel the (clearly problematic) position which was to persist for some time to come, that the spatial distribution of resources and facilities in the city was largely a result of the political system and could be addressed differently under a new political dispensation. However, in November 1990, this line of argument was likely to win support, and in fact there were no dissenting voices after my presentation.

This is not, however, to suggest that the land search and multi-nodal city adherents were convinced. Not only did this work persist both within the Regional Services Council and the Provincial Administration, but the adoption of the Urban Problems Research Unit principles by the Regional Development Strategy Steering Committee was to draw a heated protest from the representative of the conservative Stellenbosch Branch of the Regional Services Council – the body administering the area to the immediate east of metropolitan Cape Town. In a strongly worded letter (RSC file 1991) the Council planner claimed that blaming the problems of Cape Town on the Group Areas Act and apartheid was a 'one-sided, blinded approach, and an oversimplification'. He argued that the problems of Cape Town were due to the physical constraint provided by the Table Mountain chain in the west and the mountain range to the east, together with the centralization of opportunities in the eccentrically located central business district (CBD). This site, he argued, could in no way accommodate the growing population, and it was necessary to decentralize the population along the lines of the old METPLAN idea of nodal development. Clearly the way in which the spatial problems of Cape Town were framed could lead to very different spatial solutions.

Even planners within the Regional Services Council, however, could increasingly disregard positions such as these. During 1991 and 1992 the country was moving into the negotiations phase of the political transition. In November of 1991 there was an agreement between the main political parties to start talks, and in December nineteen parties attended the Convention for a Democratic South Africa (CODESA) in Kempton Park, Johannesburg. In early 1992, National Party leader de Klerk obtained a mandate from white voters to continue with the process of reform and work towards a new constitution for the country. In the meantime more legal pillars of apartheid had come down: in June 1991 the Group Areas Act, the Natives Land Act, the Separate Amenities Act, and the Population Registration Act were scrapped.

Back in the November (1990) meeting of the Regional Development Strategy Steering Committee, however, Cape Town City Council planner de Tolly had been concerned that a regional development strategy for Cape Town should not take a purely physical form. His arguments that a growth management approach demanded both spatial and policy ideas met with agreement, and a small working group (including de Tolly and myself) was set up to draft a Framework Document which would set out the elements of a growth management strategy. By May of 1991 a draft document was produced which recommended that policies be formulated in terms of six 'frameworks': spatial, economic, environmental, social, legal and institutional. The document also argued that process was as important as the product in any planning exercise, and that the work of the Committee could go no further without consideration being given to the issue of participation. It was this issue which now threatened to stall the metropolitan planning process completely, not so much because of the arguments in the Framework Document (which had, after all, been made a number of times before), but because it was becoming increasingly obvious to the Regional Services Council planners that the days of imposing plans on communities without consultation were over. Unless this planning process could gain a measure of legitimacy, it was 'dead in the water'.

The Regional Services Council planners were not the only group to come to this realization. Cape Town City Council planners working on the municipal structure plan, metropolitan transport planners working on a transport strategy, and WESGRO, which had initiated an economic planning process for Cape Town, had all been grappling with the problem of how to achieve effective participation. It was still a relatively new concept, even for the 'liberal' Cape Town Council, as de Tolly recalled:

> you must remember that in the early 1980s you were not allowed, as a staff person working for the City [Council], to get into participation until the Committee had actually approved the report for distribution. Not allowed!

I came back from Toronto which was absolutely horizontal, open, transparent, everything, to an environment where you could not speak with the public . . .

(Interview 4 1999)

Communities had, moreover, been critical of the way in which they had been approached to participate in four separate, but clearly overlapping, planning initiatives. The idea of a conference, at which the four planning initiatives could be presented to community, union and non-governmental organizations, was originally sparked off during consultation processes conducted by the consultants busy with the South East Structure Plan (the poorest part of the city), when communities argued that the exercise should be seen in the wider context of planning for the city as a whole.

The result was the landmark[4] Caledon Conference, held in June of 1991, and named after the small Western Cape town in which it took place. It was well attended by community, union and political organizations. Representing the ANC was Basil Davidson, a one-time University of Cape Town planning student, keenly interested in how local planning officials were responding to the demands for a different planning philosophy, and destined to play an important role in the metropolitan planning process, both at the Caledon Conference and thereafter.

Inexplicably, the Cape Town Regional Services Council planners presented only their work on the sub-regional structure plans and land identification and said nothing about the Regional Development Strategy Committee. The reasons for this decision can only be guessed at, but as Theunissen was later to admit, 'it was a mistake' (Interview 1 1998). The Regional Services Council was taken to task by the community groupings, with Davidson as the main spokesperson, for trying to pre-empt broader-scale planning initiatives by going ahead with local-scale planning. They were instructed to halt all work on sub-metropolitan structure plans, to direct the land identification consultants to search for smaller pieces of land guided by a normative planning framework, and to focus their efforts instead on an overall plan for post-apartheid Cape Town. This plan was to be termed the Metropolitan Development Framework, or the MDF, and had to be undertaken *jointly* by the Cape Town City Council and the Regional Services Council, a clear message that the legitimacy of the Regional body was low. Both the Cape Town City Council and the Regional Services Council were further committed to prioritizing job creation and to liaise with community groups in all further planning exercises. A representative forum of community groups was set up (termed the Progressive Development Forum) to effect this liaison.

These instructions were taken seriously by the Regional Services Council and moves were made to act on them immediately. The balance of power had clearly swung, to some extent at least, away from the tall institutional offices of central Cape Town and towards the rubbish-strewn and violence-wracked townships and informal settlements of the Cape Flats. The Regional Development Strategy Committee was renamed the MDF Interim Committee (Interim, because it was recognized that a plan could only be considered final once it had been approved by 'the people'). New consultants were appointed to take forward the work of devising an MDF. This was to be a significant step. The firm of consultants appointed differed considerably in character from those which had been appointed by the Regional Services Council in the past: a large, liberal firm, many of whose staff had been trained at the University of Cape Town planning school, and who could be expected to bring into the MDF the particular approach to planning which was now on the ascendancy. The move did not, however, please the Cape Town City Council planners, who saw in the popularly imposed demand for a joint planning venture the chance to reassert their influence in the realm of metropolitan planning. De Tolly was to comment (Interview 2 1998) that the appointment of the consultants had gone ahead without their consent, and without taking into account the extensive and superior planning skills within the planning department of the Cape Town City Council. But for the Regional Services Council, the appointment of these particular consultants, on their payroll, allowed them to retain some of the balance of power *vis-à-vis* the local authority. It was a move which was to cause extensive conflict between the planning partners in the future.

Taking forward the mandate of the Caledon Conference

The rest of 1991 and most of 1992 saw little progress on the MDF. With the mandate of the Caledon Conference, the Regional Services Council planners and the consultants felt able to make a start on the substantive work of the met-ropolitan plan, but they were not keen to take it too far without reporting back to the Progressive Development Forum (PDF). This proved to be a serious obstacle, however. Meeting after meeting was set up with the PDF, in order to present to them the progress with the MDF, but meetings were either cancelled, or community representatives arrived to declare that they did not have a mandate. Theunissen (Interview 1 1998) felt that the reasons lay in the lack of legitimacy of the Regional Services Council and the lack of capacity within the community organizations. This perception is probably correct. Regional Ser-vices Councils were, by this stage, regarded as highly discredited bodies that were functioning as an instrument to prop up racially separate local authorities. As far as community organizations were concerned, capacity was low: many had lost leadership to the umbrella political organizations and the various negotiat-ing forums, and the turbulent conditions in the townships made proper organi-zation and mandating procedures very difficult. They were also finding it difficult to come to terms with a new mode of struggle, and with the shift from an oppositional role to a developmental role which this implied. Metropolitan planning was a new and different site of political engagement, and the inher-ently non-collaborationist nature of Western Cape politics meant that organi-zations embraced the developmental role with far greater hesitancy than they had in other parts of the country (Interview 5 1999).

The MDF Interim Committee continued to meet regularly during this period, mainly to receive reports of the repeated efforts to get community approval, and to debate the issue of the overlapping work on land identification within the Province, which had proceeded with apparently little concern for community opinion.[5] Much of the work which was taking place at this time was on the design of a planning process, using facilitator David Shandler who had been appointed to the project in 1991. This proved to be a major undertaking. Using the Harvard Business School strategic management approach they produced 'such an intricate design process. You must have seen it – columns of activities which were running in parallel with time frames. We spent about a year designing that process' (Interview 5 1999).

With the PDF clearly a failure, both the Cape Town City Council and the Regional Services Council attempted to arrange their own participation process, but these were limited and one-off affairs. One meeting with community-based organizations (in May 1992) attracted two ANC members, four civic representatives (from the South African National Civics Organization – SANCO), two trade union representatives and one local civic representative. The squatter communities were notable by their absence, and the rest of the 43 people at the meeting were local planning officials, consultants and representatives from NGOs. A SANCO representative at the meeting pointed out that the City Council and Regional Services Council did not have the required legitimacy to take forward a metropolitan planning process, and suggested the linking of the process to a new, independent, representative forum under discussion at that stage: the yet-to-be-named Western Cape Economic Development Forum. This possibility had already been proposed to the Regional Services Council planners by facilitator David Shandler, who was also facilitator for the Forum process, and it met with their interest. It appeared to offer the only real opportunity to produce a plan which would not meet with immediate community rejection, and they and others at the meeting endorsed this idea. How the planning officials of the City Council and Regional Services Council attempted to legitimize their plan through the Western Cape Economic Development Forum is the subject of the next chapter.

Conclusion

What becomes evident in this chapter is how the long-standing discourse coalition which accepted the spatial problem of Cape Town as its excessive size, and the spatial solution as one of deconcentration into racially defined nodes, is challenged by a new, emerging discourse which rejects the proposition that Cape Town is too large, and argues instead that what is required is internal spatial restructuring to achieve a compact, higher-density and spatially integrated city. The story-line of the new discourse also differs in terms of its assertion that spatial change needs to be supported by change in non-spatial arenas, although quite how spatial and non-spatial intervention should relate to each other is not addressed.

The spatial forms promoted by the two discourses are diametrically opposed: outward development is countered by inward development, and separation of both land uses and racial groupings is countered by integration, and mixed and compact development. But there are also important commonalities. Both discourses are essentially modernist: both are based on the assumption that it is possible to envision an alternative and more desirable future, and to achieve this future. And both, as discourses produced by urban planning professionals, conceptualize space as an element of reality that can be objectified and manipulated, to particular social and economic ends. These understandings about planning had been present in the planning discourse which prevailed in the apartheid years (see Chapter 1), and they remained unchallenged by the new discourse.

Given the apparent importance of racial segregation to the overall apartheid project, the fragile nature of the pre-existing discourse coalition is evident, and perhaps surprising. The replacement of one spatial form with another presents itself as a far less conflictual issue (for the planners, at least) than the question of whether the planning process should be controlled by the metropolitan or the municipal authority. Real material concerns relating to the potential to exercise power, and questions of status and even potentially individual income, are bound up with this question of control of the planning process, making it a particularly strategic issue for the planners concerned. How conflict over the question of controlling the process becomes intertwined with differing interpretations of the new discourse is taken up in later chapters.

Thus, the process by which the new spatial planning discourse is inserted into the ongoing planning work of the Regional Services Council can be described as largely circumstantial. There is no grand imperative, no directives from 'above', no point at which a 'new truth' is embraced, and no inevitability about the proposition and acceptance of a different spatial model. Events could just as easily have taken a different turn. Much depended on the actions of Cape Town City Council planner, de Tolly, who through lobbying action, conference organizing and attendance at meetings (sometimes unofficially) raised the possibility of an alternative discourse. Much also depended on Regional Services Council planner, Theunissen, who made space (on meeting agendas, for example) for the new discourse to be heard, even though work more closely associated with the previous discourse – the search for land for low-income housing – continued under his direction. Much depended as well on the presence of particular academics at the local university, and their development of a new story-line which eventually came to resonate with that produced by political opposition movements. Terms such as 'integration', 'one-city' and 'redistribution' could circulate between spatial planning and political discourses and give an appearance of unity between the two – allowing a strategic political positioning of those planners who chose to adopt the new discourse. For the planners of the Regional Services Council, adoption of the new planning discourse potentially allowed them a better chance of continuing to exercise power over the process of metropolitan planning, and the productive value of this strategy became clear in subsequent years.

3 Legitimating the plan

The Western Cape Economic Development Forum

Between 16 June 1989 (the start of the metropolitan planning process) and 1992, the attitude of planning officials within the Regional Services Council towards the issue of public participation in planning had been radically transformed. At the 16 June meeting, the chair of METPLAN had proposed that a metropolitan structure plan be drawn up and approved in terms of the minimum requirements of the 1985 Land Use Planning Ordinance of the Cape Province (RSC file 1989c). This Ordinance, still in effect today, provides for a structure plan to be drawn up by a local authority and then made available for 'inspection and the lodging of objections or the making of representations ... at the office of such a local authority' (section 4(5)). The plan and any objections received must then be forwarded to the Provincial Administrator (section 4(6)) who can approve or reject the structure plan. Usually the availability of the plan for inspection, in the local authority offices, was advertised in the local newspapers, carried in small print and at the back of the paper.[1] Clearly it would have to be an alert, literate and informed public to take advantage of the opportunity for participation offered by this legislation.

Yet only two and half years later, the planners of the Regional Services Council had reached the conclusion that the preparation of a metropolitan plan could not proceed without the sanction and involvement of both community-based organizations and private sector bodies in metropolitan Cape Town. And until a process could be established through which this involvement could be secured, all work on the plan was to be labelled clearly as 'interim'. Even consultants working on the Regional Services Council sub-regional structure plans were instructed to start again, and advised to follow a 'strategic planning process' in which public participation was a central element of the planning process right from the start (RSC file 1992b).

The sanction and involvement of community and private sector stakeholders in the metropolitan planning process was ultimately achieved through inserting the planning process into a newly established regional development forum, set up in order to formulate and strategize a common economic and social vision for Cape Town. On the surface, at least, it would appear that all the preconditions were in place to ensure the most open and democratic planning process yet experienced in Cape Town's planning history. But was it? Before examining the details of the 'forum period' of metropolitan planning, it is necessary to review the broader context within which this experience was taking place.

The transition to a liberal democracy in South Africa

The attempt by the Regional Services Council and the Cape Town City Council to subject the emerging metropolitan plan to a thorough public participation process coincided with the period of national-level negotiations between the ruling National Party and the ANC, which ultimately took South Africa through a political transition and into democratic elections in April 1994.

Linz and Stepan (1996) argue that the nature of any political transition is fundamentally affected by the characteristics of the previous regime. Transition in South Africa fits their categorization of an authoritarian government (operating in a context of a robust civil society, a functioning legal system and state bureaucracy, and an institutionalized economy) which faces a crisis of legitimacy and an unavoidable demand for the extension of democratic rights. The initiation of the process of transition, in such circumstances, results not from a willingness on the part of the ruling group to share or transfer political power, but from the challenge offered by opposition forces. This challenge is such that it becomes clear to at least elements of the authoritarian regime that piecemeal reform is unacceptable and the extension of democratic rights is the only alternative to political and economic collapse. Also typical of this type of transition, however, is a political opposition which lacks the strength to overthrow the government and take political power by force. The usual outcome of such a stalemate situation is that pacts are entered into between regime moderates and opposition moderates, both of which are able to contain their respective hard-liners.

In the case of South Africa's transition, the ruling National Party had managed to retain the support of the military, large sections of business and a significant proportion of the 'white' electorate.[2] The conservative elements within the ruling group had, during the 1980s, become increasingly organized and active, but they were sufficiently small, numerically, not to pose an overwhelming threat. However, efforts to contain the opposition campaign to 'make the country ungovernable' had stretched state resources to the limit, and international economic pressure, in the form of sanctions and the refusal to roll over government debt repayments, was seriously affecting the health of the economy and capital's political support (Ginsburg and Webster, in Ginsburg 1996). On the side of the opposition, mass mobilization had been achieved, but there were many organizational weaknesses and a resource shortage, and it was recognized that the government could not be forced into an unconditional surrender (Ginsburg 1996; Marais 1998). On this side, too, a range of different political positions was loosely grouped under the umbrella of 'the opposition'. The ANC leadership were able to present themselves as the moderates of the opposition: for many of the leadership the prime task of the transition was the achievement of a liberal democracy (Ginsburg 1996). More radical positions represented by the South African Communist Party and the trade union movement agreed to submerge (but not abandon) their specific demands and join a formal alliance under the leadership of the ANC.

Moderates on either side of the colour line shaped the South African transition, although the balance of power swung unevenly between the two. In December 1991, nineteen political parties attended the Convention for a Democratic South Africa (CODESA) and signed a declaration of intent. Six months later this process deadlocked when it appeared that the government may have been involved in underhand attempts to provoke violent conflict in Johannesburg townships. The ANC called for a resumption in mass action and the unions mobilized large-scale stayaways. In September 1992 the ANC and the government agreed to continue with talks, and the proposal from South African Communist Party leader Joe Slovo for a 'sunset clause', in which power would be shared between the ANC and the National Party for a period of five years after elections, paved the way for power-sharing in a new Government of National Unity. In June of 1993 an election date was agreed on, and in November an interim constitution was accepted, entrenching, in a final constitution, principles which could not be violated, and providing for a non-racial, multiparty democracy with a Bill of Rights and nine provincial governments. The latter was a coup for the National Party and the Inkatha Freedom Party, providing each with the opportunity subsequently to secure a provincial power base, the former in the Western Cape and the latter in Natal. The ANC also agreed to the protection of private property rights, a demand strongly voiced by capital, and to refrain from purging the civil service, thus leaving the old institutions largely intact (Marais 1998).

Economic change was not on the agenda. Significantly, the ANC had entered the negotiations process without an economic policy. The first attempts to shape an economic position for the opposition movement had come from the trade unions, in the form of a 1990 document by the COSATU Economic Trends group. This put forward a position which could generally be described as 'growth through redistribution', with an emphasis on meeting basic needs. This was met, according to Marais (1998), by a concerted effort on the part of organized business, and some individual firms, to promote a position more in line with international neo-liberal thinking: specifically, what emerged was a 'battery' of scenario presentations and policy documents, which promoted reduced government expenditure and subsidies, the relaxation of exchange controls, and privatization. COSATU persisted with its emphasis on redistribution, and finally made COSATU support of the ANC in the elections conditional on ANC acceptance of a redistributive economic policy. However, the policy document which finally emerged, and was accepted by the ANC just prior to the elections, was a diluted version of the original union position.

The Reconstruction and Development Programme (RDP 1994) can be described as 'being all things to all people', containing elements of neo-liberalism, Keynesianism and a 'people-driven' process. The basis of the programme lies in infrastructural investment, which, it is argued, will begin not only to meet basic needs but also to stimulate economic growth in areas such as the construction industry and domestic appliance manufacture. Funds for this public investment programme were to come, not from higher taxes, loans or reduced expenditure in other areas, but from a more 'rational and effective' way of using existing resources. While this kind of statement may have addressed the concerns of capital and those intent on promoting a 'freer' economic system, it also ensured that the RDP was to be severely hampered by resource constraints.

Significantly, the RDP also gave direction to city planning. Using the rhetoric which was becoming increasingly popular, not only amongst planners in Cape Town but in other cities as well, it argued for the need to break down 'apartheid geography' (RDP 1994, 83) through more compact cities and good public transport. It also argued for the need to 'redress the imbalances in infrastructure, transport and basic services', to 'promote access to employment opportunities and urban resources', to promote 'densification and unification of the urban fabric' and to locate housing near to employment opportunities (RDP 1994, 86). Those planners in Cape Town's metropolitan planning process, who were aligning themselves with the emergent spatial position, could now claim that it was backed up by national policy.

Forums as arenas for debate and policy-making

The spirit of the national political transition process, characterized by negotiation, consensus and compromise, as well as strategizing and the building of new power bases, set the tone for the flurry of new policy-making in this period. All pre-existing policy was seen to be tainted in some way by apartheid ideology, demanding new policies to be forged in almost every economic, social, infrastructural and institutional sphere. The primary institutional vehicle for this policy-making was the stakeholder-based forum. Forums usually consisted of representatives of the main stakeholder groupings, including government authorities, business, communities, and non-governmental organizations, and were seen as arenas in which new policies could be negotiated for implementation in the post-election period.[3]

Policy forums emerged from a situation in which the government retained responsibility for the taking and implementing of decisions, but recognized that it lacked the legitimacy to do this. By participating in forums, the 'statutory organizations', as official structures were called, were able to influence the form of policies without actually conceding power and, potentially, able to co-opt opponents. The 'non-statutory organizations' saw forums as a way of ensuring that the National Party did not use public resources to boost their own pre-election popularity, that credit for any project implementation accrued equally to all parties, and that policy debates were hammered out prior to the election – allowing immediate implementation thereafter (Shubane and Shaw 1993). At the local level, some non-statutory organizations also tried to link the issue of improving service provision to longer-term demands for physical and financial restructuring and redistribution across the city (Turok 1994). These forums were therefore expected to play a role which went beyond that of just debate. As such they would conform to what Bryson and Crosby (1996) term 'arenas' for shared-power situations, in that they could distribute access to participation in policy-making and could potentially change economic and political relations. Forums, in terms of Bryson and Crosby's descriptive framework, are conceptually separable from arenas and act primarily as places for the creation and communication of meaning.

At the national level, forums were engaged in policy-making in the spheres of economic policy, housing, transport, drought relief, violence and peace, electricity, food and nutrition, education and training, youth development, water and sanitation, and local government. There were also tripartite forums, involving labour, business and government, concerned with the restructuring of particular industries (Shubane and Shaw 1993). Particularly important, for the purposes of this discussion, were the economic development forums which emerged at regional and local level from 1992 onwards. During 1992 and 1993, seven regional development forums emerged in different parts of the country: all were considered to be 'home-grown' in the sense that they had emerged as a result of local initiatives, although in most cases lobby groups such as the Consultative Business Movement and IDASA (Institute for a Democratic Alternative in South Africa) had led the way in their formation; most were concerned primarily with economic and development issues; and most were seen as inclusive debating and policy-shaping forums, rather than implementing agencies, for local economic development. It would appear that business interests were particularly concerned about being seen as role-players in an arena in which, in the past, regional development had been almost entirely state-directed, business had had little influence, and policy had been based largely on the principle of state subsidies to particular areas (Bekker and Humphries 1993).

The Western Cape Economic Development Forum (WCEDF), launched in December 1992 after an eight-month negotiation period, was considered to be one of the more successful and inclusive of the regional development forums. It certainly opened up a major opportunity for the Regional Services Council and the Cape Town City Council, which saw it as a vehicle through which a mandate could be gained for their faltering metropolitan planning process. Quite what kind of mandate it was able to deliver, and how this shaped the planning process, needs now to be considered.

Establishing the Western Cape Economic Development Forum

In the Western Cape, business interests had for some time attempted to influence the course of regional economic policy, via an investment promotion and business lobby group called WESGRO. WESGRO describes itself as an association for the promotion of economic growth in the Western Cape. It was established during the 1980s as a non-profit company and was supported by regional government, leading private companies and chambers of business (WESGRO 1992). In 1990 WESGRO launched a project entitled Growing the Cape, aimed at collecting information on the Cape economy and identifying trends and opportunities. As part of this process it had made contact with a range of other groupings, including labour and community-based organizations, and had presented its initiative to the Caledon Conference of 1991 (see Chapter 2) in the hope of receiving a wider mandate for its work. In April 1992 WESGRO organized a large conference at which it planned to feed back the results of its work and gauge the level of support for its findings. The conference was attended by over 300 people, including representatives of the 'non-statutory organizations': the future economic development of Cape Town was apparently viewed as important by a wide range of groupings.

One of the main initiators of the WESGRO project, economist Wolfgang Thomas, subsequently explained how the idea of a forum emerged from this conference (Interview 6 1998). The organizers of the Growing the Cape project felt that the initiative should not stop at the production of a document: South Africa's Leading Edge?, as it was termed. The chair of one of the conference breakaway groups was primed to suggest that the process be taken further, and the idea of a forum evidently emerged from the subsequent discussion. The idea was put to the conference as a whole, and accepted. A similar initiative had recently been started by the Consultative Business Movement (representing larger companies in Cape Town), as it was doing in other parts of the country, but it was persuaded to buy in to the WESGRO plan.

The Forum was thus clearly not a 'grassroots' initiative in Cape Town, given that the idea and the initial organizational steps had been taken by organized business rather than by the labour movement or civic associations. Nonetheless, the spirit of the national negotiation process was pervasive and, over the next few months, ideas for a forum structure were put in place which would be difficult to fault in terms of their intentions to create as democratic and inclusive a process as possible.

Immediately after the Growing the Cape conference of April 1992, an interim steering committee was formed. It had representatives from organized labour (COSATU), business, civic associations (SANCO), local authorities and the provincial administration, the state-initiated regional development advisory committee, WESGRO, and the ANC (the only political party to be involved). In a 'terms of reference' document produced by this steering committee in September 1992, the motivation for the Forum was set out. In tune with policy documents emerging from the various national-level forums, it began by distancing itself from past apartheid policies which had 'systematically excluded the majority of the people of the region from full participation in the various levels of regional administration and its economy' (EDF 1992, 1). Then, still in tune with national thinking, it emphasized the need to consider both economic growth and redistribution. The Forum was motivated as a way of bringing together important actors and constituencies in the region to devise development strategies and monitor their implementation (the Forum was thus seen as more than a talk-shop), to 'empower' community groups, and to enhance the 'legitimacy and effectiveness' of development strategies.

Membership of the Forum was to be drawn from the major organizations and interest groups having an interest in regional (not local) development: the region in this case was defined to cover the area under the jurisdiction of the Regional Services Council, and could be considered to include the broader metropolitan area. Four categories of organizations, which would have voting rights on the Forum, were defined: labour bodies, business bodies, civic institutions and political parties, and local and regional authorities. Each of these four categories would be represented by no more than 20 persons. Two categories of organizations would have non-voting rights: development, service and funding bodies with 14 members, and central government departments and parastatals, with 11 members. Other organizations could apply to join the Forum, and a 'credentials' committee would screen these applications.

The Forum was to operate at three levels. The highest level of decision-making would take place in the Forum plenary on which all member bodies would be represented. The plenary was to elect a steering committee of 16 people, four from each of the voting constituencies. This would meet four times a year. The chair of the steering committee would rotate amongst the four groups, with each group nominating its chair. This body would meet monthly. The third level of the Forum was made up of six commissions, each to be concerned with a specific sectoral issue. Ultimately these were: the Development Strategy Commission, seen as a 'fast-track' overarching group which would establish a common 'vision' for the other commissions; the Urban Development Commission; Economic Growth and Restructuring; Rural and Agricultural Development; Short-Term Job Creation; and Education and Training. The terms of reference and focus of each of these commissions was to be approved by the plenary.[4]

A number of other provisions was agreed on which were aimed at making the workings of the Forum as democratic as possible. Decisions were to be reached through consensus, or only after this route had failed repeatedly, through an 80 per cent majority vote. Quorums had to be met for any decision-making. Communication could take place in any of the three major regional languages: English, Afrikaans and Xhosa. A Code of Conduct was adopted which required members to negotiate in a 'spirit of mutual trust', not to take action on issues on which consensus had not been reached, and to make information and knowledge freely available. Finally, the need for capacity building was recognized, and an extensive training course, mainly for people from community and labour organizations, was arranged during 1993. The Forum provided administrative support for the plenary, steering committee and the commissions.

Ultimately, enthusiasm for membership of the Forum was high and most invited organizations responded. There were also many applications from additional smaller groupings and NGOs, and from some private developers, to join. It is important, however, to ask what might have been the motivation for involvement on the part of the various groups, as this could make an important difference to the way in which established structures operated in reality.

Participants in the Forum

The strongest party in the Forum was, according to a member of the Forum executive, the labour movement, represented by COSATU (Interview 7 1998). At both national and local levels COSATU saw itself as the intellectual vanguard of the transition, concerned both with shop floor and wider social issues, and positioned to guard the interests of both workers and poorer communities. In the Forum they saw the opportunity to replicate, at the local level, the kind of role they were playing in the National Economic Forum which was the promotion of a national redistributive economic and social policy. They were, apparently, well-organized and disciplined in terms of taking forward mandated positions.

For those in government bodies at all levels, the achievement of a measure of legitimacy for state-initiated projects was a strong motivating factor. As one political commentator put it in 1993:

> It has become well-nigh impossible to discuss, plan or implement development in South Africa without engaging with, or at least having to take account of, civic associations. Civics have managed to become perceived as being able to strengthen, prevent or obstruct development initiatives.
>
> (Heymans 1993, 1)

Certainly government bodies were the most consistent attendees at meetings, although they were amongst the few groups who had the capacity to do this. As later events in the Urban Development Commission showed, the Forum potentially represented a convenient 'one-stop-shop' to gain a public mandate for government plans and projects of all kinds.

The impact of business upon the Forum was less clear. Thomas (Interview 6 1998), of WESGRO, did not see business as pushing any particular 'line' in terms of Forum policy, and indeed it may have been difficult for them to do this, as the interests of the various sectors of business were very diverse. Thomas felt that they were ambivalent about the importance of the Forum (after all, it had neither statutory powers nor much in the way of resources) and saw it primarily as an opportunity to network with other non-statutory groupings.

Certain civic and political groups (the ANC in the latter case) clearly did see the Forum as being of some importance, although their involvement was often constrained by capacity problems and by the ongoing violence and organizational difficulties in the townships, which inevitably occupied the bulk of any ANC meeting agenda (Interview 7 1998). But by the end of 1992 it was becoming clear that national-level negotiations would proceed and would probably result in democratic elections. Involvement in a Forum such as this gave the non-statutory organizations a chance to influence government spending in the run-up to elections, to make sure that credit for progressive actions fell where it was due, and to begin to direct post-election policy. As the SANCO representative argued:

All our membership lives in the townships and there is no work out there. People have to travel all the time to central points like Claremont. So we said, let's get the jobs out there. We want factories and security. We understood all those things.

(Interview 8 1999)

Seekings (1996) notes that at this stage civic associations, in particular, were increasingly participating in decision-making around development issues. Even in the post-1994 election period, civics were encouraged by their national leadership to retain control over local development issues, rather than cede them to the newly elected local authorities: this reflected a growing tension between the ANC and the civic movement over whether it was possible to distinguish between politics and development. It did not appear, however, that this was a tension which made itself felt amongst Forum representatives. The SANCO and ANC representatives worked closely together and comfortably stood in for each other at meetings (Interview 7 1998).

A further constraint was that the civic movement in Cape Town was divided along lines relating both to race and to urban permanence. The support base of the Cape Housing Action Committee (CAHAC) had always been concentrated in the 'coloured' townships, and while the South African National Civics Organization (SANCO) cut across racial groupings, it represented mainly people living in the formal township areas. The squatter groupings (under the Western Cape United Squatters Association – WECUSA) had not initially joined the Forum, despite a special delegation by members of the Forum executive to try to persuade them to do so. There had, for some time, been tensions (many of which had been instigated by state and police actions) among the residents of African townships, many of whom tended to be longer-standing residents of Cape Town with perhaps fewer ties to the rural areas, and residents of the informal settlements. This, together with the primary focus of WECUSA on issues of housing and land in the south-east sector of the metropolitan area, meant that they had not attended many of the workshops on metropolitan planning and economic issues. According to Davidson,[5] then executive member of the Western Cape ANC, they probably did not see much to be gained from participating in the Forum.[6] And when they did finally join, in 1994, they saw their role as essentially that of a 'watching brief' (Interview 7 1998). Thus the voices of the 'poorest of the poor' were not directly present on the Forum.

There was also no formal or informal National Party representation on the Forum. As one Forum participant explained:

I know the personalities now, after the event . . . and there was no National Party support. There was a definite distancing there. There was nobody really active in the Forum that could say I am a card-carrying National Party member. Whether that was by default or by design? . . . it wasn't by default, they don't do things by default. There was simply no advantage to be gained by participating in the Forum ... how would their electorate feel about it? Would they enhance their electoral position?

(Interview 9 1999)

The Forum's Urban Development Commission and the metropolitan plan

The end of Chapter 2 left the metropolitan planning process at a point where, in May 1992, meetings between the Regional Services Council and various community and business representatives made it clear that a way had to be found to gain broad legitimacy for the plan. The idea previously raised by the Regional Services Council's facilitator, and raised again at this meeting (specifically by a representative of the national civic organization, SANCO), was that the planning process should fall under the emergent Western Cape Economic Development Forum.

This clearly represented a major step for the current 'owners' of the planning process: the Regional Services Council and the Cape Town City Council. The proposal was that control of the planning process be handed over to a non-statutory body which (as became clear during the course of 1992) was to be set up in a way which was intended to allow equal power-sharing between the region's main stakeholders – community and political organizations, the unions, business, and local government. The possibility that the planning process would be 'hijacked' by one or more of these other groupings, who would then hold the Regional Services Council to a commitment to honour the outcome of a participatory process, certainly existed.

A very real concern about placing the prospective metropolitan plan under the new Forum was one of timing. There was a general recognition that it would still be some months before the Forum was properly constituted, and that the reaching of consensus on a plan might take a long time after that. For the representatives of political and community-based organizations attending the meeting with the Regional and City Councils (in May 1992), there was a worry that unilateral actions could be taken by government departments which might constrain future planning. The particular worry, expressed by Davidson, present at the meeting as an ANC representative, was that key parcels of well-located, publicly owned, empty land could be sold off, which would pre-empt attempts to make land available for low-income housing close to existing work opportunities. There was support for this from other civic and labour organizations which saw this as a serious issue, and a working group was established consisting of members of both statutory and non-statutory organizations, to make a proposal on how to link the metropolitan planning process to the Forum.

The first recommendation of this group, originating again with Davidson, was that a set of interim planning guidelines be produced and presented at a workshop to community-based and other organizations (RSC files 1992c). The task of preparing these guidelines fell to the Regional Services Council consultants, as this was seen essentially as part of the process of preparing a longer-term metropolitan plan.

Planning the interim

At this point in time, no real work had yet been done on the metropolitan development framework. There appeared to be general consensus amongst the Regional and City Council planning officials and the Regional Services Council consultants on the broad nature of the 'planning problem' in metropolitan Cape Town. This was the conception of the problem that had been accepted by the Regional Development Strategy Steering Committee in November 1990: that there were important problems relating to the physical form and structure of the metropolitan area (caused largely by the physical planning legacy of apartheid), but that there were also problems in environmental, economic and institutional arenas. To the extent that ideas about how to address these problems had been put forward, they had not moved much beyond the physical principles accepted by the Regional Development Strategy Steering Committee in 1990: that there was a need to integrate the 'divided city', to compact development and prevent sprawl, to focus on public transport and to allow for a greater mix of land uses.

During the rest of 1992 the consultants worked on a document first entitled 'Proposed Guidelines for Planning and Development in the Cape Metropolitan Area Prior to the Adoption of the MDF'. The Cape Town City Council planners rewrote most of it. It contained a problem statement, a statement of planning ethics, planning goals, a set of physical principles and some directives for short-term planning action. The document was circulated to a lengthy list of central and local government departments, service organizations and community and labour organizations for comment, and a large-scale workshop was held in November 1992 to receive feedback. Perhaps the most telling comment was that received from the Provincial Administration. Their letter pointed out that: 'As the guidelines are very general, they do not seem to be controversial and it is expected that more controversy will arise once more specific proposals are made' (Provincial Administration 1992). This was in fact the case. The document advocated a vision for metropolitan Cape Town based on notions of redistribution and sustainability, together with efficiency and accountability. In the particular political climate of the time (at the national level, compromise had just resulted in a power-sharing arrangement, to come into effect after the elections) the vision presented a 'middle of the road' approach which may have been difficult to counter.

At the well-attended November (1992) workshop, many of the points raised, particularly by the community and labour bodies, had to do with the political ownership of the planning process. There was a request that the Regional Services Council take their name off the front of the document, and that arrangements to place the process under the new Forum go ahead as speedily as possible. From the side of the central and provincial government departments, there was general support for the document, but concern that the development of public land would be frozen. This was, in retrospect, the key controversial issue: the NGO Development Action Group and COSATU (labour) wanted all decisions on the sale of public land referred to the new Forum, but state departments refused to commit themselves to this. By the third draft of this document, in June 1993, the statement on the sale of public land had been considerably softened. There was an injunction to 'act to keep future options open' and a reference to future guidelines which would be drafted by the Forum.

But while the Interim Guidelines document (as it came to be known) managed to avoid treading on any toes, it did, nonetheless, represent a major departure from any previous city-wide planning statement in Cape Town. The idea that planning action should be grounded in a set of ethics, and that these ethics should specifically articulate concerns for redistribution and environmental sustainability (recognizing that the interpretation of these terms can be wide) was new. Also new was the nature of the spatial principles set out. Acceptance of the concepts of compaction, intensification and integration was a clear indication that the multi-nodal, racially based, spatial model of the past, and as promoted in the official Guide Plans, had been sidelined.

Setting up and operating the Urban Development Commission

The Urban Development Commission was set up to be as open, inclusive and balanced in terms of its membership as was its parent body, the Western Cape Economic Development Forum. Drafts of its structure and terms of reference were well circulated amongst all stakeholders of the Forum during the latter part of 1992. It was agreed that an interim steering committee be set up, comprising representatives of the following: labour; business; civic and political organizations; local, regional and provincial government; central government and parastatals; and service organizations. The interim steering committee met on 2 March 1993. It elected Davidson as its chairman, and as its deputy chairman, Peter Tomalin, then Deputy Chief Director for Planning of the Regional Services Council. Decision-making was to take place in terms of the rules of consensus which applied to the Forum as a whole, and the Forum Code of Conduct applied to each commission as well. Davidson, as chair, was also on the steering committee of the Forum, and regular report-backs were required from the Commission to the Forum steering committee and plenary. All major Commission decisions and products had to be ratified by the Forum as a whole.

One of the main tasks of the Commission was to deal with the process of gaining consensus on the metropolitan spatial development framework. It is significant that earlier efforts to begin to deal with spatial planning in conjunction with issues of the economy, society, the environment and institutions, were halted by the allocation of specialized tasks to the various Commissions. In the process of setting up the Forum, spatial planning again became separated from its broader context, and was again viewed as an element to be manipulated in its own right.

Some members of the Urban Development Commission believed that the production of the metropolitan spatial development framework should be debated as widely as possible. To this end a number of large-scale workshops were organized. The first of these (in April 1993) was to ratify the Interim Guidelines document: 72 people from a wide range of organizations attended (this did not include SANCO or the squatter organizations) and gave comment, some in writing. In June 1993 the overarching fast-track Commission (the Development Strategy Commission) held a very large workshop of all Forum members to reach consensus on a vision for the future of the metropolitan area: written inputs were demanded from each stakeholder grouping, and these were to include a spatial vision as well as economic and social ones. These vision statements were to guide future work in all the Forum commissions. Then in August and September 1993 the Urban Development Commission tasked the Regional Services Council planning consultants with organizing a series of six workshops of about twenty people each, drawn from all stakeholder groupings. Each workshop went through a similar process of 'cognitive mapping': people were asked to identify those parts of the city they felt 'worked well' and those that did not, and this information was synthesized and reported back at a combined workshop. The purpose of this was to try to understand how different groups viewed the city and, ultimately, to define whose vision was being promoted. These ideas were incorporated into a document.

A year later, in August and September of 1994, the Urban Development Commission held two large, open workshops. Stakeholders were to come with their own proposals for future spatial metropolitan development, and with comments on the document produced by the consultants during the preceding year. An independent person, paid with funds raised independently by the Commission, was used to synthesize the results of the first workshop and present them to the second workshop for ratification. Areas of consensus and areas of difference were recorded.

Thus, by the end of 1994, it was possible for the Regional Services Council to claim that a spatial metropolitan development framework had been produced which had been subject to a very thorough and inclusive participation process, and which had a wide community, labour and business mandate. Certainly it would appear that every effort had been made to secure this mandate. However, to understand exactly what happened during this process requires a closer look at how power relations operated within and through the various structures and processes described above.

Conclusion

Processes occurring within institutions and organizations outside the realm of the metropolitan spatial planners begin, in this period, to influence more directly the actions of the planners themselves. The progress of negotiations between members of the ruling National Party and the ANC indicates that a change of government is likely, and that changes in policies, rules and resourcing strategies will follow. In particular, the 1994 ANC policy document, the Reconstruction and Development Programme, states the intention that there will be such changes in all aspects of government. The progress of national negotiations also lends 'weight' to political opposition groups operating at regional and local level. The expectation that individuals within these opposition groups will soon take up positions (perhaps in government) which will allow them to exercise greater power, means that the demands of these groups are taken more seriously. The demand by local civic and township-based organizations in Cape Town that they be involved in any official planning for the metropolitan area is not a new demand, but at this point in time the planning officials of the Regional Services Council consider it important to pay heed to it. It is this question of how to manage a participation process which stalls the planning process for many months, and eventually leads to agreement by the planners that, as an exercise in spatial planning, it should be taken forward under the Western Cape Economic Development Forum.

The insertion of the metropolitan planning process into the work of the Urban Development Commission of the Forum has a further important effect, and that is to assist in the building of a broader discourse coalition around the idea of an integrated, compact city form. The Forum itself is made up of a wide range of groupings, some of which had, in the past, been in direct conflict with each other – for example, business and trade union organizations, and civic associations and government officials. But in the context of the Forum, these groups are aligned and homogenized by what is perceived as a common concern with the future development of the metropolitan area. Emerging 'national' policy discourse as expressed in the Reconstruction and Development Programme, and by the range of national policy forums in operation, is an important informant to the work of the Forum. However, the common factor which secures the presence on the Forum of these groups is, I suggest, the idea that a locally specific trajectory of change could be formulated through a consensus-seeking process, and implemented.

It is this alignment of power relations in the context of the Forum which assists in the strengthening and widening of support for the compact city position. Through the various Forum workshops and meetings, individuals from a wide range of organizations and institutions (excluding representatives of the National Party, who do not participate in the Forum) are exposed to this particular discourse and the spatial plan, or map, for metropolitan Cape Town, which indicates how its aims are to be achieved. On paper, at least, there is now support from a wide range of stakeholder representatives on the Forum for the compact city position. The nature and potential strength of this support is explored in the next chapter.

4 'No-one disputed that there should be a physical plan . . . '

The participation process in practice

At the start of 1992 Regional Services Council planner Peter Tomalin had taken over the task of chairing the Metropolitan Development Framework Co-ordinating Working Group (MDF-CWG). This was the group which had been formed after the Caledon Conference of mid-1991 (see Chapter 2) and was made up of planning officials from the Regional and Cape Town City Councils, the Provincial Administration, the Regional Services Council planning consultants, and a representative from the Chamber of Commerce. Tomalin was a graduate of the University of Cape Town planning school in its early days. He had since worked in local government for some twenty years, mainly in the Regional Services Council and its predecessor (the Cape Divisional Council). He has been described by other planning officials in metropolitan Cape Town as 'politically astute': that is, he understood planning to be a politically imbued arena and used this understanding to get things done without alienating other major players in the game. At this point in time he held the position of Deputy Chief Director for Planning, answerable to an engineering department head.[1]

In 1992 Tomalin found himself faced with a serious dilemma. On the one hand it was clear that the metropolitan planning process could not proceed in any meaningful way without the agreement and involvement of non-statutory organizations in metropolitan Cape Town. These organizations had, moreover, demanded that the planning process be placed under the control of the new Urban Development Commission of the Forum and that the Regional Services Council even remove its name from documents which were produced as part of the process. On the other hand, Tomalin was aware that the conservative Council body, with its appointed National Party chair, would never agree to the handing over of the planning process to the Forum (Interview 1 1998). Despite the fact that political negotiations were proceeding at the national level, and that it was becoming clear that some kind of power-sharing arrangement with the ANC was on the cards, the National Party appeared to feel sufficiently confident about its power base in the Western Cape not to have to make major concessions to the political opposition.

Tomalin took the decision to walk a highly risky tightrope between his Council and the non-statutory organizations. He felt that if he officially described what was happening as the placing of the public participation of the metropolitan development framework 'under the auspices' of the Urban Development Commission, rather than 'under its control', then he had an official loophole. In any event, he felt it wise to keep the whole matter off Council agendas if possible. However, in the eyes of the Urban Development Commission, the planning process was indeed being placed under their control: the MDF-CWG was in fact to become a Commission working group, answerable directly to the Commission and Forum plenaries. It was, therefore, entirely possible that Tomalin and the Regional Services Council could lose control of the process. But reflecting on this possibility, Tomalin said he felt 'a fair degree of confidence that this would not happen' (Interview 10 1998). He proved to be correct.

Cracks in the coalition

Proposals for the structure and functions of the Urban Development Commission were prepared by a small group of representatives from statutory and non-statutory organizations during the course of 1992.[2] There were a great many issues which the group, and others involved with establishing the Forum, thought should be dealt with by the Commission: housing, land, services and infrastructure, transport, the environment, and, of course, land-use planning in the form of the metropolitan development framework. The fact that interim planning guidelines were being developed also meant that the Commission needed to monitor all larger-scale planning projects to check that they conformed to the guidelines. Then there were requests from authorities that the Commission give sanction to, or participate in, their own larger-scale planning projects. There were at least two requests, at different times, from the Regional Services Council that the Commission become involved in the production of its sub-regional structure plans, and a request from the long-time consultant to the Provincial Administration that the Commission comment on his proposals for a project to identify land for low-income housing – an issue not yet relinquished by the Province. This, together with the fact that some 54 Forum members wanted to be part of the Commission, necessitated the formation of a number of working groups and the multi-tiered structure described in Figure 4.1. It was a structure which was to be very demanding in terms of stakeholder representation, and it soon became apparent that it was only those organizations with resources and person-power which could sustain input at all the various levels.

The working group in charge of proposing the Commission structure also recommended that where working-group tasks were already being carried out by an existing project team or technical committee, that they continue to play this role. The working group was recognizing that the Forum would not be able to employ its own consultants and that voluntary members could not do detailed planning or technical work either. What this did mean, however, was that work on the metropolitan development framework would be carried forward by the Regional Services Council's MDF-CWG, through its already appointed

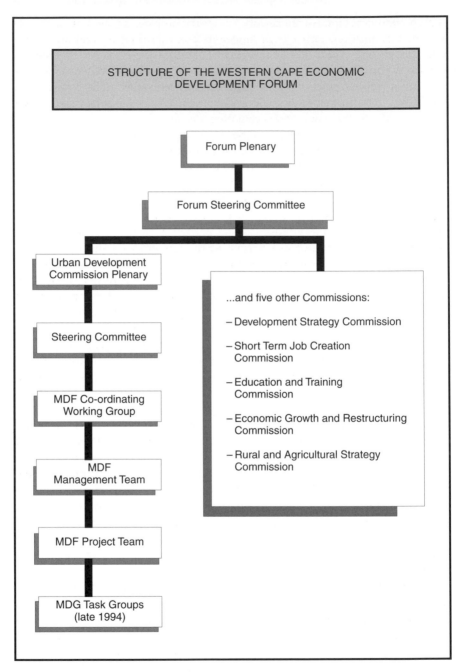

Figure 4.1 The structure of the Western Cape Economic Development Forum and the Urban Development Commission.

consultants. Furthermore, the Interim Guidelines document, already in a well-advanced state prior to the formation of the Forum, was to be accepted as providing a guiding vision to all future work on the metropolitan development framework. There was thus to be a high degree of continuity between the planning ideas and individuals who had been in place prior to the establishment of the Forum, and the ideas and individuals that were taking forward the process under the Urban Development Commission.

The decision had been made at the Forum level, prior to its establishment, that each Commission would pick up the costs of its own operation, and it was expected that stakeholder representatives would be remunerated by their organizations for work done on the Forum. This was not a problem for government officials, but it was a major problem for many of the other organizations, and a great deal of work was done voluntarily. Davidson, the chair, was in a particularly difficult position: his employer at the time, the NGO Development Action Group, was not prepared to pay him for time spent on the Commission, and paid him on a time-related basis for his work at the NGO (Interview 7 1998). Chairing the Commission was an extremely demanding role and demands on his time meant that Davidson could often not attend meetings or fulfil functions. Tomalin, as deputy chair, was generally able to step in for him.

With all these parameters in place, the Urban Development Commission was finally able to hold its inaugural meeting in May 1993. Discussions on the formation of working groups began, and it was confirmed that the Regional Services Council's MDF-CWG would become the Commission's metropolitan development framework working group, with the addition of civic, labour and NGO representation.

At the first plenary of the Commission, however, it became clear that it had bitten off more than it could chew (UDC minutes 1993). It was already being swamped with requests from local authorities and private developers to comment on, and agree to, various projects. Commission members argued that they could not act as a glorified local authority nor could they be used to bypass public participation processes. Nonetheless, responding to these proposals seemed to be one way to have an immediate impact on urban development, and so dealing with these requests began to occupy much of the Commission's time and energy. The metropolitan plan was by no means the central focus of Commission work.

Meanwhile, in the MDF-CWG, tensions were beginning to emerge between members. The NGO representative on the group was Kim Van Deventer, a planner who had graduated from the University of Cape Town planning school a few years before. Her intended role was to advise the union and civic representatives on the committee, but in May 1993 both organizations had made it clear that they did not have the capacity to send people to MDF-CWG meetings, and that Van Deventer should represent them. She agreed on condition that she met with the organizations frequently to report back and receive mandates (Interview 11 1998). A principled and outspoken person, Van Deventer was concerned that the balance of power on the committee was not even.

Tomalin chaired the meetings, and the rest of the membership was made up of four Regional Services Council planners and their consultants, two Cape Town City Council planners (one of whom was de Tolly, introduced in Chapter 1), two metro transport planners, the Provincial Administration consultant, a Chamber of Commerce representative, Davidson (as chair of the Commission), the facilitator Shandler, and Van Deventer herself. With the absence of the civic and labour organizations from the group (and an ongoing lack of interest on the part of squatter organizations) it was heavily biased in favour of the statutory organizations and their consultants.

In June 1993, discussions between Cape Town City Council planners and Van Deventer led to a restructuring of the group to try to spread the distribution of power. Using as a justification the need to speed up the process of producing a metropolitan development framework before the elections in early 1994, the facilitator proposed a management team with single representatives from the Regional and City Councils, business and the community and political organizations. This implied a more even numerical balance among the various stakeholder groupings. Under the management team was to be a project team consisting of the Regional Services Council consultants, plus other planners who had expertise in metropolitan issues, plus other subject specialists (MDF-CWG minutes 1993a). This could be interpreted as an attempt to shift the monopoly on document production away from the Regional Services Council consultants and to allow greater influence by the Cape Town City Council planners (hence the emphasis on the need for expertise in metropolitan planning), and possibly also the NGO planners.[3] Van Deventer, at this June meeting, emphasized that any work produced by this new structure would have to be endorsed by the Commission, which would in turn give the MDF-CWG a mandate to proceed. This was certainly the Commission's view of how lines of authority should be operating. It was not the official Regional Services Council view, but nonetheless Van Deventer's statement drew no objections and was minuted accordingly.

Tomalin may have been concerned that the restructuring of the membership of the MDF-CWG would shift control of the process away from the Regional Services Council. But he certainly did not express a worry about this, and in fact a month later it was becoming clear that the restructuring had made little difference to the status quo. The management team was being chaired by the Regional Services Council consultant (the head of the firm, in this case), and a complaint routed via the facilitator, that his management style be tighter and that he should follow accepted directions, may have indicated that other members of the management team were not satisfied that they were fully involved (MDF-CWG minutes 1993b). A further complaint, via the facilitator, that specialist skills on the project team had not yet been broadened, also indicated that work production was still largely in the hands of the original consultants. As Madell, then one of these consultants, pointed out:

> We had the working group (the MDF-CWG), but then we had an inner working group. I don't know if the others knew that we were doing that.

['*Yes we did*', *wrote Van Deventer after reading this quote*.] So the real working group would meet once a week, but then we had this other group, which was the consultants (we shouldn't have met, you know), and this is where the differences came in. We were spending seven days a week on it, we took over the third floor (in the consultants' office), and of course we came with preconceived ideas, by the time the real working group met.

(Interview 3 1999)

Van Deventer, meanwhile, was concerned that her inputs were not being taken seriously, and Davidson, the Commission chair, had to intervene. His warning that the labour and civic groups were unhappy that Van Deventer was not being heard, and therefore felt uneasy about the product and the process (MDF-CWG minutes 1993c), subtly reminded members that legitimation of the planning process still relied on a buy-in from the non-statutory organizations. The fact that the next meeting of the MDF-CWG was arranged, for the first time, to take place at the NGO offices rather than at those of the Regional Services Council, may well have been an attempt to reassure the non-statutory groups that they were still important.

It was at the November (1993) meetings of the MDF-CWG that tensions really threatened to stall the process entirely. The tensions were not, as may have been expected, between the statutory and non-statutory groupings, but between the old adversaries, the City Council and Regional Services Council planners. It was precipitated by the tabling of the first draft of what was to become the metropolitan development framework. The document was entitled: 'The Way Forward, Interim MDF Draft Report No. 1', and had been produced largely by the Regional Services Council consultants. Cape Town City Council planner de Tolly was adamant that the document was lacking not only in terms of structure, focus and style, but also that he had fundamental philosophical problems with its contents.

There are differences of opinion as to the basis of this dispute. Regional Services Council planners and the consultants felt this was an expression of the old rivalry between the Regional and Cape Town City Councils over which authority was best placed to undertake metropolitan planning. Cape Town City Council planners argued that their differences were substantive and philosophical. Van Deventer tried to explain it as follows:

you had people coming from that structure planning world and people (the Cape Town City Council and NGO planners) from another world that had not ever produced a structure plan and couldn't see the logic of that approach. A lot of time people were missing each other in discussions . . . There was an institutional culture clash between the Regional Services Council and the Cape Town City Council . . . Then there were real personality problems, some of it was power-politiking, some of it was personalities not getting on.

(Interview 12 1999)

The Cape Town City Council planners were not disagreeing with the principles and general spatial ideas set out in 'The Way Forward', but rather with how these principles and spatial elements should be presented graphically and how they should be taken forward to the stage of implementation. In fact many of the spatial elements in the plan (the urban edge, activity corridors, compacted development and new nodes) were the same as those put forward by the Regional Services Council consultants. What was at the heart of this dispute was whether planning is only about the production of grand plans and visions, or also about formulating implementable strategies, of which physical considerations are just one aspect. Cape Town City Council planner de Tolly believed in *strategic* planning: 'I was very obsessed, through my Canadian work, with getting away from fixed end-state planning' (Interview 13 1999). For him, a strategic planning approach also had important implications for the way in which the plan was depicted in graphic form. In the interview he jabbed his finger onto a copy of the plan for Cape Town (Figure 4.2) which had formed part of the Cape Town City Council submission to the Forum's 'visioning exercise' (City Planner's Department 1993). What is different about this graphic, compared to the one finally compiled by the consultants, is that it intends to show action areas rather than a picture of how metropolitan Cape Town may look at some point in the future.

The differences between the two approaches (the one strongly influenced by blueprint planning and the other a strategic planning approach) were therefore relatively subtle. Non-planner Shandler, the facilitator, was aware of the implications of the consultant's plan, but he interpreted the differences as gender-based.

> The [consultant's] plan was operating at a level which seemed to fly above the world and never engage with it ... It's a particularly masculine phenomenon. It's the phenomenon of the man who is very good at conceptualizing ideas but not very good at implementing them. I mean I am describing myself! ... What was interesting about the women planners in this process is that they were much more practically oriented. They always asked: How can it happen? How can I test this? It was putting a wonderful structure, a wonderfully masculine framework superimposed on the city. It didn't bear any relationship to it, but the logic was perfect.
>
> (Interview 5 1999)

With this lack of general clarity about why and how the two approaches were different, it was little wonder that the dispute could be attributed to 'personality differences' or 'institutional jealousy'. In the end de Tolly and the other City Council planners (together with Van Deventer) felt that they had been sidelined in the final production of the document and that the City Council name should not appear on the cover. They insisted that a disclaimer be printed and pasted on every cover to say that the document did not reflect a consensus position.

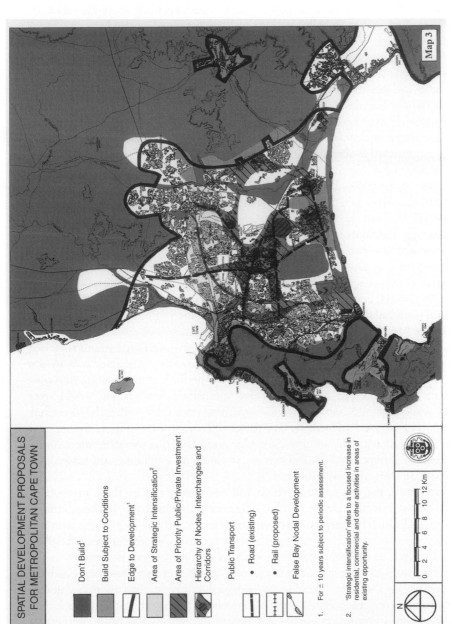

Figure 4.2 The Cape Town City Council vision for the future of Cape Town.

Source: City Planner's Department (1993).

What is interesting about 'The Way Forward' document is that it was intended to reflect a new spatial approach to the development of metropolitan Cape Town, based on an extensive process of general work-shopping and consultation with Forum stakeholders. It had been informed by the Interim Guidelines document (finalized in April of that year), by the overall visioning workshop organized by another Forum Commission (the Development Strategy Commission) in June of that year, by presentations to the Urban Development Commission steering committee and plenary, and by the six workshops held by the Regional Services Council consultants in August and September of 1993. Throughout these processes, there had been no major disagreement from the non-statutory organizations with the spatial principles or elements which had been put forward to direct future metropolitan growth, and certainly no attempt to put forward an alternative.

Some reservations had been expressed. The Chamber of Commerce was worried that the ideas did not take sufficient account of economic forces. Van Deventer also saw the ideas as unrealistic from an economic point of view and argued that proposals to build low-income housing to much higher densities (in the form of low-rise walk-ups) would price housing out of the reach of the lower-income groups (Development Action Group 1993). Cape Town City Council planners accepted that growth on the urban edge should be contained, that an internal open space system be defined, that compaction of development should occur, and that new 'nodes' should be defined to encourage commercial and economic opportunities in those parts of the metropolitan area which were lacking them. It was around the last spatial element (corridors) where they had more important differences: they argued that corridors could not be defined a priori, but that the preconditions for them (in the form of good public transport systems) should be put in place and that intensified development would, over time, respond to this opportunity. Commenting on a draft of this chapter, Cape Town City Council planner de Tolly added the following note in the margin: 'We disagreed with the untested corridor emphasis, the transport inputs were inadequate, there was inadequate environmental emphasis and there was nothing on the visual environment.'

In essence, the spatial ideas which had been promoted by the University of Cape Town (via the Urban Problems Research Unit and the teaching department), and which had been carried into the planning process by planners who had studied there, remained unchallenged and unchanged. Certainly most of the planners involved in the process were products of this institution, and even some of those involved in other capacities (such as Davidson and Van Deventer) had been shaped by this thinking. It could also be argued, correctly, that the non-statutory organizations had been only marginally involved. Their presence on the Urban Development Commission steering committee and plenary had been intermittent and partial, and on the MDF-CWG, where many of the central debates had taken place, they had had no direct influence. Van Deventer had found it almost impossible to arrange report-backs and discussions, and, where these had occurred, it may well have been the case that debates did not reach broader organizational membership (Interview 11 1998). At the six August/September workshops, only 21 of the 134 people attending had been from civic, labour or political organizations. One squatter representative had attended one of the workshops.

However, even if the non-statutory groupings had been as fully involved as was intended, it is questionable as to whether they would have been able to come up with an alternative proposal for how the metropolitan area should be planned. There were reports that many of the documents produced as part of the process had been written in a highly technical language which was not accessible to many people (EDF minutes 1993), suggesting that the reasons for poor involvement may have been more complex than initially appeared. Van Deventer reflected that civic and union members had agreed quite readily with the way in which planners had framed the spatial problems of metropolitan Cape Town: they could identify with issues such as long distances to work and public facilities, and barren townships. But they found it difficult to relate to the four spatial concepts (nodes, corridors, edges and the open space system) which, planners claimed, were intended to address the problems (Interview 11 1998). Understanding the link between concrete day-to-day problems and abstract and large-scale spatial ideas appeared to be a problem for those involved who were not trained planners. There was a tendency amongst organizations such as these, therefore, to classify planning debates as 'technical' and best left to the 'experts'. In this case the experts trusted by the organizations were the NGO planners. The SANCO representative reflected this feeling when he said:

> I think we would never deny the importance of planners, believe it or not. They were welcome because they had the skills, they know what they are talking about, you know, maps and so on . . . Yes, this was a technical exercise. It had to be. Everything is technical – when you build a house it's technical. Forget about politics.
>
> (Interview 8 1999)

As a result there was, simply, no capacity or incentive to conceive of, or articulate, a challenge to the spatial paradigm then on the ascendancy. It appeared to be the most rational and politically acceptable alternative. The broader question which remains, however, is whether or not the non-statutory organizations would have seen the need for any form of long-range, metropolitan plan. Planning consultant Madell suggested otherwise:

> There was a lot of push to do an overall plan, a master plan. If the non-statutory bodies had been more organized maybe they would not have gone for an overall plan at all. Maybe we would have had an action plan, or a programme tied to the Reconstruction and Development Programme. When this process started it was always the case that there must be a plan, no one disputed that there should be a plan, a physical plan. And us all being physical planners . . . it came about.
>
> (Interview 3 1999)

Participation in practice, 1994

By early 1994 most organizations on the Forum were gearing themselves up for the forthcoming April elections. Campaigning and lobbying activities were occupying many of the Forum stakeholders, some of which had been taken by surprise at the speed of the transition. No one could be entirely sure if the outcome would be peaceful power-sharing or chaos, and a spate of right-wing bomb attacks in the months prior to the elections made many people fear the latter.

The first MDF-CWG meeting of 1994 was highly conflictual (MDF-CWG minutes 1994a). Van Deventer complained that the minuting of meetings was insufficient and that key differences were not being reflected. Cape Town City Council planners wanted to pursue the issue of who had finally been responsible for 'The Way Forward' document, and were also unhappy that the document had been widely distributed both to Forum members and to many other official departments. After what the minutes term 'a long debate' it was agreed that 'The Way Forward' document should not be reworked but should be considered as a basis for discussion, so as eventually to produce a consensus document. In the meantime, there seemed to be at least two good reasons to suspend the process. Davidson argued that little real involvement of the Forum was likely until after the elections. Tomalin felt that 'a cooling-off period would be beneficial' (Interview 10 1998). It was left to the Commission to take up the initiative again once the elections were over.

By the time the steering committee of the Urban Development Commission met again, in June 1994, a number of factors had changed. The smoothness and peacefulness of the elections had exceeded all expectations, but while the ANC had gained a clear national majority, the National Party was the clear winner in the Western Cape (largely as a result of the support of the 'coloured vote') and it dominated the Provincial government. The predictions of those Regional Services councillors, who had believed that their power base would be largely unshaken, had proved so far to be correct.

The future of the Forum, however, was in question. The problem had been raised some time previously that it would be difficult to justify the continuation of the Forum once democratically elected institutions were in place. Thomas, of WESGRO (Interview 6 1998), had raised the possibility that it could be transformed into a social and economic advisory council to the provincial government. But initial discussions with both the new National Party provincial premier, and the head of the Provincial Department of Economic Affairs (a portfolio held by the ANC) indicated that *neither* welcomed the idea of interference from an outside body. At the level of the Urban Development Commission, Davidson was trying to extract himself from politics and survive on planning consultancy work (Interview 7 1998).

However, it is at this point that progress on the metropolitan development framework surged forward with a new sense of purpose and direction. When pressed, Tomalin admitted that at this stage he firmly took over the reins again

(Interview 10 1998). At the first Commission steering committee meeting in late June 1994 (UDC minutes 1994) it was agreed that more workshops should be held to discuss 'The Way Forward' document. All Commission stakeholders should come to the first workshop with a written statement on their view of the future of metropolitan Cape Town, in response to 'The Way Forward'. This workshop would deal with the issues which had to be addressed. Funding was to be raised from an outside source (the Development Bank of South Africa finally made a grant) and an independent person taken on to synthesize the results of both workshops. Further accusations that the Regional Services Council consultants were monopolizing the process had to be avoided if progress was to be made.

The first of these workshops, in September 1994, drew large-scale attendance, but it was clear, in terms of metropolitan planning, where most of the interest (and perhaps capacity) lay. Forty-seven per cent of those attending came from local authorities and the Regional Services Council, and a further 13 per cent from central government departments; 14 per cent were from community and political organizations (with one squatter representative); 7 per cent were from business and 1.5 per cent from the unions. NGO members and representatives from other local forums made up the rest.

A number of groupings made written representations. The newly merged Chamber of Commerce and Industry supported the idea of holding the urban edge and concentrating development in nodes and corridors within the existing city, but wanted high mobility routes (freeways) to continue to function efficiently. It was more concerned with reducing bureaucratic planning procedures and using public resources to create opportunities for the private sector. SANCO (civic) comments, typed with a seemingly old typewriter on four A4 sheets, were largely a restatement of material in Urban Problems Research Unit publications. The Cape Town City Council product was a large and professional-looking document (City Planner's Department 1994) – perhaps the metropolitan plan they had wanted to produce all along. It started off by analysing the context in broad terms, spatial and non-spatial, and including an understanding of economic dynamics. It then dealt with spatial ideas, framed in a somewhat different way from 'The Way Forward', but ultimately settling on a fixed urban edge, a metropolitan open space system, and public transport investment in strategic routes associated with higher-density housing and mixed use. The document also identified strategic public land, and identified actions to be taken in relation to township upgrade and informal settlements.

The second workshop, a couple of weeks later, was highly structured. The first two-and-a-half-hour session, entitled 'Ideal Spatial Structure', was divided into discussions of the four spatial elements: urban edge, the open space system, corridors, and nodes. The proposed locations for these were mapped, and those attending the workshop were asked either to agree or to voice objections. The subsequent workshop report stated that there were no objections to the four spatial elements. However, those local authorities present which did not have a node or a corridor in their area, wanted them. In a form of planning by bureaucratic consensus, which was to become a main feature of the planning process in the subsequent period, it was agreed that 13 more nodes and nine more corridors could be proposed! Unresolved issues such as these were delegated to small technical task teams, made up of planners from the City and Regional Councils, the consultants, and the Provincial Administration.

The MDF-CWG resumed its meetings in the offices of the Regional Services Council in October 1994. It was reported that the Commission had mandated that the MDF-CWG could continue. A Regional Services Council planner suggested that their consultants be directed to revise 'The Way Forward' document, taking into account the ideas from the workshops and the conclusions of the technical teams. There was no disagreement from the Cape Town City Council planners (MDF-CWG minutes 1994b).

In November, the consultants tabled a revised version of 'The Way Forward', now called the first draft of the Metropolitan Spatial Development Framework (or MSDF). The differences between this document, and the one which caused a breakdown of the process a year before, were not significant. Yet no major objections were raised, and there were even comments that the document was a great improvement, and that the process should not be held up further (MDF-CWG minutes 1995). Van Deventer explained why this had happened:

> In the end it become quite a pride thing about getting it [the MSDF] adopted at all costs. And I know the approach from the Regional Services Council side was that we'll keep going and they will get tired and fall by the wayside. And it's true – that is what happened. And I think part of what made me let go was thinking, well they are going to come up against problems in implementing it . . . so therefore don't keep pounding away . . .
> (Interview 12 1999)

The opposition, it appears, had dissipated.

At the end of January 1995, it was reported to the MDF-CWG that the chairs of the Urban Development Commission and the MDF-CWG had agreed that the former should collapse into the latter. The Forum was in the process of transforming itself into what was termed the Provincial Development Council, and the commissions were being disbanded. The metropolitan planning process was firmly back in the hands of the Regional Services Council, but was now able to claim a sound community and business mandate. Tomalin was undoubtedly relieved that his risk had paid off.

The intention was that the plan should be passed into law through the Land Use Planning Ordinance within the next few months. This was not to be, however. The local government restructuring process, which swung into action immediately after the elections, created a whole new set of powerful local government stakeholders, who still had to be convinced that the plan was a good idea. It is to this part of the process that the next chapter turns.

Conclusion

There are two, overlapping, arenas in which the development of the spatial planning process can be tracked. The first arena, centred on the Forum, involves the broadening of the discourse coalition around the compact city approach, to include metropolitan organizations representing business, the unions and civic associations. It is a matter of importance to the planning officials (from both metropolitan and local authorities) that this happens, as it will serve to increase the status of the plan, and Regional Services Council planner Tomalin takes significant personal risk to ensure that the planning process is located within the one institution (the Forum) which will allow coalition-broadening to occur. Broadening the coalition does not, however, imply that the planning officials no longer wish to exercise power over the process. Tomalin, at least, enters the Forum process with a conviction that the continued exercise of power will be possible, although he could have had no clear idea of how this would be achieved.

Planners have traditionally used the power of persuasion as a means of promoting particular planning positions. Their status as experts, and their ability in the fields of data presentation, graphic production, and the framing of arguments, can all be brought to bear in the persuasionary effort. The consensus-seeking process launched within the Forum is no exception, with the Regional Services Council planning officials relying largely on their consultants to manage workshops involving slide presentations and glossy documentation. A second set of circumstances which allows the planning officials to continue their central role in the process is the structure and operation of the Forum itself. While the Forum has been designed to achieve the equal involvement of statutory and non-statutory organizations, and open and democratic operation within the various committees and sub-committees, the imbalance in terms of resources and capacity between statutory and non-statutory members renders it an inequitable structure. The difficulty experienced by civic, union and political opposition members in particular, in attending meetings and workshops, and in understanding and responding to technical reports, inevitably reduces their ability to exercise power in the planning process. Even the ANC chair of the Urban Development Commission has his attendance at meetings limited by considerations such as these.

These factors have implications for the nature of the coalition which is built around the compact city position. There is agreement amongst the Forum members about the framing of the spatial problem of Cape Town, and there is agreement about the principles and goals which should guide a new plan. Problems such as long and costly travel distances to work, as a result of sprawling and fragmented urban development, are part of the everyday experience of poorer residents of Cape Town, and goals such as integration and equity coincide with the political rhetoric of the incoming government. There is much less evidence that Forum members understand either the need for a metropolitan plan in the form presented by the consultants, or its implications. Their agreement with the plan, and hence their presence in the coalition, depends, I would argue, far more on the trust they have in particular planners than in their full commitment to the plan. Their presence in the coalition can therefore be regarded as more tentative, or fragile, than it might otherwise have been.

The second arena in which the progress of the spatial plan can be tracked is that of the planning officials and consultants involved in plan production. The question here, given the apparently high degree of consensus around the plan within the Forum, is what is the basis of the intense conflict amongst the group of planning professionals involved in day-to-day work on the plan? At issue here is the form taken by the plan, and the extent to which it has the characteristics of a comprehensive 'blueprint' plan (the position of the Regional Services Council planners and their consultants), as opposed to the 'strategic' plan favoured by the municipal planners and the NGO planner. The conflict here is about more than the form of the plan itself – it represents a broader site of struggle around which group of planning officials (metropolitan or municipal) should control the metropolitan planning process. The tactics of power in this situation move beyond the persuasionary to include a range of additional mechanisms which, as NGO planner Van Deventer suggests, eventually wear down the opposition.

The efforts of the Regional Services Council planners to produce a particular form of plan appear to be part of a conscious strategy. The consultants are concerned about the extent to which the plan will gain support within other government institutions, assuming (as they do) that this body of officials will remain largely unchanged after the election of the new democratic government. Believing that these officials were more likely to feel comfortable with the comprehensive, blueprint plans of the apartheid days (this is reflected in a comment by consultant Madell in Chapter 8, p. 121), the consultants feel that adopting this form of plan improves the chances of plan acceptance in these quarters. Significant continuities with past planning are thus perpetuated, even though the planning goals represent a sharp break with the past.

5 South Africa post-1994

New systems of government and planning

In April 1994, South Africa's first national democratic elections took place in an atmosphere of unexpected peace and harmony. The ANC won a landslide victory, with its 62.7 per cent of the vote placing it well ahead of the National Party (with 20.4 per cent of the vote) and the Inkatha Freedom Party (with 10.5 per cent of the vote). Only in the KwaZulu-Natal Province and the Western Cape Province did opposition parties achieve a majority, and as a result the Western Cape Provincial government became the last stronghold of National Party rule. Nonetheless, the political and symbolic threshold into a new South Africa had been crossed (Marais 1998) and the new Government of National Unity[1] set about its task of legislative and institutional reorganization.

There is no doubt that this reorganization was slow in the making, sometimes contradictory, and frequently contested. But the extent of legislative and institutional change, which occurred in South Africa in the post-1994 years, was remarkable and concerned itself with almost every facet of society. Moreover, transition was undertaken simultaneously at both national and subnational level, making South Africa unique amongst those political systems which have undergone political transition to democracy (Swilling 1997).

This chapter interrupts the story of the metropolitan planning process in Cape Town in order to set out the nature and scale of certain of these post-1994 changes. It shows that important aspects of the context within which the planning of metropolitan Cape Town was occurring were changing dramatically. Changes in the government's macro-economic policy, and in the structure and functioning of local government, became factors which the metropolitan planners took into account in their attempts to produce a metropolitan plan.

Shifts in macro-economic policy

The Reconstruction and Development Programme (RDP) was intended to set the agenda for the new Government of National Unity. As a manifesto for change it was described as an 'icon of the new South Africa' (Munslow and Fitzgerald 1995, 42), and as a development framework aimed at the complete reordering of politics, the economy and society (Marais 1998).

The origins of the RDP lay, prior to 1993, within the trade union movement, but thereafter the ANC and other organizations within the opposition movement participated in redrafting the policy document. This proved to be a highly contested process, as 'the stridency of the Base Document was gradually excised or checked, as weaker "compromise" sections were pushed to the fore at the expense of its more radical injunctions' (Marais 1998, 179). Thus, Marais comments, the RDP became less of a policy framework for the democratic forces and more of a framework for the spectrum of parties in the Government of National Unity, and the business sector. It mixed 'neo-liberal prescriptions with some residual Keynesian regulation, corporatist processes with a "people-driven" approach, ostensibly firm commitments to redistribution with stern macro-economic strictures' (Marais 1998, 179). However, it ultimately claimed to reflect a consensus between 'right' and 'left' political positions and was able to claim at least rhetorical support from all sectors of South African society.[2]

Nevertheless, the popularity of the RDP was short lived. It proved very difficult to implement, for reasons, according to Marais (1998), relating to the reluctance of incumbent officials to change, a lack of skills and capacity in drafting RDP business plans, the lack of integration between the various line Ministries, and the different ideological position within agencies such as the World Bank and the Development Bank of South Africa. Two billion rands ($333 million)[3] in unspent RDP funds were rolled over from 1995 into the 1996/7 fiscal year, and in March 1996 the RDP Office was closed, with RDP Minister Jay Naidoo admitting that 'very little has happened in the last two years' (Marais 1998, 191).

The government's new macro-economic strategy – Growth, Employment and Redistribution (or GEAR) – was released in March 1996. According to Marais (1998, 161), GEAR's prescriptions 'lit the faces of business leaders but shocked many within the ANC alliance . . . critics immediately dubbed the plan neo-liberal'. Another commentator referred to the policy as 'cautious Thatcherism' (Pilger 1998). Economic growth was to be achieved through private sector investment, stimulated by slashing government spending, containing inflation, reducing corporate taxes, phasing out exchange controls, restraining wage increases and speeding up privatization. While GEAR was sometimes justified as simply attending to the 'development' side of the Reconstruction and Development Programme, it was clear that there had been a major about-face in government policy (Figure 5.1).

Local government transition in South Africa

The post-apartheid vision for local government in South Africa was based on a development of the clauses on local government contained in the RDP of 1994. Its broad role was enshrined in the 1996 Constitution, and developed further in two policy documents, termed the 'Green Paper' and the 'White Paper' on local government (Ministry for Provincial Affairs and Constitutional Development 1997, 1998).

Figure 5.1 South Africa's changing macro-economic policy.

Source: J. Shapiro (1996) *Zapiro: The Madiba Years*. Cape Town, David Philip. Reproduced with permission of the author.

The RDP called for democratic, non-racial and non-sexist local authorities, the amalgamation and reorganization of racially separate local bodies, integrated budgets and financial systems, cross-subsidization from wealthy to poorer areas, and the fostering of a 'development' culture within local administrations. The Green and White Papers drew a vision for local government which, in the first instance, was to be developmental. It called for the maximizing of social development and economic growth of communities, and for planning and managing development in a spatially and socially integrated and sustainable way. Implementing this vision implied a dramatic break with the previous form of local government, and in order to appreciate the magnitude of this change, it is necessary to outline the process through which it occurred.

Negotiating a new local government system

The breakdown in the system of local government in many African, coloured and Asian urban townships during the late 1980s and early 1990s had undoubtedly played an important role in bringing the apartheid government to the negotiating table. A system of racially separate local government had been a cornerstone of late-apartheid policy, embodying the principle that different racial groups should 'govern themselves' and supporting the ideal of spatially segregated residential areas. This element of apartheid policy (as with many others) had never proved to be entirely workable, and local government had been subject to many adjustments over the years in attempts to make it both economically and politically more effective (see Heymans and Totemeyer 1988). But by the end of the 1980s, the prevailing system of local government was being challenged by the main political opposition demand for universal franchise and by the collapse, in many areas, of the racially defined organs of local representation. A rent-and-services boycott had taken hold in the townships during the 1980s, placing financial pressure on the white local authorities often responsible for servicing these areas, and resulting in increasing levels of debt. Many white local authorities had begun informal negotiations with alternative township power structures (primarily the civic associations) around the issues of service payments and infrastructure maintenance and development, and were entering into various forms of power-sharing arrangements with them.

It was largely in response to the multitude of local initiatives, taking place in towns and cities around the country, that the demand was expressed for national agreements and legislation on the future form of local government. The national Local Government Negotiating Forum sat during 1993 and 1994. Representatives of the 'non-statutory alliance' were led by SANCO (the civic umbrella body, South African National Civic Organization). 'Statutory' representatives were drawn from local government associations, professional organizations, and from the provincial and national levels of government. Membership of the Forum was confined to those organizations which were nationally constituted, were not political parties, and which had an interest in local government, but both sides liaised closely with their respective political parties, and in the case of the non-statutory alliance, with the union movement as well (Robinson 1996).

Negotiations in this Forum were by no means conflict-free: a wide range of political opinion was represented, from the small, conservative, National Party-controlled towns to the radical civic and labour movements. At times it appeared as if battles over the future of local government would derail the entire constitutional process (Cameron 1999). Robinson (1996, 211) points out that 'the establishment side made repeated efforts to promote initiatives likely to preserve the status quo until the very last stages of negotiating new local government legislation'. Ultimately, there was compromise between the non-statutory demand for immediate unitary, non-racial local government structures exercising authority over all resources (the 'one city – one tax base' demand), and the conservative position in favour of more independent and powerful local authorities, with some redistribution taking place via overarching bodies – a refinement of the pre-existing, supra-local, Regional Services Council system. Cameron (1999) characterizes the negotiations as being essentially between the National Party's decentralist vision of local government and the ANC's centralist vision, which implied strong metropolitan authorities and much weaker municipal structures. The National Party was primarily concerned that if strong metropolitan governments were politically dominated by the ANC, then they could be used to adopt redistributive policies which would affect white residential areas negatively. It also hoped, through the promotion of the idea of strong ward structures, to ensure that white communities could protect their privileges by setting zoning and planning norms, controlling the supply and use of community facilities, and financing local projects (Robinson 1996). Within the non-statutory alliance, achieving consensus on the overall shape of local government had not been easy. Tensions between the centralist position of the ANC and the far less centralist position of the civic movement, which had its origins in mobilization around local, township issues, played themselves out in this and subsequent rounds of debate over the future of local government.

A process for the transformation of local government was set out in the legislation which emerged from the Local Government Negotiating Forum and was subsequently passed by parliament in the form of the Local Government Transition Act of 1993. The compromise lay in the rate at which the changes would be introduced and the nature of interim power-sharing arrangements. The distribution of powers and functions between the metropolitan and local authorities was left to the local negotiating forums to decide.

Three phases of local government transition were laid out in the Act. In the first 'pre-interim' phase, which started with the passing of the Act, existing racially based local authorities were abolished. Schedule 1 of the Act provided for the establishment of local government forums, drawn equally from statutory and non-statutory organizations. It was the task of these forums to nominate pre-interim councillors who would serve on a temporary basis until the first open and democratic local elections of 1995/6. These pre-interim councillors were also drawn equally from both statutory and non-statutory organizations. The forums were further charged with deciding on the number of seats on the pre-interim councils and, broadly, the model of local government to apply in either metropolitan or non-metropolitan areas. During this period, new municipal and metropolitan boundaries were drawn by Provincial Demarcation Boards (see Cameron 1999), with the municipal boundaries arranged so as to twin wealthier parts of an urban area with poorer parts and thus allow for cross-subsidization. Clearly this was set to become a highly political debate as it would potentially affect not only wealthier (and usually white) ratepayers in the form of higher rates and lower levels of municipal services, but also the party political composition of the new councils – thus the incorporation of African areas into a previously white municipal area could usually be relied on to increase the proportion of ANC voters.

Phase two of local government transition, as laid out in the 1993 Act, was called the 'interim phase'. It started with the municipal elections in 1995, which in the Western Cape were delayed until May 1996 because of disputes over demarcation. During this phase the new, elected local councils and reorganized administrations were to begin operating, although under the power-sharing arrangements agreed to in the national forum. Under these arrangements, 40 per cent of seats on a local council would come from proportional representation of political parties and 60 per cent from ward-based representation, but with 50 per cent of ward seats reserved for representatives from former white, coloured and Indian areas and 50 per cent from former African areas.[4] At the metropolitan level, 40 per cent of representation was proportional, but the other 60 per cent was nominated by the Transitional Metropolitan Substructures from within their own ranks and weighted according to the number of registered voters (Cameron 1999).

The third, or 'final phase', was programmed to begin in 1999,[5] at which time new elections would be held, power-sharing arrangements would fall away, and a fully developed vision for local government would have been worked out at the national level and enshrined in new legislation.

One of the most significant aspects of the post-1994 system of local government, as set out in chapter 3 of the 1996 Constitution, was the provision of a system of co-operative government in which the national, provincial and local levels are 'spheres' rather than 'tiers' of government. The intention, according to the 1997 Green Paper on Local Government (Ministry for Provincial Affairs and Constitutional Development 1997), is that the three spheres of government should each be distinctive and have equal status, and should have the power to define and express their own unique character. Divisions of powers and functions between the spheres (where not directly assigned by the constitution or national legislation) have to be negotiated.[6] This, the Green Paper argues, is a major change from the previous system, whereby levels of government were arranged in a hierarchical system with power concentrated at the national level.

However, it has never been entirely clear if the intention here was just the decentralization of powers and functions to local government, or the devolution of political power as well, and it is likely that the centralist–decentralist tension within the opposition movement contributed to this ambivalence. Some interpretations, at least, appear to suggest the former. The RDP Minister explicitly viewed local government as 'the hands and feet' of the RDP (Chipkin 1997), and the Urban Development Strategy, published by the same ministry, described the primary responsibility of local government as ensuring 'the delivery of services at community level within an agreed planning framework' (Ministry of the Office of the President 1995, 45). As Chipkin (1997, 71) has pointed out, reluctance to devolve political power to local government, and allow it to become a *de facto* equal and distinctive sphere of government, may be explained by the nature of the negotiated political settlement. This required that new local government structures inherited officials from the former local authorities. As a result, many of the new authorities came to be staffed by an 'old guard' bureaucracy, unfamiliar with and sometimes hostile to changed policies (Figure 5.2). Affirmative action, and the appointment of more African and coloured officials (assumed to be sympathetic to the new political programme) within bureaucracies, were intended to change this situation, but this was slow in the making. The overall result is that policy-making in all functional arenas remains highly centralized, and local government is assumed to fulfil its democratic mandate through the implementation of national policy and the delivery of services.

Figure 5.2 Perceptions of the South African bureaucracy.

Source: J. Shapiro (1996) *Zapiro: The Madiba Years*. Cape Town, David Philip. Reproduced with permission of the author.

But the extent to which local government in South Africa is currently able to play even a narrow, service-implementing role, has to be questioned. In 1995/6, local government expenditure accounted for only 10.5 per cent of total public expenditure (Central Statistical Services 1998) relative to national government, which accounted for 39.4 per cent, and provincial governments, which spent 40.2 per cent. Only 11.2 per cent of total government expenditure on utility services is contributed by local government, reflecting the primary role of other government agencies in providing service infrastructure (Savage 1998). Local government income is derived primarily from local sources: 85 per cent of income is from trading services (water, electricity and sanitation) and, to a far lesser degree, from property rates and local levies (Ministry for Provincial Affairs and Constitutional Development 1998). Only 15 per cent of local income is from grants, and this has been declining in real terms since 1991/2 (Savage 1998). At the local level, persistent rate-and-service payment boycotts and bad debts amounting to 32 per cent of aggregate municipal income (Savage 1998) have further constrained local government revenue, and have plunged many local authorities into financial crisis.

The White Paper on Local Government concludes that 'the local government system is still structured to meet the demands of the previous era' and that 'a fundamental transformation is [still] required' (Ministry for Provincial Affairs and Constitutional Development 1998, 16). The proposals contained within the White Paper, and now enshrined in legislation,[7] are currently bringing about another major reorganization of local government. In the metropolitan areas, the bulk of powers and functions are being located in the metropolitan authority, and municipalities will be downgraded to sub-councils or ward committees with very limited delegated powers. The number of councillors will be reduced significantly. Local authorities are urged to expand the ways in which their services are delivered, and to consider privatization, contracting out and partnership arrangements.

Cameron (1999, 109) has described the first round of local government change, in which '80 years of municipal apartheid was negotiated into the dustheap of history' as having 'fundamentally altered the shape of South African local government'. The proposed second round of change may be only slightly less significant in terms of its impact on the face of local government.

Local government transition in metropolitan Cape Town

Within South Africa, strong regional differences exist. The particular demographic, social and economic history of the Western Cape (see James and Simons 1989) gave rise to a system of local government which, in many ways, functioned differently from local government elsewhere in the country. In particular, the demographic dominance of the coloured population,[8] both within the broader Western Cape Province and the metropolitan area of Cape Town, the somewhat favoured status of coloured people within the racial hierarchy of apartheid,[9] and the dominant concern, within the various local government reform efforts under apartheid, as to how to accommodate coloured people within the structures of local government (Todes *et al.* 1989), have shaped both the past and present functioning of local government.

In metropolitan Cape Town there was, prior to the political transition, a highly fragmented and racially based system of local government, consisting of 61 local bodies. At the metropolitan level, the Regional Services Council was part of a nation-wide system of supra-local authorities introduced in 1985 in order to channel funding to African and coloured local structures. The aim was to make them financially viable and hence politically more acceptable. While the Regional Services Council allowed for multi-racial representation, voting was heavily loaded in favour of wealthier, white areas, and the institution was chaired by a Provincial government (and hence National Party) appointee. There were 19 white local authorities. The Cape Town City Council was the largest, playing in effect a 'core city' role by providing certain services to the other bodies in the metropolitan area. There were six local councils, remnants of the pre-1985 system of local government: these covered semi-rural (white) parts of the metropolitan area and fell directly under the Regional Services Council. There were seven Black Local Authorities covering the main African residential areas of metropolitan Cape Town. These potentially had powers and functions similar to the white local authorities, but because of their complete lack of financial viability[10] and their political illegitimacy, they were weak and relatively ineffective bodies. Finally there were 29 Coloured Management Committees, also potentially with powers similar to those of white local authorities, but also, due to their lack of economic and political support, playing no more than an advisory role to the white authorities.

By the end of the 1980s, the Coloured Management Committees and Black Local Authorities in Cape Town were still in place but were weak and highly discredited bodies. In many other parts of the country, African councillors had been forced to resign or had become targets of civic protest (Heymans 1993; Cameron 1999). Some of Cape Town's white local authorities were openly bypassing these structures and were drawing civics and unions into stakeholder processes around local issues. It was clear that the existing structure of local government would require major reform.

In mid-1992 the NGO, IDASA (Institute for a Democratic Alternative in South Africa), launched a series of public seminars in Cape Town on the future of local government. They attracted a great deal of interest from a wide range of groupings, and when they were over, the IDASA regional director, David Schmidt, was asked to co-ordinate a small group of influential individuals to take the process further. This group in turn expanded its membership to include five representatives from statutory bodies and five from non-statutory bodies. In mid-1993, Cape Town, following in the path of several other South African cities,[11] launched its own local government negotiating forum[12] to debate the future shape of its local government. Schedule 1 of the 1993 Local Government Transition Act, which provided legally for forums such as these, necessitated some adjustment in the Cape Town forum membership to include wider representation. But with the Forum already up and running, it was able to sign a formal agreement in 1994 on the shape of 'pre-interim' local government in Cape Town.

The agreement on local government, which emerged from the Cape Town Forum, differed somewhat from the final position taken in the national Local Government Negotiating Forum in that it favoured a relatively weak metropolitan structure and strong municipalities. Clauses in the local Forum agreement stated that the metropolitan authority should 'only address those matters which could not by their nature be effectively addressed by the TMSs' (municipalities) and that the TMSs should 'retain maximum control over local decision-making and implementation' (Cameron 1999, 116). This was an outcome which had clear implications for the interactions between the metropolitan planners and those of the Cape Town City Council.

The reason for this compromise on the part of the non-statutory organizations was, according to Cameron (pers. comm.), that it was necessary in order to retain the participation of the rather numerous National Party-aligned municipalities and statutory organizations in Cape Town, which were supporting the decentralist position within the conservative faction of the national forum.[13] However, in the final decision-making process around the division of powers and functions between metropolitan and municipal levels of government, which took place in the 'pre-interim' period of local government transition, this position was softened somewhat. This was due possibly to the realization on the part of the new municipalities that the cost of additional powers and functions would, at least partially, have to be met from their own income sources. The new Cape Metropolitan Council remained a relatively weak metropolitan authority, although somewhat less weak than had been envisaged in the Forum Agreement.

In April 1994 a Western Cape Demarcation Board was appointed by the Provincial Administrator, after consultation with a multi-party Provincial Committee (Cameron 1999). Members of the Demarcation Board were described by Cameron (1999, 117) as 'overwhelmingly white, male and Afrikaans', and there was a small minority of ANC-aligned members. Consensus was thus not easily achieved. The metropolitan boundary was contentious because the smaller outlying (and relatively wealthy) towns of Paarl, Stellenbosch and Wellington did not want to become part of the metropolitan council, and thus potentially be affected by efforts to redistribute resources to the large concentrations of poorer people within the metropolitan area. The final boundary of the new metropolitan council was not rational in a functional sense – it contained an area much smaller than the previous Regional Services Council and excluded a number of the peripheral settlements, such as Stellenbosch and Paarl, which were economically closely tied to the metropole and would logically have belonged within it.

The boundaries of the new municipalities within the metropolitan area were even more contentious (see Cameron 1999), the primary issue being how to incorporate the poverty-stricken African residential areas, which held about a third of the total metropolitan population and whose political sympathies lay almost entirely with the ANC. Both the Cape Town City Council and the non-statutory members of the Demarcation Board supported a 'bipolar' resolution to this problem. The older African townships of Langa, Nyanga and Gugulethu, together with the informal settlements around Crossroads and Philippi, would be twinned with the wealthiest of the former white municipalities: the Cape Town City Council. The newer African township of Khayelitsha would be combined with a number of the wealthier, National Party-supporting, former white municipalities. This proposal was strongly rejected by the latter and was overridden by the Provincial National Party Minister for Local Government. The Minister announced, in May 1995, that all African residential areas would be contained within the Cape Town City Council area, leaving the National Party-inclined municipalities free of African areas. He also altered the composition of the Provincial Committee which was to approve the final boundaries, introducing two new National Party-supporting members in order to ensure that his proposals would be accepted. It took a personal intervention from President Mandela and an amendment to national legislation to prevent such gerrymandering, before the original bipolar proposal could be put to the Provincial Committee and accepted. At this point, opposition from the Tygerberg Municipality was halted, when it realized that while there was little numerical difference between the older African townships on the one hand and Khayelitsha on the other, the net cash-flow deficit of Khayelitsha was some three-and-a-half times less than the older areas, and its infrastructure was far newer and in better repair (Cameron 1999, 145).

Ultimately the 61 existing local bodies, reduced to 39 at the start of 'pre-interim' local government, were further reduced to six large municipalities (see Figure 5.3). The African areas were divided between the two wealthiest existing municipalities. The previously dominant Cape Town City Council lost certain of its richer, white residential areas to the south, and gained the older African townships. The Tygerberg municipality gained large new lower-middle class, coloured areas, and Khayelitsha. The other four municipalities, all of which had less in the way of a lucrative commercial rates base, were demarcated to contain the remaining smaller pockets of lower-income settlement. Disputes over boundary issues delayed democratic local government elections in Cape Town until May 1996, and at this point the six new municipalities and the Cape Metropolitan Council became the organs of 'interim' local government. Under the power-sharing arrangements agreed to in the national forum, 40 per cent of seats on local and metropolitan councils would come from proportional representation of political parties and 60 per cent from ward-based representation, but with 50 per cent of ward seats reserved for representatives from white, coloured and Indian areas.[14] The National Party gained political control of five of the municipalities and the Cape Metropolitan Council, and it was only in the Cape Town Municipality that the ANC gained a majority on council.

The third, or 'final phase' of local government transition was programmed to begin in 2000, at which time new elections would be held, power-sharing arrangements would fall away, and a fully developed vision for local government would have been worked out at the national level and enshrined in new legislation.

New systems of planning in local government

The system of spatial planning inherited by the 1994 government was also clearly in need of major reform. It was, in the words of the Commission set up to devise a new planning system, 'fragmented, unequal and incoherent' and 'reflected minority interests' (National Development and Planning Commission 1999, iv, 4). In the years immediately after the new government took office, two pieces of legislation were introduced which were intended to change the face of planning in South Africa. The first of these was the Development Facilitation Act of 1995, and the second was the concept of integrated development planning, inserted into the 1996 Local Government Transition Amendment Act No. 97 (second amendment).

The Development Facilitation Act (1995)

The RDP policy document recognized the need to develop a new legislative and regulatory system for 'development planning' in order to make the RDP a reality

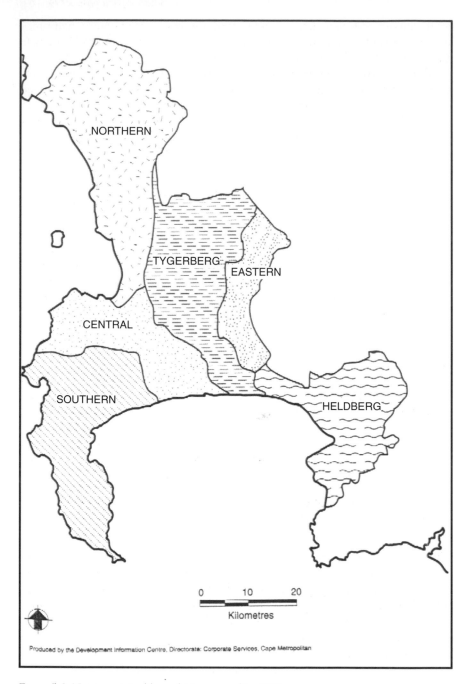

Figure 5.3 New municipal boundaries created in 1996.

Source: Cameron (1999).

(RDP 1994, 141). In particular, it stipulated that new legislation must allow for the defining and fast-tracking of strategic reconstruction projects, and for granting recognition to the planning efforts of the new interim local councils. After the elections the RDP Office moved swiftly to enact the first piece of legislation to deal with this issue.

The Development Facilitation Act of 1995 introduced 'extraordinary measures' to facilitate land development and service delivery, and provided for a Development and Planning Commission to advise further on a new system of land development (Office of the President 1995, 2). The Act had its origins in a local government and planning think-tank established in Cape Town in 1991 which, with the help of Canadian IDRC funding, pulled together a network of progressive organizations, activists and academics (Harrison 1998). It was also strongly influenced by debates taking place within the National Housing Forum, where the business lobby group, the Urban Foundation, was playing a determining role. It was, according to Harrison (1998), this latter group which stressed the need for flexible, non-bureaucratic mechanisms to promote land development and which introduced the idea of legislated 'performance criteria' to guide land use planning. Chapter 1 of the Act contains a list of 'General Principles for Land Development', applicable at both national and provincial levels,[15] with the spatial principles reflecting the spatial philosophy then on the ascendancy: land uses should be integrated and mixed, and urban development should be compact and environmentally sustainable. A more traditional, and directly interventionist, planning approach was promoted by the RDP Office, and this finds its place in Chapter 4 of the Act which provides for 'Land Development Objectives'. A tension therefore exists in the Act between these two positions (Harrison 1998). Chapter 4 sets out the requirements for more conventional land use plans at the local government level, but is not binding on the provinces. Certain of the provinces, including the Western Cape, have since developed their own provincial planning legislation.[16]

Integrated development planning

The 1996 Local Government Transition Amendment Act (Republic of South Africa 1996a) introduced the concept of 'integrated planning, budgeting and management'. It required all metropolitan and municipal governments to draw up Integrated Development Plans (or IDPs) for their area of jurisdiction. 'Integrated planning' meant that planning should take into account all conditions and circumstances and should involve all role-players. Explanatory documents emphasized that the term 'integrated' meant that the objectives of not just one administrative directorate should prevail, but that the objectives and plans of all directorates should be brought together and related to each other, and to the budgeting process. Specifically, the Act required that the areas of land use planning, transport planning, infrastructure planning and economic development planning should be integrated to inform the IDP. The product was intended to consist of a budget, a set of priorities or projects and a spatial plan.

For spatial planners in South Africa it appeared, initially, as if this legislation offered them the status they required to make a contribution to the effort of urban reconstruction and development. Planners here, as elsewhere, had long complained that the primary reasons their plans so often failed to be implemented was that there was insufficient integration between functional departments within public authorities, and that there was insufficient linking between plans and the budgeting process. The RDP acknowledged these concerns. It set out the need for land use planning to play a central role in the implementation of the RDP, emphasizing as well the need for 'collaborative, integrated planning and decision-making' and frameworks that 'must be tied to the budgeting process' (RDP 1994, 141). The concept of IDPs appeared to offer a solution to these problems. But the IDP process ultimately took on a form which was somewhat different from that expected by the spatial planners.

IDPs and public management

The idea of promoting integrated and co-ordinated planning and budgeting, as set out in the RDP of 1994, has established international precedent. Harrison (1998) points to the re-emergence internationally of integrated development planning and 'networking', after a decade or so of atomistic and project-focused planning. In Britain, pressures for more devolved and integrated government (Vigar and Healey 1999) resulted in a plan-led regime (in the 1991 Planning and Compensation Act) with land use planning set to provide this integrative role. And the World Bank shifted its position in the early 1990s from a project-based approach to one which emphasized 'integrated development' (Harrison 1998). Contact established as early as 1992 between key personalities in South African local government policy forums and staff at the British University of Warwick Business School (Local Government Centre), may explain to some extent the cross-pollination of ideas (Interview 14 1999), as would the many World Bank Urban Sector Missions to South Africa during the early 1990s.

Integrated development planning as put forward in the RDP was intended, in the first place, to overcome the fragmentation which was occurring in policy-making and spending at the national level. While some individuals in the RDP Office saw this as an exercise in institutional planning, others, such as planner Dr Laurine Platzky, initiated an attempt to co-ordinate departmental efforts through a national spatial plan. Harrison (1998) describes how the RDP Office found it immensely difficult to achieve intersectoral collaboration, and ultimately succeeded mainly in provoking resentment from national line-function departments. The rapid shift in overall state policy from a more left-leaning, planning and interventionist position, to a neo-liberal and market-led one soon after the 1994 elections, made the achievement of integrated planning at the national level even more difficult. When the RDP Office was closed in April 1996, it was acknowledged that the achievement of a national spatial plan was not possible.[17]

The idea of integrated development planning did not die here, however. With the closure of the RDP Office, a number of the staff moved to the Department of Constitutional Development, where the 1996 Local Government Transition Act was in the process of being finalized. The requirement that local authorities should prepare integrated development plans to guide and co-ordinate their actions was hastily inserted into the legislation (L. Platzky pers. comm.), and this concept thus shifted from being a national concern to a local one. The aim that a spatial plan should form part of an integrated development plan was also retained. The requirement of a spatial plan was set out in the Act, and was given high priority in the IDP guideline document issued by the Department of Constitutional Development. This document (Department of Constitutional Development 1997) described how the 'Land Development Objectives' of the Development Facilitation Act were the central part of preparing an IDP. 'The IDP process involves drawing up LDOs and some additional planning, to finally produce an Integrated Development Plan' (Department of Constitutional Development 1997, 10).

This view of IDPs was contested, however. The counter-position, articulated by the Deputy Director-General of the Department of Constitutional Development at a 1997 seminar in Seapoint, Cape Town, was that 'the IDP is a process, not a product. They are not physical plans but business plans.' It is this latter position which increasingly became the dominant one, as local government policy-makers grappled with the problem of its inherited bureaucracy 'characterized by hierarchical line departments, poor co-ordination between line departments and authoritarian management practices' (Ministry for Provincial Affairs and Constitutional Development 1998, 8). These features were seen as a major obstacle to the call for local government to become 'developmental' (Ministry for Provincial Affairs and Constitutional Development 1998, section B)

Savage (1998) argues that what the White Paper on Local Government sought to introduce was the kind of public sector reform which has been seen elsewhere in the world in recent decades.[18] Termed New Public Management, it is based on the assumption that bureaucratic inefficiency lies at the root of local government problems. To counter this it advocates the introduction of private sector management techniques, competitive, market-based organizational structures and mechanisms, and the use of performance measures, or indicators. The latter has also been termed 'management by results'. New Public Management formally 'arrived' in South Africa at the Mount Grace Conference of November 1991, organized by the South African-based New Public Administration Initiative. The Conference delegates adopted the Mount Grace Resolution, which reflected an intention to break with the previous paradigm of 'control-oriented and rule-driven public administration' (Fitzgerald 1995, 511). Fitzgerald (1995) refers to the influential American guide to 'reinventing government' (Osborne and Gaebler 1992) which specifically considers the introduction of the 'entrepreneurial spirit' into local government, but argues that it needs to be adapted to the South African context where both entrepreneurial and developmental considerations are important. It has been this initiative within the South African public sector which has become intertwined with a view of IDPs as a tool for *institutional* planning and management,[19] rather than just a way of achieving effective spatial planning. And it has been this approach to public management which subsequently swept into many local authorities, including the Cape Metropolitan Council.

It could of course be argued that a concern with institutional efficiency and effectiveness would not necessarily negate spatial planning. But the interpretation of IDPs as a public management tool, rather than a spatial planning tool, potentially affects the role of spatial planning in a number of more subtle ways. Rhodes (1997) has pointed out how an indicator-driven, management-by-results approach to public management (termed in the UK 'managerialism') has been subject to wide-ranging critique and a search for new approaches.[20] The basis of the critique lies in the tendency for managerialism to, in fact, encourage line bureaucracies and hierarchical control in authorities, and work against the creation of interorganizational links where there is a need to negotiate shared purposes with stakeholder groups outside of government. Where the approach has resulted in the transfer of local public services to public utility companies, or to the private sector, the growing lack of co-ordination of local government actions has become a cause for concern, and has resulted in a call for 'joined-up' (or integrated) local government. There are already indications that the current round of local government reform in South Africa, which involves the establishment of strong metropolitan governments, will be premised on the philosophy of managerialism. 'Egoli 2002', Johannesburg's local government plan, involves the splitting off of a number of services to public utility companies, and Cape Town may follow suit. It is possible, therefore, that the particular view of public management gaining ascendancy in South Africa will simply exacerbate the existing tendency towards functional and departmental fragmentation, work against the spatial co-ordination of policy and expenditure, and reinforce the role of spatial planning as just one of a number of separate policy-making arenas within local government.

Conclusion

The dramatic changes, which occurred in local government and in the national spatial planning framework after 1994, significantly alter the context within which the metropolitan planners of Cape Town are managing the production of their plan. All planning work within the bureaucracies is slowed considerably by the reorganization of institutions and personnel, and by high staff turnover. New and frequently inexperienced local councillors are asked to approve matters about which they often have little understanding, and which are prepared by officials whom they do not always trust. The relationship between the metropolitan authority and the new municipalities alters as well. While metropolitan planning is now clearly the task of the new Cape Metropolitan Council, there is ambiguity over the extent to which this can infringe on the planning actions of municipalities, and the new requirement for consensus-seeking between metropolitan authorities and municipalities is unfamiliar to planners at both levels. Complicating these new relationships is the new party-political nature of the councils, which aligns the Provincial and metropolitan councils with certain of the municipalities, but not with the Cape Town municipality (which is ANC-dominated).

Within the metropolitan authority, the work of individual departments is fundamentally influenced by the flurry of national policy directives, affecting every substantive area of local government work. Relationships between national and local line-function departments are tightened in this process, perhaps at the expense of intra-governmental co-ordination. Particularly important in terms of national policy initiatives is the emergence of a new direction for local government: the idea that it should be forward-thinking and 'developmental' (rather than simply administrative), and that its line-function work should be integrated through the new IDPs. Meeting this requirement involves the spatial planners in negotiating new relationships with other metropolitan departments, a process which in turn begins to affect their status within the metropolitan authority.

Encompassing all these changes is a rapid shift, after 1994, in the discourse of development emanating from the national level of government. From the interventionist, equity-driven rhetoric of the RDP (reflecting in many ways the earlier modernist, welfare-based discourse of First World social democracies), the rapid shift to a neo-liberal philosophy of development by 1996 brings about a realignment in a range of policy positions. The metropolitan planners, who had bolstered their discourse coalition-building by calling attention to the compatibility between the RDP and the framing of their plan, suddenly find themselves having to negotiate a new discourse which places the goal of 'entrepreneurial government' alongside that of the need to manage redistribution, and which is as much concerned with 'global positioning' as it is with addressing poverty and unemployment. The next chapters turn to the question of how the metropolitan planners pursued their efforts within this unpredictable and rapidly changing context.

6 Dusting off the old planning legislation

Can we make the metropolitan plan legal?

By the beginning of 1995 South Africa's new Government of National Unity, eight months old, was in full operation. In the Western Cape (the only province where the National Party secured political dominance), the Economic Development Forum was busy transforming itself into a Provincial Advisory Council. Its various commissions, including the Urban Development Commission, had ceased to function. The Regional Services Council had been renamed the Cape Metropolitan Council. A new set of 'pre-interim' metropolitan councillors was in place but, as in the previous period, the majority of these were National Party members. The contingent of officials was largely unchanged.

In the planning department of the new Cape Metropolitan Council, officials were left in possession of the Urban Development Commission's draft document entitled Metropolitan Spatial Development Framework – a guide for spatial development in the Cape Metropolitan Region (Feb. 1995), and now had to consider what to do with it. This was not a contentious issue for the planners of the Cape Metropolitan Council. The processing of spatial plans followed a traditional route. The new metropolitan plan had to be given legal 'teeth', or statutorized, so that future applications for development and local-level planning could be made consistent with the metropolitan framework. The Land Use Planning Ordinance of 1985 (LUPO) provided for the statutorization of regional, sub-regional and local structure plans which in turn had to conform with the nationally binding 'Guide Plans'. As such, LUPO had originally come into existence as part of a system of top-down, national control over settlement in urban areas, which was tied to the project of establishing racially separate areas within towns and cities. In 1995, LUPO was still in place.

In terms of LUPO, the draft plan had to be circulated for comment to local authorities (LUPO 1985 sec. 4(2)), had to be advertised for objections to the general public, and could thereafter be approved by the Provincial Premier. Cape Metropolitan Council planners were hopeful that this would take no more than six months, particularly given the extensive involvement of local authorities and other stakeholders, which had already occurred. It was, however, to take many years and cause unprecedented tension between metropolitan and local level authorities, in part because the new institutional and legislative context unfolding in the post-election period was not compatible with traditional methods of planning and control. In the process, the energies of the planners came to focus inwards on the various technical requirements needed for legislative approval, as opposed to the previous period during which stakeholder involvement had been a central concern.

While statutorization of the plan was one source of tension between the metropolitan and local authorities, another was the substantive content of the plan. There was broad agreement on the nature of the spatial problems which the plan identified, but there was much less agreement on the spatial proposals contained in the plan and what exactly the plan was attempting to control or promote.

This chapter relates how the planning effort again became embroiled in bureaucratic processes, and how the major changes in the institutional context, in particular the introduction of 'pre-interim' and 'interim' local government in Cape Town, bedevilled the planners' efforts to statutorize the plan speedily.

Processing the MSDF (round one)

In April 1995, the long-standing Co-ordinating Working Group within the metropolitan authority resumed its meetings. With the Urban Development Commission now disbanded, it was in the hands of this group to take forward the metropolitan planning process. Membership of the committee was generally unchanged. Peter de Tolly and two of his colleagues were there from the Cape Town City Council, but de Tolly was soon to be drawn away to plan Cape Town's bid for the 2004 Olympic Games. The Provincial Council sent two members, the business and NGO representatives remained the same, and the consultants and facilitators were also unchanged. Francois Theunissen (as Branch Head of Regional Planning) was in the chair.

The immediate task for this group was to circulate the draft Metropolitan Spatial Development Framework (MSDF) to municipalities, other government bodies and to the general public for comment, and thus satisfy the LUPO requirement that all 'interested bodies' had been systematically consulted. These comments would be considered and a revised version of the MSDF would be published as a Technical Report, which would contain a full explanation of the motivation for the plan. Thereafter a much slimmer version would be produced as the Statutory Plan. Despite the extended process of participation which the plan had been through under the auspices of the Western Cape Economic Development Forum, this had not formally occurred in terms of LUPO: asking for comment in terms of the legal provisions of the Ordinance still had to take place.

Communication between the metropolitan planners and the broader group of stakeholders which had been represented on the now-defunct Forum took on a very different form. The Co-ordinating Working Group decided to 'popularize' the plan. Over the next few months, large numbers of slide presentations were given to ratepayer organizations, local forums and civic associations, a regular newsletter was started and work was begun on a video presentation.

There is no doubt that the more open and accountable style of planning, which had been demanded of the authorities in the pre-election period, remained to influence the way of working of at least this group of planners, even if the form of participation was no more than that of 'selling' a set of already formulated spatial ideas.

As 1995 passed, comments on the draft metropolitan plan came in slowly, and deadlines were extended again and again. The labour, civic and squatter organizations did not respond. A serious weakening had occurred in these organizations after the elections, and this requires some explanation.

The fate of the civic movement

A particularly significant change which occurred in the post-1994 election period was in the nature and role of 'civil society', especially that aspect of it comprising the many civic and community-based organizations which had flourished prior to 1994. If the interests of the metropolitan planners in Cape Town now turned 'inwards', to the bureaucratic demands of gaining statutory approval for the Metropolitan Spatial Development Framework, then the reasons for this must be traced not just to a lapsing of their attention to public participation but also to the changes occurring within the popular, largely township- and squatter-based organizations.

Political transition theorists have noted that transitions to liberal democracy are frequently followed by the demobilizing of those forces in civil society that were instrumental in driving the process (Ginsburg 1996). Should power be made accessible to the majority through channels other than those of liberal democratic institutions, Ginsburg notes, it could be used to effect social and economic change that is unaffordable, or affordable only at the expense of the existing powerful and privileged groups. In the case of South Africa, the demands of the labour movement were contained by various legislative measures; civic and community-based organizations faltered, both as a result of internal failings and what may be termed 'benign neglect' on the part of the government.

Seekings (1998) comments that one of the most striking changes in (post-1994) South Africa was the decline in the township-based civic movement. The largest national grouping of civic organizations, SANCO, itself acknowledged that it was in a situation approaching crisis. The Western Cape SANCO office, which used to operate from 'luxurious' and 'upmarket' premises in the centre of Cape Town, had moved to a 'ramshackle building' on the poorer side of the city centre, with 'dilapidated tables and chairs and a single computer'. They were under threat of eviction for non-payment of rent and the only part-time office assistant was paid 'intermittently' (Seekings 1998, 13). Seekings estimates that the number of people in the metropolitan area who were by that stage involved with SANCO activities (on a voluntary basis) was probably no more than about a thousand. There were other civic-type bodies which had a history of organization in Cape Town, sometimes in alliance with SANCO.

CAHAC (Cape Areas Housing Action Committee) operated primarily in the coloured township areas, WCCA (Western Cape Civics Association) in the African townships, WECUSA (Western Cape Squatters Association) in the African shack settlements and WCHDA (Western Cape Hostel Dwellers Association) amongst African migrant hostel dwellers. These organizations, as well, became much less prominent than before.

There were several reasons for this decline (see Seekings 1996, 1998). Civics, and particularly SANCO, were badly affected by the establishment of democratic local government as much of the civic leadership took up positions in 1996 as ANC representatives on the new municipal and metropolitan councils. SANCO councillors were required by civic policy to resign and were therefore lost to the organization, and those SANCO members who chose to stand as independent candidates in most cases lost to ANC candidates. Resource shortages also seriously affected civic organizations. In the 1980s many of these organizations relied on donor funds, which were seen as a contribution to the anti-apartheid struggle. With the successful establishment of a representative democracy these funds largely dried up in the post-1994 period. Thereafter, very little of SANCO's income derived from membership dues as records of membership and payment were poor. Seekings (1998, 9) also notes a declining enthusiasm for unpaid work in the civic in favour of paid councillor positions within the ANC. He quotes one civic activist as saying: 'People are falling over each other to get in there [the ANC], and it's not because they want to look after people's needs, it's because they want the money.'

A further problem had to do with the rationale for civic organization. In the 1980s there was a clear goal for civic organization in the overthrow of the apartheid government, and in the early 1990s they played an important role in the various negotiating forums concerned with the terms of transition. Since the establishment of representative, democratic local government in 1996, the civic role *vis-à-vis* that of elected councillors became less clear and there was growing friction around this issue, particularly between those in secure, paid councillor positions, and those (often previous co-activists) still in the civic movement. It had been the civic position that their role was one of 'watchdog' over government activities, but this did not provide the basis for mobilization of township residents or much new recruitment into the organizations. In all, the preconditions for thorough civic involvement with a planning process, and particularly a metropolitan planning process (which is of less immediate concern to township residents) had become far less clear, even if Cape Town's metropolitan planners *had* decided to make a major effort in that direction.

The municipalities are not happy

Within the municipalities and various other local bodies, levels of efficiency were also impaired. Officials were well aware that the deliberations of the Western Cape Demarcation Board, sitting at that time to determine new, non-racial municipal boundaries, would result in the demise of many of the existing racially based local structures, and that the boundaries and sizes of the new municipalities would look very different from the old. There were high levels of uncertainty about how municipal staff would be deployed across the new structures, and what this might mean for job security, pensions and working conditions. Within councils as well, new members were battling to find their feet. On the 'pre-interim' metropolitan body, 50 per cent of council members were from previous 'statutory' organizations and 50 per cent from previous 'non-statutory' organizations. The latter had come from township civic associations, trade unions, youth groups, and so on, and had had no previous experience of decision-making in a structure of this kind. Council itself was co-chaired by members from the two groupings and each standing committee was co-chaired. There were 160 councillors in all, making it a large and unwieldy body.

Nonetheless, most of the expected comments on the draft Technical Report of the MSDF, from official sources at least, eventually found their way to the metropolitan authority. There were some comments on the content of the planning document, and the configuration of nodes, corridors and edges that made up the spatial plan, but in general there was approval of the planning ideas it contained. Considerable concern was voiced, however, about the future status of the plan. It was quite acceptable to most of the local authorities that the plan should exist as a guiding Technical Report, which would be a statement of the desired spatial future of metropolitan Cape Town. But it was of great concern that it might take on legal status and thus in any way bind the actions and plans of municipalities. It was with this in mind that the two largest of the 'pre-interim' municipalities (Cape Town and Bellville[1]) complained that the plan was too specific in its identification of areas to be developed or protected. They urged, rather, that it should contain written principles and policies which the municipalities could make spatially specific through local planning exercises.

Theunissen was determined, however, that the statutorization of the metropolitan plan should go ahead, and he was generally supported in this by his immediate superior, Tomalin. It was not entirely surprising that the metropolitan planners felt this way. Statutorization of the plan would give them wide powers to ensure that their plan was taken note of: it would bind lower-level municipal structure plans and would bind councillors at metropolitan and local levels. It would, in effect, replace the nationally approved Guide Plans from the previous political era, and confer equivalent powers on the metropolitan authority. The statutorization of strategies demarcated on a map made the application of these powers quite specific. And legal powers attached to a map would certainly be more far-reaching and specific than powers that would derive from a set of principles or policies, which would be open to wide interpretation by municipalities. Theunissen, moreover, had been personally responsible for introducing some of the basic principles in LUPO (Theunissen 1987), and he clearly felt strongly about the value of this particular legislation. As one informant commented: 'He comes from a school which says if you have a form of statutory prescription in place you will achieve your ends.' In a feedback session on this chapter, however, Theunissen took great exception to my interpretation of his reasons for supporting statutorization:

> Now please don't think I am being defensive, but that correct fact (that statutorizing the MSDF would give it more power), to convert that into our motivation, was problematic to me. If I had been at a municipality I would have still stood by this principle, that the highest plan should be statutorized ... here our motivation was strongly the principle of statutorizing the highest plan, well all plans ... So to ignore that main motivation and say that the motivation was that it would have given us power – you see, that to me is a bit unfair.
>
> (Interview 14 1999)

Tomalin also felt strongly about the merits of legal plans, although he motivated it differently. He argued that it made the planning process more transparent:

> Without statutorization you are back to 'bottom drawer' planning. Somebody is bound to have a plan in their bottom drawer. People will always have a plan which they will consult. And I say that is an underhand way of dealing with it. Rather have the plan that has been through a public participation process and approved statutorily. Then everybody knows the plan you are using. Politicians are bound by that plan, all officials are bound, the development industry knows about the plan ... It can meet the criteria for transparency and accountability in a way that a set of vague principles can never do. I feel very strongly about that. I think as planners we are selling part of our birthright if we move away from doing forward planning and statutorization.
>
> (Interview 9 1999)

But the progress of both the Technical Report and the statutory version of it were to be slowed down greatly by the process of local government transition. Comments on the draft Technical Report were finally in by October of 1995 (MSDF-CWG minutes 1995a), but the document had to be revised and then submitted to the 'pre-interim' metropolitan council for approval. This did not happen until early in 1996, and at this point the councillors (most of whom had had no previous exposure to the plan) asked for a workshop to allow for indepth discussion. The workshop was arranged, but few councillors attended (MSDF-CWG minutes 1996a). With the next round of local elections imminent, this may have been no more than a stalling device on the part of some councillors. For the metropolitan planners, however, time was of the essence. In May 1996, the first democratic local elections were due to be held in terms of the newly demarcated municipal and metropolitan boundaries. At this time an entirely new set of elected ('interim') metropolitan councillors would take their places, and the political complexion of these councillors, and their feelings about the merits of the MSDF, were unknown. It was not impossible that they would demand a major rethink of the metropolitan plan. It was a photo-finish. The outgoing Council endorsed the plan on 24 April 1996. Tomalin, politically astute as ever, made sure the report was dated 'April' 1996 (Technical Report 1996) to signify its acceptance by the outgoing 'pre-interim' council. The 4,000 copies which were printed were not ready until the middle of June.

Planning officials had to tread carefully, however. The new 'interim' metropolitan councillors were not bound to accept decisions of this kind which had been passed by their appointed, 'pre-interim' predecessors. Neither did the new 'interim' councillors of the six newly demarcated municipalities have to endorse the support given to the plan by recently disbanded, racially based local structures. Planning officials in all these newly demarcated authorities were generally unchanged, but many of the councillors were entirely new to this form of representation. Under the first local democratic elections of May 1996, large numbers of previous civic association and community-based leaders took up positions in local government. After decades of struggle against these organs of government, they were now ostensibly in control of them. But the same officials, who had been on the opposite side of battles over rents and township conditions, were still in place, and it could be expected that councillors would regard them cautiously. Moreover, local elections in metropolitan Cape Town had, for the first time, been held on party-political lines and this changed the balance of power between officials and politicians. Not only did councillors have an eye on the next election, but they were also subject to party discipline and party-aligned debate on substantive issues. In the years after the 1996 elections, many officials were heard to complain about how the new system of representation had 'politicized' the functioning of local government and made their work much more difficult.

Facilitator David Shandler had been particularly struck by this change in the balance of power (Interview 5 1999). Prior to the 1996 local elections, the National Party's hold on the metropolitan authority had been somewhat tenuous, and they had had to be more accommodating. But after 1996 they could play a more assertive role. The National Party chair of the Executive Committee of the Council began to take an interest in the MSDF and he, together with the Democratic Party-aligned chair of the Planning, Environment and Housing Committee (the National Party and the Democratic Party were by then in coalition in the Western Cape Provincial government) began to hold regular monthly meetings with the planning officials:

> Key issues and decisions would have to be passed by the politicians. And it got to the point where Watkyns (Committee chair) would chair these meetings ... And the process was taken away from the planners and it became a political process. It became a very difficult time for the planners. They couldn't operate with nearly the same degree of confidence that they had prior to that.
>
> (Interview 5 1999)

The decision was made to proceed as follows: the planners would arrange a public launch of the 1996 Technical Report after the new metropolitan council was in place, with the councillors playing an important public role in the ceremony. The MSDF was increasingly being seen as 'the glamour project' by the politicians (Interview 5 1999), and a high-profile ceremony (Figure 6.1) would make it clear that the new metropolitan council accepted 'ownership' of the plan. And the launch was 'a big splash, an incredible splash – they made a big deal of it, it became a political event' (Interview 5 1999).

Getting the new municipalities on board was a more difficult prospect, particularly given the worries expressed before by some of the municipal planning officials that the plan would constrain their local planning activities. Moreover, under the new system of 'interim' local government, persuasion had to be the primary tactic of the metropolitan planners. This was because Chapter 3 of the 1996 Constitution had introduced the system of co-operative government in which the national, provincial and local levels are 'spheres' rather than 'tiers' of government. This implied that at the local level there was no automatic hierarchy of authority of metropolitan government over municipalities. Thus municipal councils had to be 'persuaded' to comment positively on the MSDF Technical Report if the metropolitan authority wanted to turn it into a statutory plan in terms of LUPO. Under the previous, hierarchical, system of local government, negative comments from a local authority could have been

Figure 6.1 The public launch of the MSDF Technical Report, 1996.

Source: Photograph provided by S. Pheiffer, Cape Metropolitan Council.

ignored or overridden by a Provincial ruling. What emerges here is the start of a clash between the old and new systems of planning and administration, which was to bedevil the metropolitan planning process for years to follow.

In the Co-ordinating Working Group meeting of July 1996 (MSDF-CWG minutes 1996b) it was decided to give audio-visual presentations on the Metropolitan Spatial Development Framework to the planning officials of all the new municipalities. By this time a professional slide-tape show had been prepared, setting out, first, the main problems of metropolitan Cape Town, then the consequences of non-intervention, and finally the main planning strategies, presented as obvious responses to the problems facing the city. The metropolitan planners clearly saw it as the right time to use tactics of planning by persuasion. Present at the meeting, for the first time in over a year, was the trade union representative, who had also been the labour representative on the Urban Development Commission during the Forum years. He was unhappy about the persuasive approach. With all but one of the municipal councils dominated by the National Party, he clearly feared that they would dismiss the plan as a product of a body (the Forum) on which both the ANC and the trade unions had played a strong role. The union representative's suggestion that the new municipalities simply be informed of the metropolitan acceptance of the Technical Report may well have been one that the planners would gladly have gone along with, but the new system of democratic government was not, in this respect, operating in their favour. The municipalities would have to be persuaded, and this would have to be done before the process of compiling a statutory plan went further.

Before exploring how the metropolitan planners fared in this task, it is necessary to look more closely at what the 1996 Technical Report of the MSDF contained and the message that it tried to convey.

Conclusion

What becomes evident in this chapter is that while national rules and policies have changed significantly, while formal governmental structures and relationships have been transformed, and while there are many new local politicians aligned to the ANC government, in the offices of the local authority officials power is exercised in much the same way as before. While change is significant, so is continuity.

One significant source of pressure on the metropolitan planners – that emanating from the organized township and civic groupings – has been removed. While many of the individuals previously in the civic movement are now able to exert their authority as councillors, interaction between councillors and officials is contained within an established set of rules and procedures which proves, perhaps, less threatening to officials than street marches and demonstrations. The fact that the old adversaries, the planning officials of the now ANC-dominated Cape Town Municipality, prove to be strongest opponents of the plan (aimed, after all, at addressing the spatial heritage of apartheid) is testament to the unpredictability of this relationship between officials and councillors. Thus, the prime concern for the metropolitan planners is now the other potential source of opposition – the municipalities and other functional government departments within and above the metropolitan council.

How do the metropolitan planners at this point come to use legislation as a means of empowering their plan? The alternative, after all, is to leave the 1996 Technical Report as a guiding document, and to use powers of persuasion (and perhaps, indirectly, public resource allocation) to redirect municipal planning and the pattern of development in Cape Town. The latter route would have been in keeping with post-1994 local government policy which required consensus-seeking between authorities, a policy which now ran counter to the hierarchical relationships assumed under LUPO. The explanations given by the metropolitan planners as to why they chose this route indicate the value to them of established and previously tried mechanisms of management. LUPO is a legal mechanism which they had worked with for a decade, and which one of the planners had partly drafted. Planning by consensus and persuasion offers an uncertain way forward in which loss of control is possible. Consensus methods had been successfully used in the context of the Forum, when no alternative was available, but the riskiness of the situation had been recognized. LUPO, still available as a management tool, offers a clear way forward and a predictable set of outcomes, both highly desirable in a context of dramatic change and uncertainty, and likely municipal opposition.

What is also of relevance here is the importance of process relative to product. While the spatial product of the pre-1994 planning model (the multi-nodal, segregated city) is abandoned with relative ease, this is not the case with the pre-1994 planning process, or LUPO. What becomes most significant about the post-1994 metropolitan planning effort is the degree to which the energies of the planners are focused almost entirely on the goal of statutorizing the new plan. There is no doubt that different decision-making processes offer the potential for individuals to exercise power in different ways, and will be either promoted or countered for these reasons.

7 Practices of representation

The Metropolitan Spatial Development Framework (1996 Technical Report)

The 1996 Technical Report could be called a 'classic statement in the urban design tradition' (Mandelbaum 1990, 350). It is 107 pages long, carefully argued and illustrated, and culminates in a coloured map of Cape Town indicating the desired spatial vision of the city twenty years hence (Figure 7.1). It is a heroic, modernist plan, but not uncommon in large cities, both in South Africa and elsewhere.[1]

The spatial concepts which underlie it derived only partly from the South African urban experience (see Chapter 2), but they found their political moment in the early 1990s when planners, particularly those in the bureaucracies, were searching for an alternative to the spatial form being promoted by apartheid ideologies of race and exclusion. South Africa, in the years immediately before and after the elections of 1994, may be compared in some respects to post-war Europe: the sense that a brand new and better society had to be reconstructed from the ashes of the old, was a prevailing one. Policy documents and political statements of the time reflect the importance of creating a 'vision' (and this word became almost obligatory in the introductory statements of policy papers) of an ideal future condition, which, in broad terms, was usually democratic, non-racial, sustainable and focused on the poor. The redistributionary and basic needs thrust of the MSDF was therefore entirely in keeping with the spirit of the time, and in particular with the national policy position reflected in the Reconstruction and Development Programme, or RDP (1994). What the Technical Report of 1996 reflects, however, is that by 1996 the RDP was falling from favour, to be gradually replaced by a new neo-liberal macroeconomic policy which showed growing concerns with economic growth and South Africa's relationships to its global economic partners and international funding agencies.

What follows is a description of the contents of the 1996 Technical Report: the Metropolitan Spatial Development Framework (Technical Report 1996). It is a revised version of the (February 1995) document produced by the Urban Development Commission of the Western Cape Economic Development Forum, and some of the differences between the earlier document and the 1996 version are significant. It reflects some of the comments made during 1995 from (primarily) public sector bodies and business, and changes in thinking on the

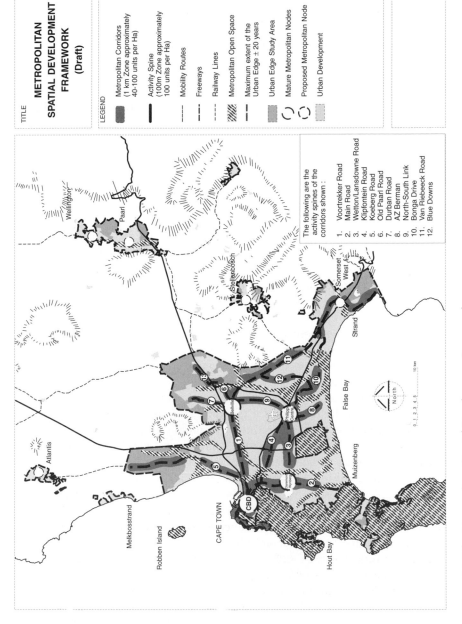

Figure 7.1 The Metropolitan Spatial Development Framework.

Source: Technical Report (1996).

part of the metropolitan planners and their consultants, on how best to ration-alize and present their plan. No description is ever entirely 'neutral', however. Fischler (1995, 14) makes the point that in our attempt to understand what planners do, we need to recognize that both the content of their discourse (spoken and written) and its form indicate how planners conceive of politics, society and the problems of the city. In the professional use of texts, images, charts or tables, Fischler argues, we need to understand persuasion as a form of power in that 'it clearly represents a means by which an actor may achieve an intended effect on another's behaviour' (Wrong 1988, 32, in Fischler 1995). In examining the contents of the Technical Report, then, I pay attention to ways in which the authors selectively organize the readers' attention, conceptually frame problems and issues in certain ways, and present facts, strategies and drawings in a way which exercises persuasive power over the reader.[2]

Justification for intervention

The preface and the introduction to the Technical Report establish the pedi-gree of the document. Text and an accompanying diagram (see Figure 7.2) make the point that the start of the planning process lay in the 1991 Caledon Conference, at which a mandate was given by civic and community organi-zations, trade union and service organizations, to proceed with a metropolitan plan. Chapter 1 has argued that work on the plan had started well before this, and that a set of spatial principles had received general support from the Regional Development Strategy Committee by early 1991. What is important here, however, is that the rooting of the plan in the Caledon Conference gives the Report a level of legitimacy amongst those perceived as the main con-stituency of the planners. It is therefore intended to operate as a persuasive device, if at the expense of historical accuracy.

Section 2 of the Report describes the study area. Section 3 is a major section that aims to establish the rationale for planning intervention. It discusses the metropolitan area of Cape Town in terms of the problems it is experiencing and the opportunities that exist to address these problems. One does not have to read far into the earlier or later versions of the Technical Report to conclude that it is addressed primarily to communities, politicians, and other policy and planning professionals, rather than to the business and investment community. In fact at a Co-ordinating Working Group meeting in September 1995, the representative of the Chambers of Commerce and Industry complained directly that the report was too 'socio-economically and politically oriented, and would not appeal to business' (MSDF-CWG minutes 1995b). A representative of the Provincial Reconstruction and Development Office, making a rare appearance at the same meeting, counter-argued that it would be incorrect simply to pursue a market-driven approach, and here the matter rested. The 1996 document was, nonetheless, changed in subtle ways which suggested that 'addressing business' was an issue of growing importance in the minds of a wider constituency than just organized industry and commerce. It is in section 3 of the Report that the

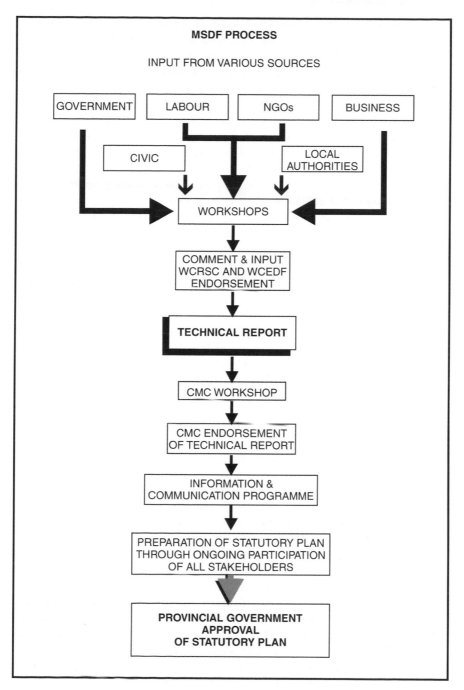

Figure 7.2 The MSDF process.
Source: Technical Report (1996).

most important changes to the 1995 version of the document occur – in broad terms there is a shift in focus from a concern with meeting the basic needs of Cape Town's poor, to a concern with economic growth.

The 1995 version of the MSDF contains a statement on the overall purpose of the plan (section 1.2) which refers to the need to

> address the historical legacy of development and deprivation under apartheid that has been perpetuated at a cost to society and the individual. The MSDF's aim is to improve the functioning of the CMR for the poor.

The statement goes on to refer to the RDP and how a spatial plan such as this one is necessary to realize its aims. The 1996 statement of purpose (section 1.3) looks rather different. It is argued that a spatial framework is needed 'to provide the context within which communities and private sector activity . . . can grow and expand'. It goes on to state that growth and development are vital to address the historical legacy of underdevelopment and deprivation. Only in the last sentence of the statement of purpose is reference made to the need to establish the basis for growth, from which 'especially the poor' will benefit. References to the RDP and to the needs of the poor, remain, but they are now downplayed and the goal of economic growth is newly introduced. Also different in the 1996 statement of purpose is that reference to the inherited problems of apartheid has been removed. In June 1995 the Chamber of Commerce and Industry representative had asked that 'political' language such as this be taken out of the document (MSDF-CWG minutes 1995c)!

The shift in the 1996 Technical Report to a more 'market-friendly' approach is particularly evident in the section dealing with the context of Cape Town. The sub-section dealing with the more positive side of metropolitan Cape Town, the 'opportunities', has been unearthed from the back of the problem statement in the 1995 document, and placed upfront. It has a new heading: 'Looking Ahead – Opportunities for Successful Spatial Reconstruction'. Two double-columned pages of new material have been inserted here, mostly pointing to the advantages of the people (emphasizing their high skill level), the place (making the point that it is an attractive place to live and locate businesses), and the economy (with reference to South Africa's entry into the global marketplace). Much of this material is sourced to a 1995 WESGRO document, entitled *The Western Cape Economy in 1995: Take-off for a Decade of Growth*. WESGRO is the business investment promotion and lobby group that initiated the Western Cape Economic Development Forum in 1993. It may also reflect the influence of several World Bank missions to South Africa in the early 1990s, which drew strong connections between the spatial structure of South African urban areas and the performance of both the urban and national economy. A 1993 Mission Report (World Bank 1993, 1) had commented that 'the Mission [also] strongly believes that the overall urban policy framework will determine the extent to which the economy as a whole is able to successfully negotiate the important transition to a post-apartheid era in an efficient and equitable manner'. Section 3.1 of the 1996 Technical Report, at least, speaks to the business sector, even if much of the rest of the Report does not.

The second part of section 3, on the problems of Cape Town, remains largely unchanged from the 1995 version, and here the basic-needs and poverty-alleviation thrust of the Report continues to dominate. These are defined in terms of relatively standard categories: poverty and unemployment, rapid population growth, inadequate social facilities, poor management of economic growth, housing inadequacies, lack of infrastructural services, health problems, and a poor public transport system. Thereafter the Report turns to spatial problems.

The issue of racial residential segregation in the city receives some prominence, and a conceptual diagram shows how the residential areas of the white population are concentrated in the west and north of the city, close to the mountains and areas with amenity, and the coloured and African residential areas are in the part of the city known as the Cape Flats, with its windswept, waterlogged and sandy environment. This is a conceptual simplification, but it nonetheless remains true that, despite the removal of legislation enforcing racially segregated residence in 1991, Cape Town in the post-1994 years continues to have strong elements of racial segregation.

Finally, problems and opportunities are depicted on a map of Cape Town (Figure 7.3). This map, which repeats some of the problems and opportunities identified in the text but adds a number of other concerns, begins to set the scene for the spatial strategies which are to follow. The older, largely white-occupied parts of the city, called the Southern Arm and the Tygerberg Arm respectively, are shown as 'the best-functioning areas' because they are physically 'integrated'; that is, they provide a 'range of accessible facilities and services' (Technical Report 1996, 17). This characterization of these areas has its roots in older publications of the Urban Problems Research Unit of the University of Cape Town (Dewar *et al.* 1976, 1990). The 1976 publication evaluated urban environments on these 'arms' positively, because they exhibited continuity of the built fabric, and were focused on stop–start movement and public transport routes which had an intensive mix of activities located along them, but the application of the term 'corridor' to these parts of the city did not occur until much later (Dewar and Uytenbogaardt 1991, 50). This form of 'evolutionary' (or unplanned) development, the publication argued, created 'high levels of convenience', 'clarity of structure' and 'integrated communities' (Dewar *et al.* 1976, 10). The identification of a spatial form of this kind as a positive urban element was not new: it resonates with earlier planning literature on the concept of linear cities and examples such as the 1948 Copenhagen 'finger plan'.

Contrasting with the well-performing 'arms' are the 'disadvantaged communities' (Figure 7.3). These are located in the planned residential areas built by the pre-1994 government to hold the coloured and African populations of Cape Town. Termed the 'construct-based' areas in Dewar *et al.* (1976), they are described as areas which have been planned according to principles of

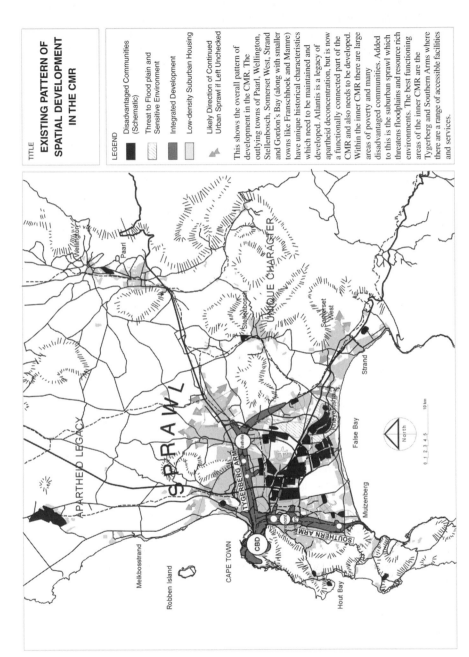

TITLE

**EXISTING PATTERN OF
SPATIAL DEVELOPMENT
IN THE CMR**

LEGEND

Disadvantaged Communities
(Schematic)

Threat to Flood plain and
Sensitive Environment

Integrated Development

Low-density Suburban Housing

Likely Direction of Continued
Urban Sprawl if Left Unchecked

This shows the overall pattern of
development in the CMR. The
outlying towns of Paarl, Wellington,
Stellenbosch, Somerset West, Strand
and Gordon's Bay (along with smaller
towns like Franschhoek and Mamre)
have unique historical characteristics
which need to be maintained and
developed. Atlantis is a legacy of
apartheid deconcentration, but is now
a functionally connected part of the
CMR and also needs to be developed.
Within the inner CMR there are large
areas of poverty and many
disadvantaged communities. Added
to this is the suburban sprawl which
threatens floodplains and resource rich
environments. The best functioning
areas of the inner CMR are the
Tygerberg and Southern Arms where
there are a range of accessible facilities
and services.

Figure 7.3 Spatial problems and opportunities in Cape Town.

Source: Technical Report (1996).

separation: separation of residential areas on the Cape Flats from areas of work opportunity on the 'arms' and in the CBD; separation of one planned neighbourhood from the next, and, within areas, separation of one land use from another. And of course, the desired separation of African and coloured people from each other, and from the white population of Cape Town located on the 'arms' and around the CBD, was a key factor which gave rise to the construction of these areas. The Technical Report, however, focuses less on the inadequacies of local planning on the Cape Flats and more on the fact that these areas contain people who are poor and unemployed, who are physically removed from work opportunity (which is assumed to mean formal jobs), and who experience poor service and housing facilities. A wide range of income groups, cultural groups and forms of accommodation are captured in this single category of area, and this begins to draw attention to the 'dual city' conceptualization which informs the framing of the spatial problems. Figure 7.3 reflects this, but Figure 7.4 shows it more clearly: Cape Town is categorized into two kinds of areas – the 'arms' and the CBD are characterized as 'areas of opportunity' and the Cape Flats as the area which 'lacks opportunity'.[3]

Marcuse (1989), in his critique of the 'dual city' concept so often applied to cities, concedes that South African cities may be one instance in which deliberate racial segregation has given rise to a literal 'two city' situation. This portrayal, with its 'implicit call for the inequality to be evened out with the benefits of prosperity at the upper end shared by those excluded from them at the lower end' (Marcuse 1989, 698), certainly fits the thrust of the MSDF problem-framing (which focuses on spatial inequities) and the redistributionary justification for its proposals. It can be argued, however, that Marcuse's worry about the reality of dual cities is as valid here as it is elsewhere. As in other parts of the world, divisions in Cape Town society exist along many lines: 'relations of production, consumption, race, income, ethnicity or color, gender, household composition, age and housing tenure' (Marcuse 1989, 703). The categorization of Cape Town into 'areas of opportunity' and areas which 'lack opportunity', or even into 'arms' and 'townships', may be a useful communicative device; however, it obscures not only the great diversity which occurs within these areas but also the nature of the relationships which occur between them and which potentially perpetuate inequalities. The danger in simplified dual city categorizations, as Marcuse points out, is that they become the basis for simplified strategies. Arguments about skewed distributions of benefits and burdens (or opportunity and lack of opportunity) suggest strategies of redistribution, from givers to receivers, from the wealthy part of the city to the poor part. In spatial planning terms they can suggest that the poor part of the city should be made to look, or function, more like the wealthy part. They suggest palliatives, Marcuse argues, but not cures.

The dual city concept, along with the normative assumptions it carries, that dualism must be overcome by integration, potentially perpetuates other simplifications as well. Robinson (1999) has pointed to the varied connections and disconnections which shape the form and experience of particular city spaces.

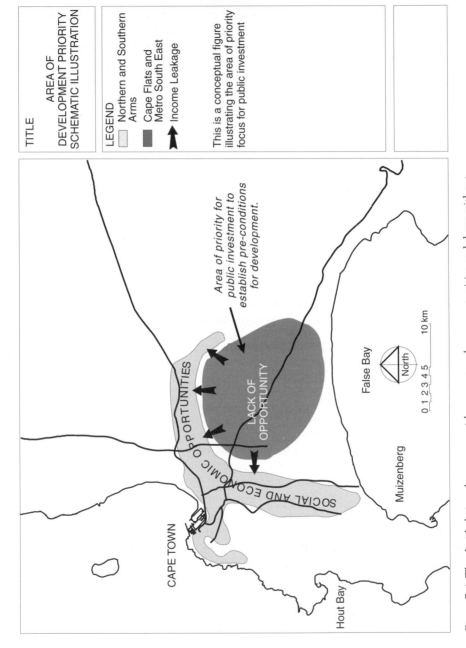

TITLE

AREA OF
DEVELOPMENT PRIORITY
SCHEMATIC ILLUSTRATION

LEGEND

Northern and Southern
Arms

Cape Flats and
Metro South East

Income Leakage

This is a conceptual figure
illustrating the area of priority
focus for public investment

Area of priority for
public investment to
establish pre-conditions
for development.

OPPORTUNITIES

LACK OF
OPPORTUNITY

SOCIAL AND ECONOMIC OPPORTUNITIES

CAPE TOWN

Hout Bay

Muizenberg

False Bay

North

0 1 2 3 4 5   10 km

Figure 7.4 The divided city: those areas with access to urban opportunities and those without.

Source: Technical Report (1996).

Graham and Healey (1999, 641) refer to the 'realities of the open, dynamic, multi-layered and dialectically-constructed multiplex circuitry of the contemporary urban region'. These dynamics have not yet been understood in the context of Cape Town; neither has the possible impact of making new spatial relationships or disrupting existing ones. Disconnection can also create opportunity (for example, for small businesses to flourish away from competition with larger, formal ones), and may be required for particular cultural practices (such as Xhosa initiation rites) which need to take place in the open but in privacy. The question of integration may be important in the replanning of Cape Town, but it is clearly a multi-faceted one.

Scenario-building

In what seems to be an increasingly common approach in planning reports and processes (see Forsyth 1999), the next section of the 1996 Technical Report sets out three 'development scenarios'. Here, as elsewhere, this involves the presentation of a number of other cities to show possible ways in which Cape Town could change in the future. The three cities chosen to represent these alternatives are Los Angeles, São Paulo and Curitiba.

The planning consultant[4] responsible for compiling the 1996 Report (the same consultant who had been appointed by the then Regional Services Council in 1991 to assist with the MSDF process) explained why these particular cities had been chosen (Sturgeon, pers. comm. 1999). Los Angeles represented the archetypal sprawl city,[5] demonstrating the consequences of allowing low-density residential development to continue: these were pollution, poor public transport, a marginalized urban population, a vast and costly road infrastructure, loss of agricultural land and a lack of public open space. It was exactly these characteristics of sprawl and private transport dependence which the Technical Report identified as underlying many of Cape Town's spatial problems, and Los Angeles served as a 'warning' of what might come if these trends were allowed to continue. The planning consultant explained that the Los Angeles case was particularly useful in countering the pro-freeway stance of many of the local transport engineers. It had also been used for these purposes in Newman and Kenworthy's 1989 book on automobile dependence, and both the book and the case were well known amongst South African planners.

São Paulo was chosen because, according to the planning consultant, it was a 'third world' example, with high population growth rates and poor management, and because it had 'tried to be a Los Angeles but had failed' (Sturgeon, pers. comm. 1999). In the Technical Report, São Paulo is referred to as 'The Tidal Wave Scenario', because it was unprepared for the rapid growth of a predominantly poor population. The outcome, according to the Technical Report, was the movement of the wealthy into high-rise inner city apartments and the marginalization of the poor on the urban periphery where access to services, housing and jobs is limited. South African planners had been exposed to the São Paulo case through the visits there of one particular Johannesburg urbanist who had subsequently given a number of slide-talk shows around the country and had suggested that South African cities were likely to follow this path.

The third example, Curitiba, is called the 'What Works Best Scenario'. The MSDF consultant explained how Curitiba came to be chosen as a scenario.

> I was in a doctor's waiting room and I picked up a *Time* magazine which had an article on Curitiba as a successfully planned city. I immediately made a connection between the types of strategies which Curitiba had adopted (compaction, densified, public transport-based corridors, a public open space system and environmental management) and the spatial principles which were in the MSDF. Here were good examples of MSDF-type strategies which had been implemented and appeared to work.
>
> (Sturgeon, pers. comm. 1999)

Over the next few years groups of Cape Town planners made trips to Curitiba to view the success story at first hand, and important differences began to emerge between the apparently favoured groups who had made the journey and those who had not. Cape Town City Council planner Peter de Tolly clearly felt that they had been excluded from the organized visits for political reasons:

> [W]e didn't go to Curitiba, we weren't invited. It was very simple. And when they came back, there was now a new Curitiba alumni association, you see, and if you had been, you were a convert. Something about . . . 'well we had crossed the Rubicon of public transport and many of our colleagues had not . . .' This is a quote – I do remember those things quite clearly. I always kept saying that this whole 'grabbing' the corridor and settling on the corridors in the face of a lot of the transport evidence . . . it didn't make sense to me. It makes sense to draw up a scenario, but then you must test it.
>
> (Interview 4 1999)

Those who had been to Curitiba did come to recognize that aspects of that city did not quite fit with the principles of the MSDF. For example, the population living at high density along the Curitiba transport corridors was middle-income, while the MSDF proposed to locate lower-income people in these areas of high opportunity. How to achieve low-income, high-density housing in a situation in which the national public housing subsidy specifically promotes low-density, site and service housing on individual erven, is a problem which persists to the present time. But these details were glossed over in the scenario construction.

The three scenarios were graphically imposed on the landscape of Cape Town (Figure 7.5). The Los Angeles and São Paulo scenarios give 'shock' images of what the future of Cape Town could be without appropriate intervention. In the Curitiba scenario, corridors and spaces are drawn to resemble the final MSDF plan very closely. This, however, was not simply a case of deriving a spatial model from one context to apply in another. Curitiba functioned as

WHAT THE SCENARIOS COULD MEAN FOR THE CMR

THE SPRAWL SCENARIO

(LOS ANGELES)

The CMR grows through discrete pockets of low-density suburbia attached to the edge

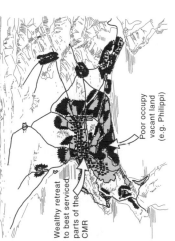

The CMR continues to grow in uncontrolled sprawl extending as far as Piketberg in the North. This is accompanied by poor public transport and inner city decline with associated social and economic problems.

THE TIDAL WAVE SCENARIO

(SÃO PAULO)

Wealthy retreat to best serviced parts of the CMR

Poor occupy vacant land (e.g. Philippi)

The wealthy of the CMR retreat to the best-established, serviced and wealthiest parts of the CMR, while the poor occupy peripheral and vacant land and live in unsanitary conditions on unserviced land.

THE WHAT WORKS BEST SCENARIO

(CURITIBA)

The City is structured through a range of high density public transport corridors

Vital green spaces are protected & used effectively

A determined attempt is made to improve public transport, and provide for affordable low-income housing and opportunities for economic development.

Figure 7.5 Three possible scenarios for Cape Town.

Source: Technical Report (1996).

a useful scenario because it supported a set of spatial ideas for Cape Town which had already been formulated. One of the consultants confirmed:

> My thinking was that Curitiba was very much an add-on, it was more a way of selling the thing [the MSDF]. The visits to Curitiba only happened way after [the corridor proposal was in place], and when everybody came back very little was changed in the document or in the concept. It was just used as a way of reinforcing it.
>
> (Interview 3 1999)

Presenting scenarios in this kind of way served to give the impression that the planners had scanned a range of possible alternatives and had made a rational choice, and likewise that the Cape Town public was faced with choosing from these three alternatives. But there is no doubt that the choice had already been made. The consultant was clear that the images functioned as an important persuasive device, and that they helped to make the MSDF a 'saleable commodity'. They also, he believed, served to educate non-planners about the ways in which the spatial form of a city would affect their day-to-day lives, as 'many people had never made this connection'.

The framework for metropolitan planning

Section 4 of the 1996 Technical Report sets out the vision and the values on which the plan is based. The vision statement was produced in a plenary session of the Western Cape Economic Development Forum in 1993, and remains unchanged. It has a primary focus on meeting basic needs and on achieving integrated and sustainable urban development. The four 'development principles' which inform the plan continue this theme – they are: equality of opportunity, social justice, sustainable development, and openness and accountability. The development principles are elaborated into ten 'goals',[6] which in turn inform a set of 'spatial' and 'non-spatial' guidelines.[7] Facilitator David Shandler (Interview 5 1999) explained how the starting point had been influenced by the Strategic Management Approach developed in the months after the Caledon Conference of 1991. It required the initial development of a vision, and then a SWOT (strengths, weaknesses, opportunities, threats) exercise. Thereafter possible interventions are identified and evaluated. But, he explained, there always tends to be greater emphasis on the problems than the opportunities. Starting with the problems it becomes

> a vision driven model ... a linear one, work from the problem to the ideal outcome. Not to expectations but to an ideal vision ... One of the problems with the MSDF is a striving for perfection. And trying to be perfect is setting yourself up for failure ... Grand plans are always striving for perfection.
>
> (Interview 5 1999)

Planners are frequently challenged to clarify the way in which they derive their goals. The set of goals contained in the Technical Report of 1996 was agreed to by the Urban Development Commission of the Western Cape Economic Development Forum some years previously, and could thus claim a level of legitimacy. The goals had been drawn up prior to this process, however, and most, in fact, had their origins in the University of Cape Town Planning School. Here it was taught that planning is normatively driven, and that all planning action is guided by the overarching and universal ethics of social justice and environmental sustainability. The goals which found their way into the Technical Report could be traced via this academic route, back to some of the Founding Fathers of planning (Geddes, Mumford) and to influential writers such as Kevin Lynch, Jane Jacobs, David Crane and Christopher Alexander. They are general goals, reflecting the planners' view of well-performing urban environments, and the desire for balance and equity.

Section 5 of the Technical Report sets out four 'structuring' elements which comprise the spatial aspect of the plan. They are: the definition of a fixed urban edge, the demarcation of an open space system within this edge, and the identification of centres and routes which are to function as 'nodes' and high-density, public-transport-carrying 'corridors'. The question which can be raised here is: how did the planners arrive at these proposals?

One answer to the question is that the way in which the spatial problems of metropolitan Cape Town were framed made these solutions appear as natural or inevitable. The problem of urban sprawl into high-value agricultural land could be prevented by stopping further development in this direction. This in turn would bring about compaction of the existing metropolitan area (considered desirable in order to counter problems of fragmented and inefficient development), and hence the need to hold existing important open spaces. The problem of inequality and a lack of integration between the poorer and wealthier parts of the city could be overcome by linking the two (via corridors) and by creating replicas, in the deprived areas of the city, of those elements (centres and corridors) which represented economic opportunity in the wealthier areas. In each case, the strategies can be read as obvious responses to the identified problems.

Another answer to the question of how the planners arrived at their proposals could be that the scenario-generating exercise had produced an example that should clearly be emulated. The Curitiba approach is presented as workable in practice, and easily applicable to the context of Cape Town. Its strategies appear tailor-made to address the spatial problems that the Report identifies.

An argument has been constructed which flows logically from problem identification, through a scanning of alternatives, to the presentation of strategies. Planning documents should obviously be logically coherent in this way; they would be very confusing to read if they were not. The point that is being made here, however, is that arguments such as these are framed in particular ways, and could conceivably be framed in other ways. A different approach to problem identification could lead equally logically to very different outcomes.

As Madanipour (1996, 183) has pointed out, such professionals operate within particular 'design paradigms' which constitute a 'set of ideas and images that designers develop and promote for a better environment'. Design paradigms, like epistemological ones, are social products and can change over time (Kuhn 1962).

The strategies themselves (the edge, spaces, nodes and corridors) may appear as obvious responses to the spatial problems of Cape Town. But they did not emerge *de novo* in the minds of the planners as they contemplated these problems; neither were they inspired by cities such as Curitiba. Some of the planners had been presented with these ideas during the course of their planning education at the University of Cape Town, and were simply applying what they had learnt. The idea of containing urban development through the holding of open space on the urban edge had appeared long before in Abercrombie's 1944 plan for London and its green-belt, and before that in the ideas of Ebenezer Howard and Raymond Unwin (see Hall 1988). It is compatible with the 'classic Abercrombie tradition' of viewing the city as a self-contained object set within the 'container' of the landscape (Graham and Healey 1999, 636–637). The strategy of concentrating development along public-transit corridors had featured in early plans for cities such as Copenhagen and Vienna. The design tradition of New Urbanism, with its emphasis on defined edges, pedestrian movement systems, formative public spaces, higher densities and mixed land-use (see Calthorpe 1994) can be traced from the work of Leon Krier in the mid-1970s (Madanipour 1996) and manifests itself in the increasing number of plans for 'neo-traditional' environments. Toronto, for example, in the period 1989 to 1992, adopted metropolitan plans dominated by the concept of the 'intensified city'. High-density development was proposed in order to reduce car use and the urbanization of rural land, and car-oriented retail strips were to be transformed into pedestrian and transit conducive 'main streets' with continuous store façades and upper floor apartments (Filion 1999)

Within South Africa itself, researchers in the national Council for Scientific and Industrial Research had, since the late 1980s, promoted the idea of the public transport-based activity corridor as an answer to movement problems within the larger urban areas. A report commissioned by the Council in 1990 (Chittenden and Associates 1990), entitled *Activity Corridors as an Urban Strategy*, and focusing on the application of this strategy in Cape Town, was mentioned by a number of planners involved in the MSDF process as being 'very influential'. Furthermore, a draft metropolitan plan had been drawn up for the Witwatersrand metropolitan area in 1993 (Gapps Architects and Urban Designers 1993), promoting corridors and nodes as urban structuring devices. As consultant Cecil Madell remarked: 'they [on the Witwatersrand] were far down the track in relation to us and there was the perception that we needed to catch up with this kind of process' (Interview 3 1999).

Thus, at the time the MSDF strategies were being formulated (and this process had begun in work presented to the Forum in 1993), these particular strategies already had a lengthy track record and, moreover, had growing support both internationally and within South Africa. They formed a 'design paradigm' which the consultants were able to draw on.

The last question raised by section 5 of the Technical Report is: how did the spatial strategies of edge, open spaces, nodes and corridors find their location on a map of metropolitan Cape Town?

The primary intention behind the demarcation of the urban edge is to protect land of agricultural and ecological value, and thereby to counter urban sprawl (Technical Report 1996, 57). Certain of the edges, such as that defining the boundary of the Table Mountain Chain, were broadly uncontested: this edge had been held for many years. The definition of the open space system also raised little objection.[8] However, the definition of the outer edge was soon made subject to other considerations. One consideration was the new metropolitan boundary which had been defined in 1996. In some areas the edge had to be 'pulled in' to coincide with the administrative boundary, as there was no agreement in place with the neighbouring Councils to define an environmentally logical edge which deviated from the administrative one. A second consideration was the worry, by the Tygerberg Municipality in particular, that the edge would restrict its expansion possibilities. This municipality had been experiencing strong pressure for high-income residential development onto the rich agricultural lands of the Tygerberg Hills, a trend which was favourable from the point of view of its municipal rates base. As a result the 1996 Technical Report shows an urban edge drawn wider than it is in the earlier (1995) version of the document. Political considerations had overridden environmental ones.

The configuration and identification of nodes and corridors were, from the start, inspired by a different logic. Within the planning programme of the University of Cape Town, students had been taught to develop conceptual diagrams describing desirable spatial relationships. The 'grid', in particular, had been promoted as a spatial organizing device which had the potential to achieve the urban qualities of equity, access and integration. Structural concepts such as these should then be 'warped' to fit the features of a particular context.[9] In metropolitan planning studios run throughout the 1980s and 1990s, students explored various ways in which Cape Town could be 'restructured' on the basis of this approach. Various Cape Town routes were identified which could become the linear elements of a grid, and points were located where the linear elements intersected to become centres or nodes.

This conceptualization of nodes and corridors, and the warping of a 'grid' to fit the Cape Town context, is not documented in the 1996 Technical Report, thus lending some mystery to their appearance on the final plan. There is little doubt, however, that the consultants, some of whom were graduates of the planning programme, were strongly influenced by the spatial forms which had emerged from this approach.[10] Three existing centres (the CBD, Claremont/Wynberg and Bellville) form three corners of a giant square which has been superimposed on the metropole (each side of the square is 12 to 15 km in length). The three centres are significantly different from each other in terms of their size and function, with the CBD, in reality, significantly larger than the other two, but in the conceptual plan they are represented by circles of equal size. The fourth corner marks the point at which a new centre (of the same order of significance as the other three) is to be developed, close to the poorest residential areas.[11] Its location coincides with a large tract of relatively undeveloped land zoned for industrial use. Philippi Industria was proclaimed industrial land during the apartheid years, but was never developed, as it would have competed with efforts to decentralize industry and the African workforce associated with it.

Two sides of the square fall on existing and historical 'corridors': the Main Road of the southern suburbs and Voortrekker Road of the northern suburbs. The lines of the grid are continued from the four corner points, both to the north and the south, in all cases except one (the line into Mitchell's Plain) following routes which could be regarded as existing corridor-type developments. The base of the square, and a diagonal through it, are designated 'new corridors'. Both these routes already carry public transport and, at points, concentrations of mixed use; over time both may have developed into corridor-type elements of their own accord. The completion of the square in the east, and likewise the grid-lines into Khayelitsha and through Blue Downs, is more problematic, as no such existing or incipient routes exist. Here 'corridors' will have to be planned and implemented from scratch. Significantly, the final strategy map shows a 'picture' or vision of how the metropolitan area should appear at some point in the long-term future. The new nodes, corridors and spaces are not distinguished graphically from the existing ones, and the graphic does not, therefore, indicate a strategy or guide for future action. While the lines on the plan are, to some degree, conceptual rather than precise, it remains a blueprint plan.

Where justification for a plan rests on an abstract geometric logic, it can then open itself to challenge from positions which propose an alternative geometry, or positions which argue that the plan ignores the realities of context. Both challenges have been faced by the MSDF. Both the Tygerberg and Cape Town Municipalities have drawn up municipal plans which start, methodologically, with the rationalization of an abstract geometry. Both, when 'superimposed' on the city, indicate locations for corridors (in the case of the Tygerberg plan) and centres (in the case of the Cape Town plan) which differ from the MSDF. While differences with the Tygerberg plan have been resolved (Tygerberg municipality shifted their corridor to fit in with the MSDF, and, in the light of the impending local government reorganization which will greatly enhance the status of the metropolitan authority relative to the municipalities, this may simply have been a case of accepting the inevitable), differences with the Cape Town Municipal plan may be less easy to resolve. The location of the MSDF corridors and nodes has also been challenged on the grounds that the realities of the Cape Town context have not been sufficiently analysed and understood. Staff from within the Social and Economic Directorate of the Cape Metropolitan Council have frequently questioned the viability of a new economic centre in Philippi, as the area is poorly serviced and crime-ridden. New economic investment, they argue, is locating elsewhere in the city and little of it is choosing locations in the designated corridors and nodes. The MSDF, it is suggested, does not understand the dynamics of the local space-economy.

Implementing the MSDF?

The final two sections of the 1996 Technical Report are very brief. The first specifies more detailed policies in relation to sectoral issues such as the environment, transport and housing. The last section, on implementation, covers only nine pages and much of this deals with the procedural and legal aspects of plan adoption. The Report makes the point that actions should be identified and projects initiated, but does not specify these. This aspect may be regarded as beyond the scope of the document, which was aimed primarily at gaining consensus around a broad strategy. But it is also indicative of a more general characteristic of this kind of planning, which sees the final output of planners as texts and documents rather than the implementation of actions or investments, and which makes the assumption that the generation of 'good ideas' will be sufficient on its own to carry a plan through to implementation. It reflects a style of planning which views plan production as an essentially technical, rational (or sometimes simply creative) operation, and implementation as part of the political process which can be left to others. It also reflects a real practical constraint on planning in that it has no investment funds at its disposal and has to rely on other agencies to carry out this investment.

Conclusion

Foucault's concept of discourse is a broad one, manifesting itself not only through 'talk' but through a wide range of practices, of which the compiling of policy documents is one. As part of discourse, planning documents such as the Technical Report of the MSDF also represent a site of struggle, in which knowledge is mobilized in the effort to establish a particular conception of the planning problem and how this should be addressed. Planning documents thus form one instrument in what may be called planners' 'representations of space' (Lefebvre 1991, 38): 'conceptualized space, the space of scientists, planners, urbanists, technocratic subdividers and social engineers, as of a certain type of artist with a scientific bent – all of whom identify what is lived and perceived with what is conceived'.

What is significant about the 1996 Technical Report is the way in which the particular discourse which has been built around the concept of the compact city is reinforced by the Report. The Report thus represents the success of the metropolitan planners (and consultants) in establishing their view of the plan over that of the Cape Town Municipality planners, who were promoting what they termed a 'strategic' approach. The form taken by the plan in the Technical Report is in fact more compatible with an approach to spatial management which intends to rely heavily on regulatory mechanisms (LUPO) for its implementation. Its comprehensive, long-range and relatively precise form potentially enables the metropolitan planners to intervene significantly in the spatial structure of the metropolitan area – an effort which they believe is necessary to remove the inequities and inefficiencies of the apartheid city.

Also significant in the document is the way in which the discourse has been broadened to incorporate the discourse emanating from the country's new, neo-liberal macro-economic policy, and the way in which the rationale for inter-vention has been adjusted to incorporate the additional concern for economic growth with the previous concern for equity and redistribution. It reflects a decision not to counter the new emerging discourse on development – which is, after all, potentially incompatible with the established one – but rather to attempt to incorporate it as part of the reason for the plan. It does not, however, change the nature or form of the plan. Hajer's (1995) notion of mutating story-lines, which can become a vehicle for discursive change, is of relevance here.

What becomes evident later in the story of the MSDF is that taking account of what is an emerging, competing, policy-discourse coalition will present far more of a challenge than the spatial planners can contemplate at this point in time. A conception of reality which is grounded in understanding the city as a pattern of land uses (which can be manipulated) is very different from one which understands it as a place where complex international, national and local economic and social relations interrelate, and where their spatial mapping may look very different from one which portrays land uses. These are two different 'regimes of rationality' that do not easily coincide.

What will tend to disadvantage the spatial planners in the years that follow is the lack of a credible body of theory (knowledge) in the field of spatial plan-ning which can convincingly make a connection between particular spatial strategies and their social and economic effects. The emergence of thinking about the MSDF, as this chapter shows, occurred through a combination of his-torically influential ideas, political considerations (the demand from each municipality for a corridor) and coincidence (the *Time* article on Curitiba). Other planning processes elsewhere in the world would probably have a similar story to tell. While the notion of a 'scientific' planning process would be equally questionable, those disciplines which can draw on what are perceived to be credible bodies of knowledge have an advantage when it comes to the exercise of power. In the future confrontations between the existing and new (urban development) discourse coalitions this becomes a relevant factor.

8 New discourse coalitions and the marginalization of spatial planning

With the MSDF Technical Report (1996) accepted by the Metropolitan Council, the main concern of the metropolitan planners, and Francois Theunissen in particular, remained the legalization of the plan by having it approved under LUPO (the Land Use Planning Ordinance of 1985). The Provincial government was the approving body. While the existence of the plan as a technical report meant that it had no more status than that of a guideline, approval would render it a statutory regional structure plan, giving it greatly enhanced status.

The stakes here were high. Chapter 5 outlined the major changes which were taking place in the country in terms of new legislation and new systems of local government. By early 1997, new Provincial planning legislation was in the pipeline which proposed to scrap LUPO and instead, grant spatial plans a rather uncertain status as a 'sectoral element' of the new 'integrated development plans' designed to co-ordinate all planning and budgeting within authorities. Moreover, in terms of the new system of 'spheres' rather than 'tiers' of government, the MSDF could be accepted as this sectoral element only if there was consensus on this on the part of the municipalities. The reactions of certain of the municipalities to the idea of statutorizing the MSDF had already made it clear that achieving such consensus was likely to be a very difficult and perhaps impossible task. For the metropolitan planners, concerned about giving the MSDF the greatest possible power and influence, the best strategy appeared to be to push the plan through LUPO before its demise (the timing of which was at any rate unpredictable) and to hope that this would give it an advantage in the uncertain times ahead. Early drafts of the Provincial planning legislation had suggested that existing structure plans could be reviewed and then deemed to be spatial 'sectoral' plans[1] under the new Act. This offered the MSDF a much easier route to future official acceptance than the difficult and uncertain one of consensus seeking.

However, the spatial planners were operating within an institutional context which was changing rapidly. There was growing competition between spatial planning and the policy initiatives of other functional departments in the Cape Metropolitan Council, which in turn were linked to developing national, sectoral policy positions. The Integrated Development Planning process within the metropolitan authority was intended to achieve a degree of integration across these policy sectors. But spatial planning found its focus on plan statutorization increasingly challenged by other functional departments with their own policy (and spatial) plans, and by access to budgets which could make these plans real. The spatial planners found themselves trying to achieve the increasingly questioned goal of plan statutorization, in circumstances which indicated their growing marginalization.

The municipal challenge to statutorization

The story broke off, in Chapter 6, at the point where the metropolitan planners orchestrated a public demonstration of acceptance of the MSDF Technical Report by their councillors (November 1996). But they decided that it was still necessary to convince the new municipal councillors, who had been elected into office in May 1996, to support the contents of the Technical Report. This, it was believed, would make the process of statutorization much easier. There was a further factor, however, which was holding up statutorization. In terms of the national legislation governing local government transition, metropolitan authorities and municipalities together constituted the 'sphere' of local government. The division of powers and duties between the metropolitan and local authorities in each of South Africa's larger urban areas had to be negotiated, and it was clearly not possible to statutorize the MSDF until the scope of planning functions at metropolitan level had been settled. It was not until October 1996 that this matter was finalized. In the meantime the Technical Report was again circulated to municipalities for comments and was accompanied by a slick slide-tape show aimed at the new councillors.

The comments trickled back in very slowly: it was not until October of 1997 that they were all finally submitted, and it was only in early 1998 that they were presented to the MSDF Co-ordinating Working Group. One reason for the slow response was the fact that a new set of elected councillors, most of whom had little or no previous experience of public office, were trying to find their feet. Lengthy education programmes had to be arranged to explain to them how departments and budgets operated and how council meetings were run. Perhaps a more important reason, however, was the huge disruption caused by the reallocation of local government employees into the six newly created municipalities and the metropolitan council. Almost a third of all local government employees in Cape Town, some 10,000 people, were affected by the move (Cape Metropolitan Council 1997), involving, for each one, new employment contracts, conditions of service, pension arrangements, and so on. The Cape Town Municipality, which had performed a number of metropolitan or supra-municipal functions prior to the reorganization, was most severely affected by staff redeployment.

When I visited this Planning Department in early 1998, the 16th floor of the 20-storey, concrete-slab municipal building, which had once housed a planning staff of some one hundred professionals and support staff, appeared to be in the aftermath of a natural disaster. Large areas of the open-plan office floor were empty, except for the occasional overturned chair and piles of old files. I was told that 75 professional and support staff had left or taken early retirement (possible at age 50) in the last year. A large noticeboard had been propped up on an old table, and magnetic staff name-tags on it had been divided into two columns – 'left' and 'still here'. The staff member accompanying me walked over to the board and shifted three more names from the now very short 'still here' column, remarking that it was difficult to keep up with departures.[2]

The new Tygerberg Municipality, by contrast, was created partially out of four small and previously white-controlled municipalities. Together these had contained some 282,000 predominantly white, middle- and upper-income, National Party-supporting people.[3] In the 1996 local government reorganization, the boundaries of this new municipality were set to include the four existing municipalities together with the lower-income formal housing areas to the south, and the large and very poor African area of Khayelitsha. The population of the new municipality was 820,000 people (Cameron 1999), with 59 per cent of this total falling into the lowest income group (earning under $200 per month[4]). The task of adjustment on the part of both officials and councillors was obviously a major one, and 'change-fatigue' was a commonly voiced complaint amongst workers in both the public and private sector. There is no doubt that the scale and intensity of the restructuring which occurred in local government during this period, together with major changes at higher levels of government, was a serious limitation on the ability of planners to undertake even mundane tasks such as commenting on an already much-debated metropolitan plan.

The comments on the MSDF Technical Report finally forwarded from the six new municipalities were mixed in nature. The four smaller municipalities suggested relatively minor changes to the content of the plan, but did not object to the idea of its statutorization. The two larger municipalities (Cape Town Municipality and the Tygerberg Municipality) objected strongly to statutorization. This objection from the Cape Town Municipality was not unexpected, given the long history of resistance by its planners (and certain other officials) to domination by the Metropolitan Council. It may also have been that the culture of 'metro-bashing' by Cape Town Municipality planners was reinforced by the political (ANC) alignment of their councillors. Such political differences clearly did not lie behind the objections to statutorization from the (National Party-dominated) Tygerberg Municipality, and their objections were phrased in a far more conciliatory style. Tygerberg, however, as the historical centre of the Afrikaner capital (Bickford-Smith *et al.* 1999) in the metropolitan area, had a particular pro-growth and business-friendly approach to development, and was undoubtedly concerned that its expansionist aims would be curtailed by MSDF principles of compaction, containment and redistribution.

Would these strong objections from the two largest municipalities stall the process of statutorizing the MSDF? The regulatory process, and the unwavering position of Theunissen as chair of these meetings, ensured that they did not.

The comments from each municipality were summarized into an abbreviated list of bulleted points, with minor suggestions and fundamental objections both being given the same degree of emphasis. The comments were tabled at a meeting of the Co-ordinating Working Group in March 1998, with the promise that they would be 'fed into' the discussions on statutorization.

A month later, at a meeting of the MSDF Statutory Working Group (established as a sub-committee of the Co-ordinating Working Group) on 16 April 1998, the summarized list was similarly tabled. The meeting was asked to accept that the list correctly reflected the concerns raised by the municipalities, and when this was agreed upon the planning consultant was asked to outline the next steps of statutorization, including the preparing of a draft statutory document which would be circulated for comment. The two Cape Town Municipality planners present at this meeting were clearly in no mood to be conciliatory.[5] One of the planners pointed out that the process proposed by the consultant did not allow for a debate about the spatial plan which was to be part of the final document. This was the plan which indicated the elements to be reinforced by law: the line of the urban edge, the MOSS (Metropolitan Open Space System), and the nodes and corridors which were intended to be the parts of the metro where new development occurred. By raising this question, the planner was essentially asking for a fundamental review of the spatial form of the MSDF, a move which could have set back the statutorization process considerably. The chair was quick to rule this request out of court. He pointed out that the metropolitan council had already accepted the Technical Report, and that while the alignments of the four elements of the plan (the nodes, corridors, edges and open spaces) could be discussed, their existence was not negotiable (MSDF Statutory Working Group meeting 1998).

While the Cape Town Municipality planner did not, at this point, say why he wanted the plan reviewed, lying behind his request were concerns which were to be raised again and again during the course of the statutorization process. One concern was that while statutorization may be an appropriate tool to control or prevent development in certain areas (such as beyond the urban edge or within demarcated open spaces), it was much less easy to understand how it could function as a tool to direct development into demarcated nodes and corridors. Much of the new development expected in these areas would be initiated by the private sector, which could not be bound by law in terms of where it would invest.[6] This is not a new issue for planners generally, and the shift away from 'master plans' in the 1950s and 1960s was largely due to the realization that statutorized maps of a desired future outcome were generally ineffective. Later on the Cape Metropolitan Council planners were to agree that planning law, on its own, could not bring about development in the nodes and corridors, and that public projects and incentives of various kinds were needed to induce investment. While some steps were taken in this direction (such as the support of a public–private utility company in the new node on the Cape Flats), nonetheless the major effort on the part of the metropolitan planners remained focused on the statutorization process.

A further issue was that a structure plan, by its nature, was supposed to be broadly conceptual and indicative, and did not, according to the 1985 LUPO legislation, have the power to confer or take away land-use rights. Yet the MSDF map, which was to be appended to the statutory planning document, showed corridors which were precisely defined in the map key as a 500-metre zone on either side of the central route. The lines indicating the corridors, as well as the urban edge and MOSS areas, although not cadastrally defined, could nonetheless, at the map scale of 1:300,000, also be fairly accurately located. Although final cadastral definition of the four elements of the plan was in the hands of the municipalities, it would not be difficult for a landowner to bring pressure to bear on a local authority and to argue, for example, that his or her land was within a corridor or within the edge, as defined in the MSDF map, and should therefore be granted development rights. It was this degree of precision of the MSDF plan which became a bone of contention between the metropolitan and municipal planners. The metropolitan planners felt the necessity to spell out as clearly as possible the form of development and control needed to restructure and reintegrate the city, but the municipal planners felt that this very clarity constrained their freedom to make planning and development control decisions at the local level. The exercise was seen to represent domination of municipal planners by the metropolitan planners, even when many of the former agreed fully with the principles of the MSDF.

Interestingly, however, the original decision to produce a plan of this kind had come not from the metropolitan planners but from the consultants. Cecil Madell, consultant planner, explained that they had felt that the University of Cape Town published reports promoting the new spatial approach had been too 'academic and conceptual'. They believed that they would have to translate them into a different form if they were to be accepted by planners in the bureaucracies:

> [T]here was a realization that there is a large stock of planners out there that are in control of government departments and local authority departments, that are used to the Guide Plan (blueprint) type of planning ... A lot of the stuff we started to draw up around the corridors and nodes, in the minds of people in the group (consultant team), there was a feeling that we are being too prescriptive, too much of a blueprint approach. But I think that was a conscious decision also, because there was a realization that we had to provide something people can relate to, particularly your rank-and-file planner from other university institutions. For the group to produce something different (more conceptual) would have been easier ... and would have met the City Council concern that the MSDF was too precise. I can remember a lot of us saying in the group constantly, the academics are not going to be happy with what we do. We were aware of that.
>
> (Interview 3 1999)

There was a resultant compatibility between the form of the MSDF and the traditional mode of processing and using such plans. Madell should perhaps have been less surprised at the outcome:

> [E]ven though one tried to do a plan which is practical, which rank-and-file planners could relate to, at that stage there was obviously also an attempt to bureaucratize the plan. For me that was the downside of the thing. It has become so institutionalized and bureaucratized that even though the approaches and principles have changed and the politics have changed, the methodology in terms of how you approach planning has not changed. People saw it as just another blueprint plan. Just put the Guide Plan aside and use this blueprint plan.
>
> (Interview 3 1999)

For the MSDF to become a statutory plan under LUPO, it was necessary first to prepare a new text (containing just the aspects of the plan to be legalized) and the map which would be appended to the document. This draft document would have to be circulated again to the municipalities for comment and approval by their council. It would then have to be approved by the metropolitan council, and thereafter forwarded to the Provincial government which would give it final approval. By April 1998, work on the draft statutory plan was still in its early stages, and the process of gaining municipal approval of it was clearly not going to be easy. In the meantime, work on the new Provincial planning legislation, which would remove LUPO entirely, was nearing completion. For Theunissen and the metropolitan planners, this was a race against time. But while the main obstacles in the race had, so far, taken the form of municipal obstructiveness, new clouds were on the horizon in terms of the growth of sectoral policy initiatives which also had their spatial implications.

Creating 'developmental' local government

The call by the White Paper for local government to become 'developmental' (Ministry for Provincial Affairs and Constitutional Development, 1998: section B) implied a reorientation of local governments away from their traditional role as administrators and service-providers. In particular, the White Paper called for these authorities to 'have a clear vision for the local economy' and to concern themselves with local economic development. This is a functional shift which occurred some time ago in countries such as the USA and Britain, and was not entirely new to all South African local authorities: the Cape Town City Council had, for example, been undertaking work in this area in the mid-1980s. But for many local authorities, and the Cape Metropolitan Council, this new imperative to become developmental, implied the establishment of new or reorganized departments and the employment of new professionals.

In the internal reorganization of the Cape Metropolitan Council which occurred in 1997, a new directorate of Economic and Social Development was established, headed by Kim Van Deventer – last encountered in Chapter 4 as

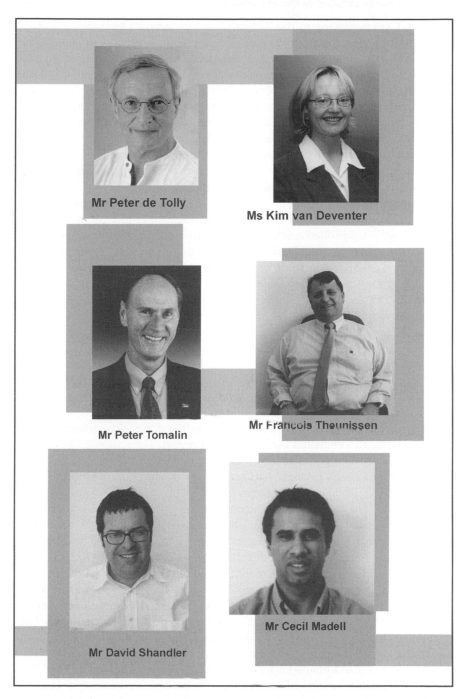

Mr Peter de Tolly

Ms Kim van Deventer

Mr Peter Tomalin

Mr Francois Theunissen

Mr David Shandler

Mr Cecil Madell

Figure 8.1 Some of the main role-players in the MSDF process.

the NGO representative on the Western Cape Economic Development Forum. A second new directorate in the Cape Metropolitan Council was Transportation and Traffic. This was not a new function, either at metropolitan or local level, but the task of managing metropolitan transport had previously been attached to the Cape Town Municipality. A third new functional area was created to deal with the environment. Neither the RDP document nor the White Paper had much to say about the functioning of local government in the area of environmental management: it was not an important item on the agenda of the post-apartheid government. However, international initiatives (such as Agenda 21), together with strong internal lobbying groups, succeeded in promoting national environmental legislation, and Environmental Impact Assessments became a requirement for almost all kinds of development. In the Cape Metropolitan Council in 1998, a new department of Environmental Management was established under the reorganized Directorate of Planning, Environment and Housing. Housing administration had been a long-time function of metropolitan government, but in the reorganization it gained a new head (Basil Davidson – chair of the Urban Development Commission of the Forum in 1993 and 1994) and a new task – that of developing a housing policy for the metropolitan area. In the Spatial Planning Department, Theunissen was placed as head, and Peter Tomalin was appointed as executive director of the three departments of Planning, Environment and Housing. Reorganizations of this kind have been common occurrences in local government in many parts of the world, although the trend in the United States has increasingly been to combine the planning and economic development functions.

All these new functional areas within the Cape Metropolitan Council were backed up by strong policy directives from functional departments at the national level, all formulated in the post-1994 period. The national Department of Transport set up a policy review process soon after the 1994 elections, with the aim of formulating a new national transport policy (see Moving South Africa 1998; Republic of South Africa 1996b). The creation of densified transport corridors was promoted as an important way to reduce travel-to-work distances and hence the cost of subsidizing commuter travel from peripheral, low-density suburbs. National economic policy for local economic development was still being formulated, but policy direction emerged in a Jobs Summit Declaration in 1998, in policy documents on Public Sector Procurement and Tourism, and in legislation relating to the promotion of small businesses. In the environmental field, the 1998 National Environmental Management Act set out environmental principles to guide all developments affecting the natural, social and economic environment, and required Environmental Impact Assessments for a wide range of developments. In the housing field, a new national housing policy was formulated in the National Housing Forum (1991–1995) and was thereafter enshrined in a policy document (Department of Housing 1994) and an Act (Republic of South Africa 1997).

The point about the newly created functional areas in the Cape Metropolitan Council is that, informed by national policy initiatives, there were clear imperatives to develop plans and policies within the functional areas concerned. And certain of these functional areas, such as transportation, were promoting particular spatial forms. Spatial planning, therefore, no longer had the monopoly on forward thinking, as it had done in the past. Increasingly, it had to promote spatial strategies in 'competition' with the strategies put forward by other directorates. This was placing pressure on spatial planning in two ways.

First, the traditional 'synthesizing' role of spatial planning was being challenged increasingly by other directorates and departments developing their own policies and spatial plans, and the ability of the Spatial Planning department to promote the MSDF as the spatial strategy for the Cape Metropolitan Council as a whole was becoming more and more difficult. Second, with the new departments engaging in current and in-depth analysis and policy formulation in their specific functional fields, they were able to suggest that the MSDF was based on a lack of detailed contextual understanding,[7] and a lack of understanding of newly developing and specialized policy arenas. The fact that the MSDF had been formulated, some years back, on the basis of a rather broad-brush analysis of the metropolitan area, using information dating largely from 1990, made it somewhat vulnerable to this claim.

The most significant challenge to the MSDF as the appropriate spatial strategy for the Cape metropolitan area came from the new metropolitan Directorate of Social and Economic Development. The growing problem of 'fit' between the MSDF and the local space-economy will be discussed in Chapter 9. Here, however, it is worth noting that an economic critique of the MSDF was articulated during the course of an analysis of Cape Town's economy, commissioned by the Social and Economic Directorate during 1998 (Metropolitan Development Consortium 1998). The Report pointed out two areas of concern. The first was that by fixing a limit on the outward expansion of the metropolitan area (through the proposal of an urban edge), the supply of land would be artificially constrained and its price forced up, to the detriment of lower-income people. The second was that a number of recent 'mega-projects' (large-scale office, retail and recreational developments) had located themselves away from the MSDF corridors, and were undermining the development of the latter. In an implied criticism of the lack of flexibility of the MSDF, the report pointed out that such unpredictable economic shifts were likely to occur, and that a 'planning by learning' approach should be taken, rather than 'rigid adherence to positions taken in the past' (Metropolitan Development Consortium 1998, 18). The head of this Directorate, Van Deventer, reinforced the view that the form of spatial planning needed to change:

> [S]patial planning is facing a future with a question mark . . . I think a lot of it is how you work with other disciplines, other departments. Because up to now it has been a protected thing through its legislation. So now spatial planning has to move out of that legal, protected spot and into a let's-sit-around-the-table-and-negotiate spot.
>
> (Interview 12 1999)

The differences between the spatial planners and the transport planners within the Cape Metropolitan Council appeared, on the surface, to be minimal. Theunissen (Interview 1 1998) voiced his opinion that 'a very good level of understanding' had been achieved between the two directorates, and Metropolitan Transport Planner Peter Clarke (Interview 15 1999) confirmed that 'in terms of the [Transport] Directorate's official position there is complete buy-in [to the MSDF]'.

However, the policy co-ordination mechanisms which were in place were less than effective. As Clarke explained:

> The main way it [co-ordination] happens is that a lot of projects are driven by steering committees on which sit people from sectors like spatial planning ... The actual work is done by the Transport Directorate and they either do it themselves or they give it to consultants ... A lot of it depends on the kind of personal commitment and input of people on the steering committee. It's a structure that allows integration, but I think it could probably work a lot better. On all these sectorally driven steering committees, one doesn't know when you produce a report whether it's been taken back to the line departments ... and properly work-shopped and got full comment.
>
> (Interview 15 1999)

Is getting comment back from other departments a guarantee that the necessary integration will occur?

> [A]t the end of the day, with all those types of co-ordinating committees, ... the people who chair are not trying to influence things or whatever, but just because they are sectorally driven, they can act as kind of gatekeepers. Not overtly, you know, but just the way the whole thing is structured. They decide what comments get incorporated and what don't.
>
> (Interview 15 1999)

It is perhaps not surprising, therefore, that important philosophical differences still remained between the spatial and the transport planners. Both spatial planners and transport planners identified the concept of 'corridors' as central urban restructuring devices. However, the corridors which made up one of the four spatial restructuring elements of the MSDF were conceived of, by the spatial planners, as taking the form of the existing historical 'high streets' which stretch from the Cape Town city centre to the east, south and west. These are stop–start routes of, at most, three lanes (one for parking) in either direction, with land uses fronting directly onto them and with frequent lower-order routes taking access to them. They carry public transport routes and volumes of pedestrians (Figure 8.2). The transport planners, on the other hand, have traditionally been resistant to this idea of 'ribbon development' as, they argue, it interferes with the efficient flow of traffic and pedestrian safety. Their interpre-

Figure 8.2 An existing 'activity corridor' in Cape Town.

Source: Urban Problems Research Unit, University of Cape Town.

tation of corridors is that they should accommodate both the 'mobility' function and the 'access' function. Some transport planners believe that a freeway should be the central route in a corridor.[8]

What makes it particularly unlikely that these differences will be resolved is the fact that the 'transport engineering' view of the urban movement system is being reinforced by provincial policy directives. The 1997 Provincial Road Access Policy (Provincial Administration 1997) contains a set of guidelines regarding the spatial planning of movement systems which remain very much within the previous, car-oriented approach to transport planning. Overriding concern for the movement of vehicular traffic, and its efficiency and safety, translates into a rigid definition of a road hierarchy and rules regarding the width and use of the road and the nature and spacing of intersections between different levels of the hierarchy. There is much support for this approach in the Cape Metropolitan Council Transport Directorate:

> There is a strong, strong feeling that the functional hierarchy of the trans-
> port system needs to be protected, so the Provincial guidelines coming out
> ... people kind of stick to that ... they are fully buying in to those guide-
> lines.

(Interview 15 1999)

The position on the movement network presented in the Metropolitan Spatial Development Framework is different. Figure 8.3 shows a hierarchy of movement routes, but the hierarchy includes a pedestrian and cycle system, and 'activity streets' are intersected frequently by lower-order routes.

This difference of interpretation came to a head in mid-1998, over the issue of whether or not a new corridor route (Symphony Way), under construction in the south-east section of the metropolitan area, could have direct access at an intersection with a metropolitan freeway which cut across its path (MSDF Co-ordinating Working Group meeting 1998). The spatial planners argued that if the corridor route did not intersect directly with the freeway, then the corridor would be bisected and its development as a carrier of mixed land use would be retarded. The transport planners were adamant that the efficiency of traffic flow on the freeway could not be jeopardized by a direct intersection with a 'lower-order' route. The impression given at the meeting was that the transport planners would have the 'final say' over this issue!

Integrated development planning

These kinds of co-ordination problems between line function departments were not new, and were exactly what the integrated development planning process had intended to overcome. However, achieving integration proved to be a particularly difficult task.

The Cape Metropolitan Council began its first attempt to draw up an Integrated Development Plan (IDP) in 1997. It was decided to adopt a three-phase process, starting with the 'setting of direction': this involved obtaining agreement on a vision for the metropolitan area, and analysing the existing trends and problems. A set of key strategic priorities would emerge from phase 1, which would form the basis for strategies in phase 2, implementation in phase 3, and monitoring and review in phase 4 (CMC IDP files 1997). At a large workshop in late 1997, involving councillors and officials from metropolitan and municipal governments, agreement was reached on a vision for the metropolitan area and on five 'strategic themes'. The vision read as follows:

> In ten years the Cape Metropolitan Area will be one of the major tourist destinations of the world, especially noted for its natural environment and supported by a harmonious, tolerant and well-governed and educated people. The growing economy will be characterised by adequate housing and a low incidence of crime, making the Cape Metropolitan Area a global economic player.

The five, theme-based, strategic priorities were identified as poverty and homelessness, strengthening the position of the metropole in the global economy, enhancing the environment, building social harmony and citizenship, and developing local governance. It would appear that the spatial restructuring of the metropolitan area was no longer seen as a priority.

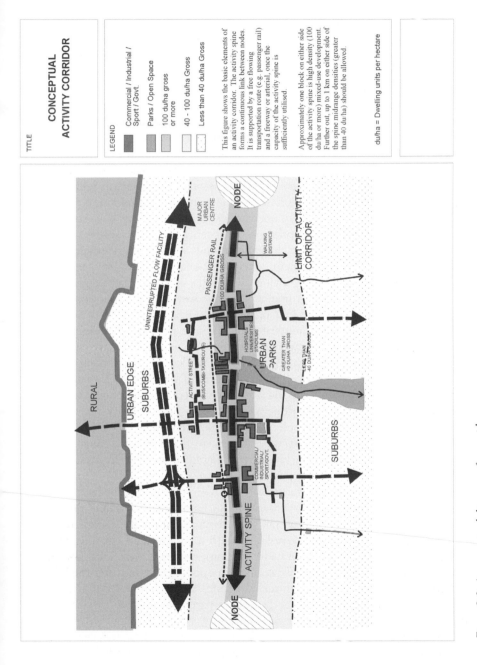

TITLE

CONCEPTUAL
ACTIVITY CORRIDOR

LEGEND

☐ Commercial / Industrial /
   Sport / Govt.

☐ Parks / Open Space

☐ 100 du/ha gross
   or more

☐ 40 - 100 du/ha Gross

☐ Less than 40 du/ha Gross

This figure shows the basic elements of
an activity corridor. The activity spine
forms a continuous link between nodes.
It is supported by a free flowing
transportation route (e.g. passenger rail)
and a freeway or arterial, once the
capacity of the activity spine is
sufficiently utilised.

Approximately one block on either side
of the activity spine is high density (100
du/ha or more) mixed-use development.
Further out, up to 1 km on either side of
the spine midrange densities (greater
than 40 du/ha) should be allowed.

du/ha = Dwelling units per hectare

Figure 8.3 A conceptual diagram of a corridor.

Source: Technical Report (1996).

The question now was how to achieve integration, at least within the Cape Metropolitan Council. The process that was followed required each directorate to link their existing projects to the five strategic priorities. This did not appear to be particularly difficult to do. It was quite possible, for example, for Spatial Planning to argue that the MSDF would spatially link the poor and the homeless into areas of urban opportunity, and that the strategies of MOSS and the urban edge would enhance the environment, and so on. The point is that this approach to integration did not require departments or directorates to change significantly the way in which they were working. If they could suggest a connection between their existing policies and programmes and the (very broad) IDP strategic objectives, then they could continue business as usual.

This process did, however, allow the production of a glossy publication by the Cape Metropolitan Council entitled *Integrated Development Planning and Management Framework* (February 1999). The vision statement had been reworded to replace the earlier emphasis on tourism with goals relating to a high quality of life, and access to services and opportunities. The five 'strategic themes' produced in the 1997 workshop had been replaced by seven areas of 'core business': effective urban management and an integrated community; resources for equity and development; services for safe and habitable communities; infrastructure to support a growing metropolis; economic development to alleviate poverty; a strong local democracy; and world-wide promotion for a winning metropolis. In the final part of the report, existing projects or areas of work within the various departments are linked to the areas of 'core business'. It is significant that, of the 40 projects which are listed, and grouped according to how they further core business, the Spatial Planning department alone is identified as having only one task: the implementation of the MSDF, with its 'key result' for the following year being the statutorization of the plan. Sixteen other tasks, to be carried out by departments *other* than Spatial Planning, are all related to the development of policy frameworks in various specialized fields (environment, economy, transport, waste water, etc.), and all would have either a direct spatial component, or at least spatial implications. The fragmentation of policy-making is clearly reflected here.

In the second attempt to formulate an IDP, the metropolitan council decided to employ an outside consultant. In an interview on the IDP process, this consultant described himself as an 'institutional man', professionally involved in 'transformation processes', and with a background in public management and political science. He had had long experience with local government negotiating forums in Cape Town in the periods before and after the 1994 elections, and knew the local political dynamics well. Undoubtedly a highly competent and committed man, he brought a particular approach to bear on the IDP process, which viewed it as a means of achieving improved organizational performance and effectiveness.[9] Spatial Planning, in his view, was simply one of a number of functional departments whose work needed to be prioritized and integrated. Moreover, it was a function which he regarded as having had a rather poor track record in the past. 'Where in this city has it had an impact?', he asked. 'The demands on local government are far more complex now than just spatial issues' (Interview 13 1999).

The second round of the IDP process began in much the same way as the first. Five 'objectives' now replaced the five 'strategic themes' of the first round. The themes – building a globally competitive city, addressing poverty and equity in service delivery, ensuring financial sustainability, enhancing account-ability, and enhancing management and administrative efficiency[10] – indicate a growing shift towards a concern with the operation of the authority itself. The new consultant was well aware that the previous approach, of trying to link departmental work to themes or core areas of business, had not worked. He was adamant that no integrated planning or budgeting had yet occurred in the met-ropolitan council. His way of integrating was to be starkly different, using (in his terms) a 'macro scoreboard'. What this meant in practice was the establish-ment of performance indicators (derived from the five 'objectives') which cut across departmental work. Monitoring and impact assessment would then be carried out to determine the extent to which departmental work was meeting the desired targets. Three 'integrated management teams' were initially set up below the level of the executive officers, and later more were created. These teams, one on 'policy', one on 'indicators', and one on 'impact assessment', were constituted as project teams concerned with meeting the objectives. This approach, the consultant argued, would directly affect the way in which work within departments happened, and would ensure a move towards integration. This attempt to produce an IDP was put on hold in early 2000 when local government entered its next round of restructuring.

Last-ditch attempts to halt the plan

From April 1998, the consultants in the MSDF Statutory Working Group were presenting drafts of a new version of the MSDF Statutory Plan. There was a tight timetable. The aim was to present the Statutory Plan to the Urbanization and Planning Committee of the metropolitan council (for information) in Sep-tember and to give the next three months over to the circulation of the draft statutory plan for comment by municipalities and the general public. A second draft would then be prepared, incorporating comments, and this draft would need the approval of the Technical Advisory Committee (a long-standing advi-sory committee set up to comment on development proposals and policies of metropolitan significance), as well as of the Planning, Environment and Housing Committee and the Executive Committee of Council, in time to be submitted to the Provincial Administration in April 1999.

Theunissen's earlier concern, that the Statutory Plan should be approved by Province before the new provincial planning legislation[11] was passed and LUPO disappeared entirely, had become less urgent. While the Planning and Develop-ment Act was almost ready to be passed, the Provincial Council had decided that the Act would not come into effect until an accompanying set of guide-lines and regulations had been drafted, and this process could take from six months to a year to complete. The more immediate worry for the metropolitan planners was that South Africa's second general election was scheduled to take place early in 1999. Not only did this imply a new set of provincial ministers, but also there was an increasingly strong chance that the ANC would capture the province from the New National Party. Quite how an ANC Provincial government would react to the MSDF was unclear, but the fact that it was being promoted by a New National Party-dominated metropolitan council could give them reason to treat it with caution, despite the progressive origins of the plan.

In the MSDF Statutory Working Group, the most significant challenge to the progress of drafting the statutory document came from the two Cape Town Municipality planners. Both were located in the development control section of the Municipality, and both were greatly concerned about how the statutorization of the MSDF would complicate their everyday processing of development applications. Both planners adopted the tactic of continually raising technical problems with the process, asking for opportunities to review the map, and suggesting that their councillors were not supportive of the MSDF. These objections may have slowed the process, but did not stall it: the Cape Town Municipality planners did not have unequivocal support from the other municipal planners, and it was not difficult for the chair of the Working Group either to answer the technical objections or to accommodate them in the drafting process. Clearly frustrated by his inability to make an impact on the procedure, one of the Cape Town Municipality planners finally stormed out of a meeting in a temper and never returned.

It would appear, at this point, that the Cape Town municipal planners decided on a change in tactics. At the Statutory Working Group meeting in June 1998 (MSDF-SWG minutes 1999), a senior Cape Town Municipality planning professional made his appearance and asked permission to report back from a recent meeting he had had with the Provincial government. His attitude was conciliatory and he complemented the metropolitan Spatial Planning team for their work on the MSDF. Information he had obtained in the Provincial meeting, he said, had important implications for the statutorization of the MSDF. First, he had been informed that the new Provincial planning legislation proposed to delegate many new powers to local government. Statutorizing the MSDF through LUPO, which provided for higher-order plans to bind lower-order plans, and for the Provincial government to have the final say over appeals against local planning decisions, would go against the spirit of the new Act and would cause confusion. Second, a new national bill (the Municipal Structures Bill of 1998) was proposing a further reorganization of local government involving the creation of powerful metropolitan authorities and much weaker 'sub-councils'. As a result of these changes, he argued, the distribution of powers and functions between metropolitan and municipal government was likely to change dramatically, and it did not make sense to continue with the statutorization process until the future was clearer. In the meantime, he suggested, the document should simply be called a 'framework' or 'concept' plan, and all references which impacted on what a municipality 'should do' should be removed.

This was a far more sophisticated attempt to halt the statutorization process. It did not, however, succeed. Officials at all levels of government had, some time ago, come to realize that in the 'new' South Africa, reorganization and change had become a permanent feature of their lives. The fact that new changes always appeared to be imminent, and that some materialized and some didn't, could now, in a way, be used as an excuse for ignoring them. Changes in laws and structures could be dealt with when they occurred, and there was nothing to be gained by putting business on hold to wait for them. Thus, the response of the Working Group chair to the arguments of the Cape Town Municipality planner was that the new Municipal Structures Bill, with its proposals for 'mega-city' government, could 'take years' to emerge. The new Provincial legislation was still under debate and the requirements of the statutory plan could be adjusted once the outcome was known. The meeting then proceeded to a discussion of the statutory map and whether or not the new municipal boundaries should be shown on it.

It had become evident, however, that the Cape Town Municipality planners were intending to stick to their guns in terms of objecting to the statutorization of the MSDF. Whether or not this could present a serious obstacle to final Provincial approval of the plan was not entirely certain. In terms of the LUPO legislation, the metropolitan authority had a right and a duty to draw up a statutory metropolitan plan and submit it to the Provincial government, with or without municipal approval. However, the new constitution had explicitly replaced the concept of 'tiers' of government with separate but equal 'spheres' of government, and now agreement had to be reached through consensus. The problem was that the two areas of legislation were existing side by side, temporarily at least, and the provincial premier could decide to evoke either the old or the new. At this point, with the general election on the horizon, the metropolitan planners decided not to take a chance, and to try to sort out their differences with the Cape Town Municipality.

The proposal was that the dispute be resolved at the 'political' level; that is, that a special committee of councillors from the metropolitan council and from the Cape Town council be asked to sit together to consider whether or not the municipality had grounds for objection to the statutorization. Two outside consultants, one a planner and the other a lawyer, were appointed jointly to review the arguments for and against statutorization and to submit their conclusions to the councillors.

As part of this process the metropolitan planners, on the one hand, and the municipal planners, on the other, were asked to set out in writing their arguments for and against the statutorization of the MSDF (The Planning Partnership 1998). The arguments put forward by the metropolitan planning staff indicated an overriding faith in legal process[12] as a means of implementing spatial planning. Their main arguments were that the metropolitan authority had a 'duty' to carry out the planning function and must do this in terms of the applicable law (LUPO); that it was a legal requirement to statutorize the MSDF (the planning consultant disagrees here – he points out that there is no such legal compulsion); and that statutorizing forward planning was 'a well-supported planning practice in the Cape' (The Planning Partnership 1998, 2). They also argued that a statutory plan would provide public and investor confidence and would 'focus development on areas of need'.

The arguments of the Cape Town Municipality planners were rooted in a different philosophical position on the role of spatial planning. Their first argument, a new one, had to do with the incompatibility between the requirements of Integrated Development Planning and statutory land-use planning. Drawing on the Local Government Transition Act of 1996, they argued that spatial planning is just one sub-component of IDPs and 'is not more important than social or economic planning' (The Planning Partnership 1998, 7). Statutorization of the MSDF, they argued, implied the elevation of spatial planning to something more important than other forms of planning. They were exactly right here: the legal backing of LUPO would have given the plan an enhanced status, and would also have allowed the spatial planners to play the overall co-ordinating role which has been traditionally entrenched in spatial planning as a discipline. It is not surprising that they continued to appeal to the rule of law. The municipal planners raised other objections which they had aired before. The top-down hierarchy of plans assumed in LUPO contradicted the equal spheres of government introduced in the new local government legislation. The precise, but not cadastrally defined, nodes, corridors and edges in the MSDF would cause uncertainty in development control processes. Finally, a legal plan may be a useful tool for controlling development, but it could not, on its own, induce development in areas such as the nodes and corridors.

The consultants, asked to arbitrate on this matter, appeared to have found themselves caught in the legal confusion of the day. They reported that the metropolitan council did indeed have the legal right to statutorize the MSDF, but that given the passing of new provincial planning legislation, the implications of the Local Government Transition Act for local government powers and for integrated planning, and the proposed further reorganization of local government, the decision to statutorize should probably be deferred. They went on to say, however, that they recognized that there may be 'political reasons indicating desirability of immediate action'. This may refer to the impending elections and a possible political change in provincial government, or to the advantages of having a statutorized MSDF in place before the demise of LUPO.

The final decision-makers in this matter were the councillors from the metropolitan authority and the municipality, with one official from each of the authorities. They were presented with the detailed arguments of the two sets of officials, the consultants' recommendations, and a covering letter from the Executive Director of Planning and Economic Development of the municipality, reinforcing the position of his staff. Attached to the back of these papers, as Annex E, was a copy of a newspaper article, dated October 1998. It announced that the metropolitan council had decided to relocate its offices from the city centre to a new, upmarket office development called Century City, 'in a location which is not a corridor, nor in an MSDF node such as Philippi East or Bellville CBD'.[13] The article was referred to by the Executive Director as indicating that there were 'differing interpretations' of the MSDF. The underlying message was clear: support for the MSDF, even within the metropolitan authority, was questionable.

In the end, neither rational argument nor subtle strategizing benefited the municipal planners. The councillors decided unanimously in favour of statutorizing the MSDF. One municipal ANC councillor, an architect/planner of long standing had, it appeared, played an important role in convincing the other councillors that this was the correct route to follow. The Cape Town Municipality planners had again failed in their challenge of the MSDF. Down, but not entirely beaten, their Executive Director ultimately recommended to his council that it support the structure plan process for those aspects of the MSDF which required strong levels of control (the edges and open space system), and that the concept of the corridors and nodes be fed into the IDP processes at metropolitan and municipal levels.

End of the 'Prague Spring'

> After 1996 there was an increasingly missionary approach to the MSDF – it became a mission rather than a rational planning process. It became political. It coincides with the politicization of the bureaucracy . . . it was about competition . . . it was about positioning for the future and the Unicity [the impending creation of new metropolitan government].
>
> (Interview 5 1999)

The three-month period allowed for municipal and public comment did not produce the results the metropolitan planners had hoped for. Three public meetings had been advertised but the last had been cancelled due to non-attendance (MSDF-CWG minutes 1999). Invitations placed in newspapers inviting public comment attracted only ten written responses – from non-governmental organizations and a few companies. The heady days of the Western Cape Economic Development Forum, when large numbers of people from all sectors of society had turned up to workshop the ideas of the MSDF, were clearly over. Of the six municipalities, two failed to submit comments in time. None of the remaining four supported statutorization unconditionally. All complained that statutorization allowed undue interference with local planning powers, that there were strong incompatibilities between the outgoing LUPO approach to planning and the incoming IDP-related approach, and that statutorizing nodes and corridors, on the assumption that this would attract development, was misguided.

There was now little time left before the June 1999 general election. As political support for the New National Party in the Western Cape wavered, so pressure began to emerge from unexpected quarters for the draft statutory MSDF to be submitted to the Province. The chair of the metropolitan council Executive Committee, closely involved in New National Party structures, had previously held back from unequivocal support for the MSDF because of the resistance to it from the New National Party-dominated municipalities. Now, however, he supported it fully.[14] Planning staff within the Province were now also advising that the MSDF be submitted as soon as possible.

In an effort to speed up the process, and to forestall at least some of the municipal objections, the metropolitan planners decided to delete from the draft structure plan all references to planning procedures. These references were in any event superfluous as LUPO contained its own procedural mechanisms which would apply automatically. In an unusual step, the reworked draft (dated February 1999) was submitted back to the Co-ordinating Working Group and to the Technical Advisory Committee simultaneously: conventionally, approval would have been obtained from the former before submission to the latter. At the Co-ordinating Working Group meeting, some of the municipal planners reiterated reservations they had with the statutory plan, but at this point it was clear that raising objections to it was a mere formality. The chair suggested that municipalities could do this at the Technical Advisory Committee meeting two days later. Only one representative attended, and the item was passed without a single dissenting voice.

Two weeks later the Planning, Environment and Housing Committee of the Cape Metropolitan Council approved the statutory plan. But the final hurdle, the Executive Committee of Council, would not be rushed. They demanded a workshop on the MSDF first. Spatial Planning staff felt that they did not want to be seen to be taking unpopular decisions on the eve of an election. Very few Executive Committee members turned out for the workshop, and shortly thereafter they approved the plan. It was submitted to the Provincial minister in April 1999, a matter of weeks before the general election.

Out in the barren and windswept townships of the Cape Flats, five years had now passed since the first national democratic elections, and little had changed physically (Figure 8.4). There had been no serious public attempt to address the spatial heritage of the apartheid city. The ex-SANCO chair (John Neels) put the blame squarely on the elected representatives:

> I blame the people sitting in Council ... they are incompetent. The moment they become councillors, they are no longer accountable ... they forgot about their powers there, they forgot all their political skills ... They should say 'you do it', but nobody does it. It's all a failure because the bureaucracy we were guarding against has been reinvented.
>
> (Interview 8 1999)

MSDF facilitator David Shandler had a view of events grounded in his understanding of the nature of the political transition:

> There was an interesting kind of 'spring', like a Prague Spring for planners, which was from about 1991 to 1994. And it coincided with the interregnum. Planning was the leading edge – of the government, of the change

Figure 8.4 Little has changed on the bleak Cape Flats.
Source: Photographed by Philip Burns.

process and in the engagement with the extra-parliamentary forces. And so it assumed a greater responsibility ... a political responsibility. It was about redefining institutions, it was about power. And other than that period, both before and after, the engineers and the finance people were dominant, and that hasn't changed. So it [planning] had its moment in the spotlight, and then it kind of disappeared. And that moment had everything to do with the balance of forces in the country, with the interregnum, and it was a perfect case of it – the old dying and the new struggling to be born. Who stepped into the breach? The planners. They were dealing with something that was not about life and death, it wasn't about day-to-day management, about streets, water and so on. It was about vision, it was about policy, but it wasn't as threatening as how people were going to deal with the new institutions, the interim councils, that kind of thing. It was a wonderful place to be at the time, and it was fifteen minutes of fame ... ! But subsequent to that what we've seen is maybe the settling of the political forces, the institutionalization of political conflict, and the re-emergence of the historical balance of power in the bureaucracy. And I'm not sure there has been much shift at all in the bureaucracy, regardless of the political change. I think it is more in the Western Cape, yes, but I do a lot of work in Durban and it's similar there, and there you have an ANC-dominated government. And it's still the engineers and the finance people who hold sway. Planners and environmentalists who are generalists, who are integrative thinkers ... nothing, they really struggle. So there hasn't been a revolution in South Africa, there has been a change of regime, not a change of the state.

(Interview 5 1999)

Postscript

At the end of 1999 Theunissen resigned and was replaced by an acting head who refocused metropolitan planning work in the direction of a large-scale urban project which could initiate the implementation of the MSDF. But this effort was put on hold as well when the next round of local government reorganization began in early 2000. In this final stage of local government transition, legislation requires the creation of strong metropolitan governments (or 'Unicities'). The municipalities will disappear and be replaced by more numerous, weaker, 'subcouncils' with delegated powers and limited functions. The shape and content of the new structures, currently under consideration by a temporary Unicity Commission, will be decided after the December 2000 local government elections. The MSDF came under increasing attack within the Unicity Commission during 2000 because of its 'blueprint' form and its incompatibility with the increasingly dominant concerns of economic growth, global positioning, and developmental, entrepreneurial local government. On 19 September 2000, the MSDF Co-ordinating Working Group held its last meeting. The metropolitan planners finally decided to submit only the goals and principles of the MSDF to the Provincial government to be statutorized under LUPO, but even this may never happen. They accepted that a new round of metropolitan spatial planning would be initiated after the Unicity was in place, but what form this will take is as yet unknown.

Conclusion

What is evident in this period of the MSDF process is the way in which challenges to the plan, in part from the municipalities, and increasingly from other functional departments within the metropolitan authority (particularly the economic planners and the transport engineers), coincide with intensified efforts on the part of the spatial planners to turn the plan into a legal document. It is possible to speculate that there is a connection between these two trends, and that the safety and privilege of legal status for the plan becomes increasingly attractive in the face of growing challenge and ongoing institutional uncertainty. In this sense, change itself helps to reinforce continuity.

Also evident in this chapter is the range of practices through which the spatial planners involved try to realize their aims of statutorization. A wide variety of taken-as-normal bureaucratic procedures, such as agenda-setting, chairing of meetings, the giving of voice to some at meetings and not to others, processing of official comments, and so on, can be marshalled to this end. The form of the plan diagram is also important as it lends itself to being a tool of regulation far more than would, for example, a set of principles or policies. Evident as well is the degree of autonomy experienced by those planners attempting to counter the plan. Power is not unidirectional and they too are able to exercise power. From the municipal planners there are expressions of anger, attempts to flatter and conciliate, the production of rational arguments about the difficulties of local land-use control, the resorting to legal arbitration, and finally the mobi-lizing of emerging discourse around integrated development planning in an attempt to challenge the very rationale for separate spatial planning. From the transport engineers there are arguments, grounded in a different technical rationality from the MSDF, which assert the imperative of traffic efficiency over that of spatial integration. These challenges add to the growing pressure on the statutorization process.

In the end, as the Postscript indicates, institutional restructuring and the prospect of municipal demise begins to close the space in which the municipal planners can mount a challenge. Ironically it is just at this point that a new acting head within the metropolitan spatial planning department refocuses efforts around the plan towards an implementational project, a move which may anyway have changed the relationship between metropolitan and munici-pal planners. But such attempts to adjust the discourse may be too little and too late.

What becomes more important than these disputes *within* the realm of physi-cal planning over the form of the MSDF, is a much more significant challenge which amounts, I suggest, to the rise of a new discourse coalition and a growing struggle for discursive hegemony over the question of the independent existence of spatial planning. An influential new discourse coalition arises out of the pene-tration of neo-liberal philosophy into public institutions, and into local govern-ment in particular. Internationally the terms 'new public management' and 'entrepreneurial government' are central to this discourse, and in South Africa it has been promoted through the recent policy papers on local government and the concept of integrated development planning based on co-ordination through the budget (see Chapter 5). In brief, the new discourse is centred on the notion of 'developmental' local government, which is client-focused and output-driven, and which can play a role at the local level in relation to national goals of global positioning and job creation/poverty alleviation.

Over the past few years, spatial planning within the Cape Metropolitan Council has had some difficulty in placing itself in relation to this new dis-course. Its monopoly in the early 1990s on forward thinking in the metropolitan authority (along with the assumption that forward thinking was essentially spatial thinking) was usurped by the idea that local government as a whole should be forward thinking (or developmental). Its monopoly was usurped particularly by those within the new Economic and Social Development Direc-torate in the metropolitan authority, which was quite specifically set up to be forward thinking, but which drew on the new emerging discourse around eco-nomic growth, the importance of the global economy and Local Economic Development (LED). It also incorporated spatial issues within its discourse (a number of its staff were, in fact, spatial planners), but as an adjunct to economic concerns. This aligned its work more closely with GEAR (the post-1996 macro-economic policy) as opposed to the MSDF which remained rooted in pre-1996 RDP thinking. The adherence of spatial planners to a form of planning which assumed that it was possible for local government to control the location of private investment, which relied for its implementation on legal controls and which saw the end-product of planning as the production of a spatial plan, lent ammunition to those who were arguing that the MSDF was outdated and bureaucratic. These very different and competing professional positions made discourse combination or co-option unlikely.[15]

A further difficulty for spatial planning emerged as a result of the introduction of Integrated Development Plans. The establishment of the budget, as opposed to the spatial plan, as the mechanism of integration, put into question the historical role of spatial planners as the synthesizing generalists, co-ordinating the spatial elements of other departments' work (even if in practice this seldom occurred). Clearly the work of spatial planning could not be viewed simply as that of another line-function department, but the IDPs left open the question of quite how spatial planning should be integrated. With their old functional role undermined and a new one not in place, exactly how planners were to locate themselves institutionally was not clear. The practice of spatial planning, and the compact city discourse, is in danger of being sidelined and is increasingly subject to arguments that its narrowly spatial concerns need to be broadened and made more relevant to contemporary economic imperatives.

9 Beyond the MSDF

Issues for planning

In the previous chapters I have tracked the challenges and difficulties of spatial planning in metropolitan Cape Town. I have shown that despite the opening of what appeared to be a window of opportunity during the early days of the political transition, late 2000 found city-wide spatial planning marginalized and delegitimized. The ability of spatial planners in the early 1990s to build a discourse coalition which synchronized with both macro-economic philosophy and political sentiment of the time, allowed them a degree of status, across the political spectrum, which they had not enjoyed before. The concept of the compact, integrated and equitable city, as an antidote to the segregated, apartheid city, proved to be an influential one: it found its way (in various forms) into spatial planning efforts in many of South Africa's major cities, and into national planning legislation. But while the new discourse around spatial form was a useful one for planners, the discourse it was displacing had contained understandings on the nature of the plan (blueprint, and focused on land uses) and on the planning process (plan implementation through statutorization) which lent power to planners in a range of important ways. Within the Cape Town metropolitan authority (and to a greater or lesser extent in other local authorities across the country) elements of the old discourse were retained and interwoven with the new. The potential for continuity within spatial planning which this offered was reinforced by the essentially modernist nature of both apartheid and post-apartheid planning. Both envisioned an ideal urban future and assumed that spatial planning could be used as a central tool to achieve it.

I have also, in the previous chapters, tried to show the relationship between political and economic changes which happen at the broader national and international levels, and events which occur within other realms of society – in this case within the metropolitan authority of Cape Town. It became clear that processes within society are complex and contradictory, perhaps especially so in a period of rapid transformation, and that generalized national shifts are rarely mirrored in a simple way in particular institutions or locales. Certainly, wider shifts did impact on the metropolitan planning process discussed here, but in ways which were rarely predictable. It was therefore possible to see how both change and continuity marked the passage of the metropolitan plan and how, at times, holding on to previous practices even became a way of dealing with change. Thus the very significant change which took place in the rhetoric of larger-scale spatial planning (from a reinforcement of segregation to equity and integration) became intertwined with pre-existing planning processes which appeared to offer spatial planners the predictability and power necessary to put the new 'vision' into effect. It was, perhaps, the steadfast adherence to these tools from the past that placed the spatial planners increasingly at odds with new dynamics of change which swept into local government in the post-1996 years. Marris captures the nature of this problem:

> the act of plan making is characteristically so different from the everyday conduct of political or economic business – at once more rational and more inclusive – that there is no structure of relationships by which it can be carried out ... Instead, it will be translated into administrative rules and guidelines, fiscal incentives, special grants and projects whose interpretation, use and cumulative effort may all be different from the plan's intentions, and all immediately subject to changes of government and policy. All that remains of the original plan is an expression of collective purpose, daily becoming more out of date.
>
> (Marris 1996, 139)

By the mid-1990s, the metropolitan planning process in the Cape Metropolitan Council found itself trapped within a discourse which was increasingly at odds with the transformations which were going on around it, and challenged by an emerging discourse coalition which redefined the role of local government and the meaning of 'development' more generally. In the notion that local governments as entities should be goal-directed and entrepreneurial, functionally integrated (via the budget) and open to performance management, spatial planning struggled to find an identifiable role. And against the post-1996 assertions that national development in South Africa should place an emphasis on economic growth and competitiveness, primarily through the efforts of the private sector, the 'social welfare' rhetoric of the metropolitan plan was increasingly seen as outdated. This left it open to challenges by staff of other functional departments who had incorporated concepts of space into their own work and could argue that they dealt with 'cutting edge' urban issues in an integrated way. The most serious of these challenges came from the economic planners, well positioned within the emerging developmental discourse, but it came as well from the transport planners who had also incorporated elements of the compact city discourse into their traditional frame of traffic efficiency and safety. It could perhaps be argued that commitment to the compact city position beyond the limited circle of spatial planning professionals had always been ephemeral, judging by the nature of the participation of community groups and organized business in the Urban Development Commission of the Forum years. Certainly at a time when the aim of achieving spatially integrated, equitable and sustainable cities is falling off various public agendas, there are no voices from beyond the public institutions to demand that it should still be there.

The question now is what attitude should planners, policy-makers and political representatives take to the problems that beset South African cities? The spatial form characterizing South African cities was described by a World Bank Mission to this country in 1993 as 'the most extreme form of spatial distortions which, one could arguably say, has not been observed in any other place in modern history' (World Bank 1993, 5). There is no doubt that this spatial heritage imposes both public and individual costs which can be ill-afforded, and that the spatial implications and informants of development policies of all kinds need central recognition. In the post-apartheid period spatial and economic disparities have persisted and become more complex as new and wider forces have made themselves felt. At the same time, the ability of cash-strapped and weakened local governments to change these patterns is diminishing, particularly given the national government shift away from an interest in reconstruction and development and towards a more market-friendly economic philosophy. Debate in the literature continues to rage as to whether, in this era of post-modernity, it is realistic to imagine that intervention in cities, to the end of some imagined public good, is desirable or even realistic (Dear 2000). Accusations of naïve modernism have been levelled at those who still hope for a better future. But to abandon all efforts to address the costs of the present form of urban development, to place a stamp of approval on the miserable and degrading conditions under which the majority of Cape Town residents (and those of other urban areas) live, and on the severe environmental conditions which result from current forms of development, seems entirely unacceptable.

While being careful not to lapse into simplistic notions regarding the dynamics of social and economic relations in Cape Town and the role which space plays in these, while remaining realistic about what intervention may and may not accomplish, and while confirming the need for any intervention to pay close attention to the complex, multi-faceted and multi-cultural nature of the experienced spatial problems in Cape Town, there would still appear to be an extremely strong case for reopening the question of what the nature of planning at the metropolitan level might be. The following sections highlight some of these considerations.

The changing nature of the Cape Town space-economy

Numerous authors have made the point that, in the latter part of the twentieth century, cities everywhere have been subject to important new forces. These have greatly complicated and diversified land-use patterns and the pattern of social and economic relations of the earlier 'modern' or 'Fordist' city (see Borja and Castells 1997; Graham and Healey 1999; Healey 2000; Soja 1995, etc.). In South African cities, many elements of this pre-existing (modern, Fordist) spatial structure have persisted, but these cities, too, have become increasingly complex, both spatially and relationally. To some degree this has resulted from the dropping of racial laws, but changes in domestic economic policy and economic structure, and the re-establishment of stronger linkages between this country and the rest of the world, have had significant effects. Evidence from the main cities of South Africa suggests that spatial divisions and fragmentation are simply taking on new forms and dimensions rather than disappearing (see Mabin 1995 on Johannesburg, and Todes 1998 on Durban).

Cape Town's economy[1] continues to be dominated by the manufacturing sector[2] (it contributed 28 per cent to overall production in 1996, relative to 21 per cent by trade, 19 per cent by services and 17 per cent by financial services), much of which has been decentralizing within the metropolitan area to locations offering larger sites and lower land costs. In this sense Fordist production patterns are persisting. However, the fastest-growing sectors are currently trade and finance, fuelled by a growing tourist industry and a concentration of finance and insurance offices and head offices. Sectors likely to grow in future are those able to take advantage of export possibilities (tourism, real estate, high tech industries, food and finance), and are likely to display a relatively dispersed locational pattern.

These economic dynamics have had a major effect on income distribution, both sectorally and spatially. Prior to 1994, South Africa had one of the worst income distributions in the world. Despite post-1994 national policies and programmes aimed at redistribution, the overall inter-household distribution of income has worsened, with the income of the poorest 40 per cent of African households being 20 per cent lower in 1996 than in 1991 (*Cape Times*, March 2000). However, African earners' share of total income has increased (Nattrass and Seekings 1997). Significant income inequalities therefore remain, although their correlation with racial categories is beginning to decrease. Change in the labour market in South Africa is one factor which continues to fuel inequalities. Here, as elsewhere, traditional manufacturing industries and mining have seen large-scale job losses due to declining international terms of trade, the removal of protective tariffs and the switch to an export-led economy. In Cape Town, textile manufacture has been badly affected by international competition, and manufacturing generally has shifted towards more capital-intensive and higher-wage areas of production (Metropolitan Development Consortium 1998). This has resulted in large-scale job losses in Cape Town, particularly amongst coloured women who were previously concentrated in the clothing and textile sectors. As a result, unemployment in Cape Town swelled from 6 per cent in 1980 to 19 per cent in 1996, and the size of the informal sector doubled over the same period (Metropolitan Development Consortium 1998). The more rapidly growing sectors of finance, trade and leisure activities tend to draw on a more skilled labour force and to generate a wealthy elite, thus exacerbating inequalities. In many respects, therefore, but not always for the same reasons, the international patterns (see Soja 1995) of social polarization, growing income inequalities, and the marginalization of an urban underclass are occurring in Cape Town and in other South African cities.

These patterns of economic development and sectoral increases in income inequality manifest themselves spatially. Apartheid cities in South Africa evidenced extreme symptoms of social and spatial exclusion as a direct result of racial segregation policies. But patterns of spatial inequity and exclusion are persisting in the post-apartheid era, although they may now be attributed to income inequalities and poverty, rather than to legal racial barriers. At a general level, the clear divisions in Cape Town between wealthier areas and poorer areas remain, and have intensified.

The Cape Town Metropolitan area, more than any other large South African city, has always been highly centralized in spatial terms. Radial corridors of transportation feed volumes of people and traffic into the dominant CBD, which still houses the largest concentration of office, retail and small manufacturing activity. The Cape Town Municipality (containing the CBD) today holds 40 per cent of the metropolitan population but generates over 80 per cent of all employment (Metropolitan Development Consortium 1998). In the other large centres of Johannesburg and Durban, inner-city areas have undergone a transformation from white to African residents (see Morris 1999, on Johannesburg), but the Cape Town CBD remains under the control of finance and retail capital, and few people of colour hold residential or commercial land here.

The spatial pattern is, however, beginning to change, and Figure 9.1 shows the dispersed and decentralizing nature of current public and private land developments. In the CBD, office and retail has been decentralizing due to 'crime and grime', traffic congestion, and the pull of attractive alternative office park locations, but it remains vibrant as a tourist and entertainment centre and as a location for the growing film industry. The historical sub-centres of Claremont and Bellville, located on two of the 'mature' corridors, have for some time attracted retail and office development, and the tendency for large-scale shopping malls to locate themselves close to wealthy suburbs on major freeway routes is also not new. The more important recent trend is towards what are known as 'mega-projects'. These are large-scale, mixed-use, retail, office and leisure developments, taking up decentralized,[3] accessible and high-amenity locations, particularly to the north of the city. Such developments are increasingly attracting commercial activities away from the historical centres and corridors, raising obvious questions about the feasibility of the corridors identified by the MSDF. But while decentralization processes have tended to blur the earlier core–periphery pattern of development in Cape Town, they have done little to change the stark contrasts between economies in the wealthier and poorer parts of the metropolis.

It is in the poorer areas of the city, particularly on the Cape Flats, that the real 'urbanization of suburbia' has taken place. Thirty-four per cent of Cape Town's labour force is classified as being in informal employment or unemployed, and given the absence of a welfare system in this country, it can be assumed that the bulk of the latter survive by generating informal income of some kind (Figure 9.2). A small percentage of these informal jobs is to be found in the wealthier parts of the city, where street-trading is given (a little) more freedom than was the case in apartheid days, and where middle-class families sometimes operate businesses from home. The bulk of informal income is generated in and from the

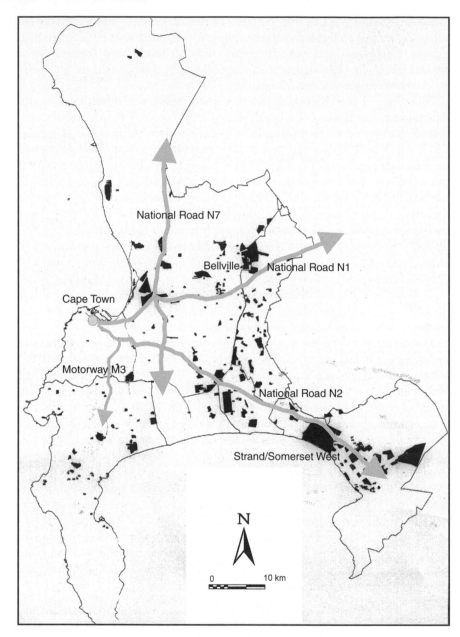

Figure 9.1 Major developments completed and proposed, June 1998–1999.

Source: Spatial Planning, Cape Metropolitan Council.

Figure 9.2 Two responses to growing poverty: the informal sector in the poorer parts of the city and increased security in the wealthier areas.

Sources: Cape Photo Library, and photographed by Philip Burns.

poorer townships themselves, on the streets, in homes or through the wider networks of gangsters and criminals.[4] But inputs to these activities are sourced from across the metropolitan area, from surrounding rural areas, and even, in the case of African curios and the gun and drug trade, internationally.

These poorer areas still hold a population that is almost entirely African and coloured. While there has been some movement of African families into previously classified coloured residential areas, and limited movement of wealthier African and coloured families into the more expensive white residential areas, the spatial pattern of race and income segregation remains largely intact. This is the case as well in South Africa's other major cities (Todes 1998; Beall *et al.* 1999).

Cape Town is now displaying some of the features which Soja (1995) attributes to post-modern urbanism, and which in this context can be attributed to growing social polarization, inequality and exclusion. In particular, crime rates have escalated dramatically (in all parts of the country), precipitating a flurry of protective measures on the part of wealthier urban residents and formal businesses: walled and access-controlled residential developments and whole commercial areas under camera surveillance are becoming as common in Cape Town as they are in Los Angeles (Figure 9.2). Inevitably it is the poorer areas, however, which bear the brunt of criminal activity, and in Cape Town the control of large sections of the townships by gangs has rendered many of these areas ungovernable. For example, the Cape Town Municipality finds it increasingly difficult to manage its public housing stock, as gangs moved in to collect the rents and allocate units. In the shack settlements, 'warlords' (or self-appointed headmen) collect compulsory monthly contributions from shack-dwellers in return for 'protection' and have organized resistance to housing upgrade projects which would remove their income source (Cape Town Municipality 1998).

Spatial patterns of poverty and wealth in Cape Town should not be oversimplified, however. Significant generation of income also occurs on the Cape Flats, often linked to illegal activity, and the economic relations which support these activities span local, national and international space. Similarly, pockets of poverty exist in the wealthy parts of the city, the povety manifesting itself in rented rooms, homelessness and a growing population living and earning on the streets. Both formal and informal economic activity is highly dispersed across the city, with different types of activities pursuing particular locational logics of their own. This in turn is generating complex and cross-cutting flows of people and goods, not necessarily confined to the city itself, and multi-purpose patterns of movement across and within the city.[5]

Graham and Healey make the critically important point that these new complexities, affecting all cities to a greater or lesser extent, have to influence the way in which spatial planners think about their work. In the past, they say,

> Planners assumed that cities were physically-integrated places, amenable to local land use and development policies ... The planners' task was to

manage the structure to remove economic, social and environmental problems ... Space, distance and the city, in effect, were reified as automatic
and determining forces directly shaping the social and economic world in
some simple, linear, cause and effect way. The desired socio-spatial order of
the city, and hence its associated socio-economic world, was then expressed
and promoted in a master plan (comprehensive plan/development plan).

(Graham and Healey 1999, 624)

They go on to argue that the tendency to view cities as single, integrated,
unitary, material objects, amenable to local land-use and development policies,
and as space–time containers, bounding the activities which go on within it, is
thrown into question by the current dynamics of change. Rather than a cohe-
sive 'uniplex' structure, the city has a 'multiplex circuitry' with the relations of
people and firms stretching across and beyond the city, uncontainable within
any particular physical form. The relationship between the spatial structure and
form of the city, and the social and economic relations which operate within
and beyond it, is a complex and frequently unpredictable one. Interventions
which are conceived in narrowly spatial terms, or are based on the assumption
that spatial interventions can direct society and economy, are increasingly open
to question. They may do no more than, as Marris (1996) suggests, provide a
temporary reassurance that the threat of disorder can be contained and that
society is really comprehensible and governable.

Implications for planning

The aim of this section is to do no more than draw together some of the threads
of the previous text, and to spell out the implications they may have for thinking about the future of Cape Town, and South African cities more generally. I
remain optimistic that the process of political transition has opened cracks of
opportunity, however small, that will allow room for thinking and action about
a better urban future. Post-modern thinking has introduced necessary modera-
tion to the grandiose and ultimately unrealistic dreams of the great urban
utopian thinkers, but it cannot exclude the possibility that, individually or col-
lectively, the citizens of Cape Town can have some determining role in their
urban future.

Experience both in Cape Town and elsewhere shows that it is not difficult to
gain consensus around the kind of broad goals for a future Cape Town put
forward in the MSDF.[6] Who would disagree that it would be good to live in a
city where the environment is sustainably managed, where decision-making is
accountable, where there is equitable access (by a largely non-car-owning population) to a choice of urban opportunities, where environments are safe and
attractive and where the population is prosperous? These are morally defensible
goals and worth striving for. But these worthwhile aims have to be tempered by
the constraints of reality. South Africa is, after all, a poor nation at the tip of a
continent which has largely been bypassed by global flows of resources. It is a

country where the reality for most urban dwellers is a desperate daily struggle for survival, and where poverty, crime and AIDS threaten every development effort. As in most other African cities, the 'reach' of government is rapidly contracting as the 'informal' becomes the norm, and the ability of the state to intervene, to plan and implement projects, and to manage development processes, is put in question. This is also a country which, like many others, is feeling the impact of global forces in various ways. There are impacts on its economy, causing some sectors to grow and others to fail, there are impacts on income distribution and there are impacts on the consumption patterns and tastes of its citizens. These in turn have an impact on the spatial dynamics of its cities. Increasingly, therefore, the city and its people are subject to forces which cannot easily be controlled and which are not easily amenable to local redirection.

The emerging position on city-wide planning (see for example, Borja and Castells 1997) takes these new dynamics into account and puts forward an approach which may well hold potential. In terms of this approach, a realistic planning response begins with a clear idea of the economic and social development role which local government is able to play. The spatial implications and informants of these ideas are of crucial significance, but it is vital that this spatial understanding remains an integrated, rather than a separate, concern. An important realization must be that planning has to be far less ambitious in relation to the economic and spatial restructuring of the city as a whole, and far more ambitious in relation to the implementation of shorter-term and more localized projects which can gradually, over time, have an impact on the space economy of the city. This is not an argument for a return to the project-based and ad hoc form of planning intervention of the 1980s which occurred largely in isolation from broader conceptions of how the wider space-economy of the city should function. That wider view is crucial as it informs the nature and location of shorter-term actions, but it is strategic and flexible. It is also important to recognize that certain urban elements still require broader-scale intervention: environmental systems can span the city and the region beyond, and the securing and management of threatened and valuable natural areas may require intervention across a large territory; public transport requires system-wide planning around modal interchange and pricing policies; well-located land which could be used to house lower-income people needs to be identified and secured; and bulk infrastructure needs to be considered in relation to city-wide patterns of development. However, efforts need to shift to immediate and implementable actions.

The form and nature of shorter-term and action-focused planning is of major importance. A second important consideration, I would add, is sensitivity to the context in which such planning occurs.

Urban transformation projects

Spatial and economic planners need to work together to develop an integrated understanding of the urban space-economy and to identify, within this, potential 'urban transformation' projects (see Borja and Castells 1997). Such projects, which are public-sector led and later partnership-based, are designed to capitalize on those sectors of the economy which have growth potential. This potential should be sought both within the formal, export-oriented sectors of the economy and within the realm of informal and locally oriented sectors. Physically, urban transformation projects need to be located with the specific aim of addressing the spatial disparities of Cape Town. They need to be positioned, initially, within the interstitial areas between the wealthier and poorer parts of the city, recognizing the fact that private investment will not commit to the areas of deep poverty. Over time, and building on what has been learnt from earlier projects, the potential to shift such initiatives into the poorer parts of the city can be explored. Urban transformation projects also need consciously to integrate surrounding areas, spatially and economically. This requires location in relation to metropolitan public transport systems and vehicle access systems, and the building of physical connections between previously physically separated townships. Urban transformation projects need to pay particular attention to the quality of the public urban environment. Such projects are mixed-use and contain important social facilities; there is constant surveillance and there are public spaces and markets which accommodate small traders.

The exact form and nature of such projects are not predictable: there are no blueprints for such initiatives. They need to emerge out of processes of thorough communication with both city-wide and local organizations and residents, in which issues of cultural specificity are high on the agenda. This focus on locationally specific projects potentially leaves the way open for a more direct response to local expressions of culture and difference, and these, too, must be central informants of project design and process. A project-based approach acknowledges that inequities and injustices cannot be addressed in the same way in each part of the metropolitan area, and that the nature and content of each project must be locally informed.

The approach has important implications for planning skills and the kinds of products which planners deliver. It is clear that the kinds of skills which planners are equipped with have to be broadened. There is a need to understand space, not as a determining variable but as an integral part of social and economic forces, and as an element which will inevitably be shaped in various ways by the ebb and flow of social change. There is also a growing need for planners to understand more about how urban economies operate, how economic actors (big and small) respond to public interventions, and how financial viability can be achieved. There is, as well, a need for planners to be more sensitive to social contexts within which they are proposing interventions. A respect for local knowledge, and for locally and culturally specific ways of acting and prioritizing, is essential. This opens the way for the formation of cross-disciplinary teams of professionals, dedicated solely to a particular project, and thus an integration of work (particularly spatial ideas) across departmental boundaries.

The plans they produce will also be different from before. Within plans which set the city-wide frame of reference, project-based plans need to view planning and implementation as occurring in parallel. The end product of the planning process is not just a document or a map: it is a set of ideas which are tested and refined as the project proceeds and as consultations progress.

This approach also has implications for the institutional location of spatial planning within local bureaucracies. The separation of spatial planning into a line-function department may have been important as a way of asserting professional identity, but it has not served the purpose of integrating spatial ideas into the work of government. While development control work may require dedicated functional space,[7] spatial planners should rather integrate themselves into other line-function departments or into area-based professional teams working on specific projects. Spatial thinking needs to become part of the work of every department, not a separate concern on its own.

Diversity and difference: acknowledging multi-culturalism

In cities all over the world there has been a growing realization that, rather than gradual processes of social assimilation and homogenization of socially diverse and often unequal ethnic and interest groups, such groups are often asserting their right to be different and to have that difference recognized (see Sandercock 1998; Fraser 1995). A politics of difference has received growing theoretical recognition in recent years, partly as a result of waves of international migration and the increasingly multi-cultural nature of many cities. In a context in which a challenge to the prevailing capitalist system seems close to impossible, social movements organized around ethnicity, gender, sexual preferences, indigenous rights and environmental issues have been making themselves heard. A politics of difference is also compatible with a post-modern view of the world which rejects single, universalized explanations and solutions and which celebrates difference, diversity and multiple, competing views of the future. It is compatible as well with an emerging literature on (post)development which comes to 'the defence of cultural difference' (Escobar 1995, 226) in place of the destructive discourse and strategy of the technicians of modernization theory.

In the light of this, questions must be asked about the nature of both a long-term vision and short-term actions in the context of Cape Town. Do, for example, the ethics of equity and redistribution require that metropolitan interventions in the poorer parts of the city look and function in a similar way to the older and wealthier parts of Cape Town, as it was perhaps assumed in the MSDF? Proceeding from a different assumption would have highly practical planning implications. It may suggest that the economic activity which is targeted for urban transformation projects includes the sort which is more likely to provide jobs and income to a largely unskilled population. It may suggest that prime locational spots are not automatically reserved for 'outside' investors, but that local business people are also given the opportunity to use such land. It may suggest that the provision of public services and facilities take account of specific cultural practices. For example, Xhosa-speaking people have a relationship with deceased family members which requires frequent and easy access to their graves: cemeteries therefore need to be smaller and more dispersed than is the case in other parts of the city. And specific open spaces may need to be set aside for Xhosa initiation ceremonies, which require privacy, visual seclusion and access to water.

These are extremely sensitive questions in the context of present-day South Africa. In the very recent past, people of colour in South Africa were subject to policies which argued that the different cultural practices of racially defined groups justified political and geographical 'separate development'. This in turn provided the justification for the entrenchment of extraordinary forms of inequity and injustice. It is therefore not surprising that early post-apartheid policy documents were so concerned about emphasizing an ethic of equality and an erasure of difference. It is nonetheless necessary now to take a step beyond this position and interrogate more closely our understanding of the concept of equality. There is growing support within the planning discipline for an ethical foundation which *adds* to the traditional (and still vitally important) concerns of equity, redistribution, accountability and environmental sustainability – a concern with the recognition of difference.

How does Foucault fit into this?

The opening of debate on a set of broad and morally defensible goals for Cape Town's future is an important first step: without shared ethics of some kind, any way forward is problematic. Experience from the early years of the MSDF process has shown that groups and organizations may commit themselves to such initiatives (and to the discourse coalition which forms around it) quite readily, although the strength and duration of such commitment is not predictable. Discourse coalitions are fragile, and are easily challenged or replaced. Where conflicts will inevitably arise is in the translation of these goals into actions and resource flows, when questions of who gains and who loses are raised. The greatest danger of the approach to metropolitan planning outlined above is that public and private resources are focused into a limited number of projects or areas which, by their very scale and nature, will be worth fighting over. In a highly unequal society such a fight is unlikely to be a fair one. The broad progressive political movement, which Marshall (2000) sees as a guarantor of the redistributionary goals of such efforts, does not exist in Cape Town (or arguably in other South African cities) at this point in the political transition. A decision to embark on this approach to planning would represent a major risk in this respect, and may well result in the exacerbation of existing disparities and inequities.

The usefulness of Foucault lies in his drawing of attention to the inevitable manifestation of power. Exploring the history of the MSDF process has clearly shown that planning cannot claim to be a technical, rational exercise, producing incontestable solutions to particular framings of the urban problem. A growing number of texts argue this position (see Flyvbjerg 1998; Forsyth 1999; Throgmorton 1996). This is not to suggest that the MSDF is irrational, but rather that the planning process was shaped by individuals, operating in a particular context, who singly or in combination exerted power in a wide variety of ways, to very different personal or public ends. It is arguable that this will be the case with any planning process. However well-designed and however well-intentioned a metropolitan planning process may be, it will present an opportunity for the exercise of power which could be simultaneously (but unpredictably) positive and productive, or negative and dominatory. This is one important conclusion which can be drawn from the Forum years of the MSDF (see Chapter 4) in which most of the preconditions for a democratic and inclusionary participation process seemed to be in place, but in which the workings of power in various forms happened to give rise to a less than satisfactory outcome. At the present time, the conditions for democratic planning processes with equitable and redistributionary consequences are far less auspicious than they were in the early 1990s, and the threat of dominatory action is far greater.

This does not necessarily mean, however, that any planning effort is futile. Normative rationality, Flyvbjerg (1996, 384) argues, may still provide an ideal worth striving for, but it is a poor guide for the tactics and strategy needed to get there. Foucault draws our attention to the need to focus on power relations in any such process, and to be able to identify and counter relations of domination wherever they may occur. Being alert to power (and its workings through rationality and knowledge), giving support to its productive and positive forms, and monitoring and revealing its negative forms, thus become important elements of the planning task, and of those planners seriously committed to ethical action. It is not, however, only the task of planners or professionals to do this. Foucault's ideas hold not only the potential to be an analytical technique, but to form the basis, as well, for public action. An awareness on the part of township-based and other marginalized groups of the workings of power, and of the ways in which professionals or business people can use knowledge to manipulate and to co-opt, would in itself be a significant counter to the threat of domination.

A final question which remains is that of how to develop the tactics and strategies needed to identify and counter negative forms of power. Foucault would reject the possibility of generalized rules or criteria which would guide action in such circumstances, and would argue instead that tactics must be context-dependent. We can learn to recognize the operation of power, I would argue, by analysing and understanding the processes of which we are already part (Watson 2000). This book represents just such an attempt. If those involved in future planning processes in Cape Town are able to reflect on their past, on how the operation of power has shaped planning in this city to date, and on how power has manifested itself in various ways and with both positive and negative outcomes, they may be in a far better position to take forward the task which still lies ahead.

Chronology

1988	METPLAN sub-committee (Investigating Land for Future Housing for the Low Income Group) receives a report from its consultant but decides to defer making a decision on it until a meeting in June 1989.
1989	June: first meeting of planning officials to discuss a possible regional development strategy, held at the offices of the Regional Services Council.
1990	Nelson Mandela is released from prison.
1990	July: workshop on a new direction for metropolitan planning, convened by the Regional Services Council.
1990	October: first meeting of the reconstituted Regional Development Strategy Steering Committee.
1991	June: Caledon Conference, attended by community, union and political organizations of Cape Town, as well as local planning officials. The aim is to initiate a process of participation in future metropolitan planning.
1991	November: national level agreement between the main political parties to begin negotiations towards power-sharing.
1992	December: launch of the Western Cape Economic Development Forum. Metropolitan planning is placed under the Forum's Urban Development Commission.
1994	April: first democratic elections in South Africa.
1995	January: metropolitan planning process transferred back under the control of the Regional Services Council. The Forum is disbanded.
1995	The draft Metropolitan Spatial Development Framework is circulated to other government departments for comment.
1996	March: national government adopts its new (neo-liberal) macro-economic policy, GEAR.
1996	May: first democratic local government elections in Cape Town, forming the Cape Metropolitan Council and six municipalities.
1996	June: copies of the document – Metropolitan Spatial Development Framework (MSDF) – are released.
1996	December: public launch of the MSDF.

1997–1998   MSDF circulated to the municipalities and the public for comment with a view to statutorizing the plan (i.e. turning it into a legally recognized structure plan).

1997   December: Cape Metropolitan Council initiates its first attempt at preparing an Integrated Development Plan (IDP).

1998   Cape Metropolitan Council planning officials begin work on preparing a draft statutory plan.

1999   April: the Draft Statutory MSDF is submitted to the Provincial minister for approval in terms of the Land Use Planning Ordinance.

2000   January: planning begins for the next round of local government reorganization, involving the transformation of the metropolitan authority and the six municipalities into one 'unicity'.

2000   September: the MSDF Co-ordinating Working Group has its last meeting, at which it is reported that only the goals and principles of the MSDF will be submitted for statutorization.

2000   December: municipal elections, ushering in the new 'unicity'.

Notes

Introduction

1 Cape Town was not the only city to launch metropolitan planning initiatives at this time. The other major metropolitan areas of Johannesburg and Durban also undertook planning exercises.

2 Adler and Webster (1995) have argued strongly against the implication that democratic transitions necessarily have to take this form. They criticize both the tendency to de-emphasize the role of mass movements in transition and the tendency to undervalue the role which they can play in achieving less conservative outcomes.

3 Drawn from Smart (1985), Hoy (1986), and Ransom (1997).

4 These ideas would not necessarily be applied to a consideration of change in society as a whole.

5 In using history it is obviously important to be wary of the simplistic use of precedent, and stressing superficial similarities at the expense of fundamental differences between one age and another, as well as historicism, which holds that each age is entirely unique and that there is no continuity (and hence the possibility of learning) between past and present

6 Narratives have a number of characteristics which separate them from history, although there are clearly many overlaps. Narratives have a temporal or sequential framework, they have an element of explanation or coherence, they have some element of the general in the particular, and they recognize generic conventions relating to the expected framework, protagonists and modes of performance or circulation (Finnegan 1998, 9).

1 'What's needed is a metropolitan plan'

1 On 16 June 1989 it was reported that hundreds of thousands of people (primarily African and coloured) stayed away from work, and many businesses closed voluntarily. The government had refused again to declare the day a public holiday (*Cape Times* 16/6/89).

2 Hereafter referred to as the Regional Services Council.

3 In terms of apartheid, urban land was classified for occupation by separate racial groups under the Group Areas Act, 1950.

4 In the metropolitan areas Regional Services Councils were governed by elected representatives chosen from the white municipalities, the coloured 'management committees', and the African councils, but with the representation weighted in favour of those areas which consumed the most services, i.e. the wealthy 'white' areas. The chair of the Council was appointed by the Provincial Administration, which by this time had ceased to be a political body.

5 A central goal of early apartheid was that African people should settle and exercise

political rights in those territories (homelands) set aside for them. Those African people present in the 'white' urban areas were intended to be there on a temporary basis to offer their labour, and influx controls were set in place to prevent 'surplus' African people from coming to or remaining in the urban areas. In 1979 this policy was relaxed somewhat as a result of the recommendations of the Riekert Commission which proposed that Africans be divided into two categories: 'qualified' urban dwellers and the 'disqualified' others, who would remain in the rural homelands. In 1986 influx controls were abolished and thereafter more subtle policies (relating to the location of jobs and housing) were used in an attempt to reduce migration to cities.

6   This was undoubtedly a gross overestimation. Migration between Cape Town and the previously termed homelands has always had a significant component of circulatory movement, and there has been extensive movement within the city as well (see Dewar *et al.* 1991) which has made permanent in-migration figures almost impossible to estimate.

7   Planning also played (and still does) a managing role with regard to the regulation of land settlement, subdivision and land speculation activity, affecting more particularly the white population and the wealthier parts of the city. It played then (and still does) a further modernizing role by planning for the provision of public services infrastructure.

8   The Fifth Report of the Social and Economic Planning Council (1942–1945). Its proposals were received with some reservation when published in 1944, but it came to influence the position on planning of the post-1948 (apartheid) government (Wilkinson 1996).

2   Cape Town as a 'compact, integrated' city?

1   It is not clear from the handwritten set of notes of a meeting, which must have taken place immediately before the 22 October gathering, who motivated for this decision to expand the group to include non-governmental bodies.

2   It could be asked why City Council and Regional Services councillors did not appear to be playing a more direct role in this debate on the future of the city. However, at that time councillors were not elected on party political tickets (although some had clear party affiliations) and many had local property and business interests – the longer-term growth of the metropolitan area was perhaps beyond their immediate and often local concerns.

3   Most planning practitioners used as their guide to planning, at the local level, the set of Guideline documents produced by the national Centre for Scientific and Industrial Research. These documents recommended a spatial model based on the suburban 'neighbourhood unit': monofunctional, low-density and car-oriented.

4   A landmark, because the metropolitan plan formally dates its existence from the time of the Caledon Conference.

5   In August 1992 a Regional Services Council planner was invited to attend a meeting on urbanization strategy, convened by the Provincial Administration. The presence at the meeting of members of the Intelligence Service, the Police and the South African Defence Force may have indicated which constituencies the Province felt that it still needed to draw into strategizing around the urbanization issue (RSC files 1992a).

3   Legitimating the plan: the Western Cape Economic Development Forum

1   The current Executive Director of Planning, Housing and Environment in the Cape Metropolitan Council, Tomalin, felt that this statement reflected unfairly on planners. Adverts of this kind *were* carried in small print in the back of the newspapers,

but this was where all such advertisements were carried. The planners, he insisted, were not trying to hide anything.

2   It should be noted that the form of democratic rights enjoyed by white, Indian and coloured people were not the same. In terms of the Tricameral parliamentary system, introduced in 1984, coloured (and Indian) people elected representatives to the national level, but in separate houses of Parliament. Under certain circumstances the white, coloured and Indian houses could meet together. African people were excluded from this arrangement entirely. At the local level, coloured and Indian people elected separate local government bodies which, in terms both of resources and powers, were decidedly inferior to their white counterparts.

3   These policy-making forums on development issues need to be distinguished from those local government negotiating forums, established around local government restructuring, some of which were convened by 'white' local authorities under the provisions of the 1991 Interim Measures for Local Government Act. The primary aim of this Act was to restore service provision to African urban areas where local councils had ceased to operate. These statutory forums were largely rejected by township civic associations as being a creation of the apartheid government and an attempt to legitimate and entrench inequalities and discrimination (see Turok 1994). Policy-making development forums were not constituted in terms of the 1991 Act and were much broader in terms of their stakeholder involvement.

4   The Western Cape Economic Development Forum was registered as a section 21 (not for profit) company, which allowed it to raise funds, and these provisions were inscribed into the Articles of Association of the Company.

5   Davidson, introduced in Chapter 2 as the ANC representative present at the Caledon Conference, was also a professional planner and graduate of the University of Cape Town planning school.

6   A representative of Chittenden and Nicks Associated, a private sector planning consultancy involved in local level planning exercises in the south-east sector of the metropolitan area at the time, explained that, at local meetings with civic and community members, there was a great deal of interest in, and awareness of, the importance of spatial planning issues. People involved in these meetings were usually younger and more progressive and aware. However, at forums where larger-scale issues were discussed, these areas were represented by the older, more conservative, but more senior, 'traditional' leaders (sometimes also described as 'warlords') who were less aware of the importance of spatial issues.

4   'No-one disputed that there should be a physical plan ...': the participation process in practice

1   The Chief Director of Engineering and Planning had two deputy chief directors, one for engineering and one for planning.

2   This was the group set up at the meeting between City and Regional Councils and community-based organizations in May 1992 (see Chapter 3).

3   In a note from Van Deventer to the facilitator, she comments that the idea of the production team was to 'enable UDC to short-cut the process by producing a document in a collective way' (MDF-CWG minutes 1993b).

5   South Africa post-1994: new systems of government and planning

1   One of the compromise agreements reached prior to democratic elections was that there would be a period of compulsory executive power-sharing (until 1999) between the political parties which won more than 5 per cent of the national vote. This was known as the Government of National Unity.

2   The programme itself was oriented towards meeting basic needs and alleviating

poverty, with its five key targets being: meeting basic needs; developing human resources; building the economy; democratizing the state and society; and implementing the RDP (RDP 1994, 7).

3　At the time the exchange rate was 6 rands to 1 US$.

4　The intention in the legislation was to protect white minorities, but in the Western Cape Province this had a rather different outcome from other cities. The arrangement served to boost the voting strength of the smaller African population, as the more numerous coloured population had to share their seat allocation with white and Asian voters.

5　These elections were subsequently deferred to late 2000.

6　This is a system which the 1998 White Paper on Local Government proposes to change: it suggests that in metropolitan areas, the municipal tier of government be abolished or considerably weakened, and that powers and functions be concentrated in the metropolitan tier in order to create more administratively and financially efficient local government.

7　The Municipal Structures Act of 1998 and the Municipal Systems Bill of 1999.

8　In 1990 the Western Cape Province contained 3.6 million people of whom 52 per cent were coloured, 25 per cent African and 23 per cent white. Metropolitan Cape Town contained 3.1 million people of which 50 per cent were coloured, 27 per cent African and 23 per cent white (Bridgman *et al.* 1992).

9　The Colored Labour Preference Policy was instituted by the apartheid government in 1954, the aim being to give employment preference to coloured persons and hence reduce the number of African workers in the Western Cape.

10　All local authority structures drew their funding from rates, house rentals and service charges in their area of jurisdiction. Because African townships had an almost complete absence of higher rate-paying commercial activity, and a very poor population, their income from this source was extremely limited.

11　The Central Witwatersrand Metropolitan Chamber had begun work in April 1991. It was chaired by the national director of IDASA (Van Zyl Slabbert) and had been set up in order to 'provide a forum for negotiating non-racial and democratic structures of local government' (quoted in Mabin 1999, 166).

12　The local government forum operated separately from the Western Cape Economic Development Forum discussed in Chapters 3 and 4, but representatives from the local government forum were present on the Economic Development Forum.

13　Local government negotiations on the Witwatersrand, South Africa's largest urban complex, also concluded, after much dispute, with the acceptance of a weaker metropolitan government. Here, however, the reasons were related to a fear by the Provincial government that the metropolitan authority would represent a large and powerful competitor, even if both structures were ANC controlled (see Mabin 1999). In Durban, the third major metropolitan area, a stronger role for metropolitan government was agreed on.

14　In Cape Town this had a rather different outcome from other cities, owing to the voting arrangement described in note 4.

15　Section 146 of the 1996 Constitution states that national law will prevail over provincial law in matters which require uniformity across the nation, by establishing norms and standards, frameworks or national policies. The principles of Chapter 1 of the Act fall into this category.

16　Western Cape Planning and Development Act of 1999.

17　Forum for Effective Planning and Development meeting, 6 May 1997. It was agreed that 'there should be no single focus point for spatial planning' (Harrison 1998, 7).

18　The New Public Administration movement in the United States dates from the Minnowbrook Conference in 1968 (Fitzgerald 1995).

19　The Municipal Systems Bill of 1999 provides for local governments to undertake 'processes of planning, performance management, resource mobilisation and organizational change' and '[link] these processes into a single, integrated cycle at the local level'.

20 The prevailing mode of governance in the UK has been termed 'institutional economics', which stresses the need to introduce incentive structures into public service provision, disaggregating bureaucracies, the contracting out of services, and consumer choice (Rhodes 1997). This, in turn, Rhodes argues, is being replaced by a new position (termed IGM, or intergovernmental management) which features problem-solving, inter-governmental co-ordination and networking, and a management which plays a facilitating and integrative role rather than a hierarchical, indicator-driven one.

6 Dusting off the old planning legislation: can we make the metropolitan plan legal?

1 The Bellville municipality became an important component of the new ('interim') Tygerberg Municipality after the 1996 local government elections.

7 Practices of representation: the Metropolitan Spatial Development Framework (1996 Technical Report)

1 Talen (1997) found, in a survey of the 50 largest American cities, that 25 had long-range traditional comprehensive plans in operation. Both of South Africa's other major metropolitan areas, Johannesburg and Durban, developed comprehensive metropolitan spatial plans during the early 1990s.

2 It is not intended to suggest that the authors of the Technical Document were at fault in doing this. Most planning and policy documents are written persuasively (in fact students are taught to do this), and most planners write this way in order to be effective.

3 Figure 7.3 identifies two other problems as well: that of urban sprawl, into areas of high-potential agricultural land, and that of the existence of Atlantis: a decentralization point planned for coloured people, initiated in the 1970s and currently experiencing high levels of poverty and unemployment.

4 The consulting firm was MLH, headed by Mr Ken Sturgeon.

5 Ashworth (1973, 62) refers to Los Angeles as a 'nightmarish sprawling anti-city peopled by a rootless and lonely crowd', and Schneider (1979) warns of the 'Los Angelization' of the earth. Both these quotes are used in Newman and Kenworthy (1989).

6 These goals are: equity and access, vitality and choice, prosperity, social well-being, uniqueness and beauty, adaptability, safety, openness and accountability, efficiency, and sustainability (Technical Report 1996, 28). Two of the goals, 'prosperity' and 'openness and accountability', reflected more recent concerns with economic growth and democratic government.

7 What are termed 'guidelines' in the Technical Report would become legal requirements if the plan takes on the status of a statutory plan.

8 The definition of metropolitan open spaces may still become a contested arena. Their preservation and maintenance demands resources and this is likely to lead to pressure for their development for urban use. In late 1998 a dispute arose between the Tygerberg Municipality and the Cape Metropolitan Council over the use of one of these spaces: Driftsands. The municipality argued that they could not afford to maintain it and protect it from land invasion, and that it should be developed as part of an activity corridor. Pressures of this kind on demarcated open spaces are likely to continue.

9 The philosophy behind this approach, and the far more detailed and nuanced thinking of which it is comprised, is set out in, for example, Dewar and Uytenbogaardt (1991).

10   The reaction of the planning programme staff to the publication of the MSDF was that the spatial concepts had been misunderstood and misapplied.

11   A recent spatial plan drawn up for the Cape Town Municipality (1999) starts with the rationalization of a grid as a metropolitan structuring element, but the assumptions with regard to the scale of the grid and the way it is positioned on the map of Cape Town differ from the MSDF. As a result, the location for the highest-order new centre falls north of Philippi, adjacent to the airport.

8   New discourse coalitions and the marginalization of spatial planning

1   Western Cape Planning and Development Act, 1999, clause 9a.

2   A more recent visit to the 16th floor of the municipal building indicated that the situation had again changed. Floor space was again occupied, although now with different faces and different functions.

3   Population figures are for 1990 (WESGRO 1992).

4   Exchange rate 2000: R 7.50 = $1.

5   From this time onwards, I was present at all Co-ordinating Working Group and Statutory Working Group meetings, and observations such as these were captured in notes I made at each meeting.

6   Theunissen, during feedback on this chapter, disagreed strongly with this assumption. He wrote in the margin: 'Of course they can [be bound by law]. I just don't follow how anyone can conclude that planning law doesn't bind investors.' They could invest in another city. 'Oh yes, but then it is whether it will invest . . . if they invest we can determine where.'

7   Blowers (1982) argues that the planning profession generally has a weak knowledge base, particularly when it comes to understanding the economic and financial environment in which it attempts to intervene.

8   Not all transportation planners would agree on how these two functions should be accommodated spatially. One group of transport planners (Burnett *et al.* 1999) describes 'activity or development corridors' as accommodating major linear transport routes like rail or freeways, large shopping concentrations, social facilities and residential accommodation. Their paper puts forward a range of possible corridor designs which 'ensure the protection of the mobility function of the higher order roads'.

9   This is a view which would be widely supported within government.

10   These objectives were put to a chief executive officers' meeting in early 1999.

11   The Provincial Council was able to produce this legislation because it has 'concurrent' powers, with national government, in the area of planning. Schedule 4 of the Constitution sets out a number of functional areas where national and provincial governments have concurrent legislative competence. Regional Planning and Development and Urban and Rural Development are included on this list. Section 146 of the Constitution, on 'Conflicting Laws', provides for certain national legislation to prevail over Provincial legislation, where national legislation requires uniformity by establishing national norms and standards, frameworks or national policies. Under this provision, Provincial planning legislation has to accept (*inter alia*) a set of planning principles contained in the national Development Facilitation Act (1995) and the concept of IDPs contained in the Local Government Transition Act (as amended, 1996).

12   Not all planning staff felt equally strongly about this, and it would appear that Theunissen felt the most strongly about it. In a marginal note on this chapter he makes reference to what he sees as 'the whole sickness of opposition to the principle of statutorization of planning'.

13   Spatial planners in the Cape Metropolitan Council explained how frustrated they felt by this decision. As a major public investment, carrying with it hundreds of jobs,

it could have given an important boost to the new Philippi node in the poorest south-east of the metropolitan area. One informant suggested that the location of Century City, relatively close to the homes of some of the top officials and councillors, was a more important deciding factor.

14 These observations were communicated to me in informal discussions with metropolitan spatial planning staff.

15 But it was not inevitable: in metropolitan Durban, spatial planning is functionally combined with economic development, and some integration of approaches appears to have been achieved.

9   Beyond the MSDF: issues for planning

1   The following information is derived from a survey of the Cape Town space-economy, commissioned by the Cape Metropolitan Council, and published as Metropolitan Development Consortium (1998).

2   In order of magnitude, this sector is made up of textiles and clothing, paper and printing, chemicals, metal and steel, food, rubber and plastics, wood and furniture, electronics, beverages and tobacco.

3   The one mega-project which does not fit this picture is the waterfront development. It lies close to the Cape Town CBD and is partly responsible for the continuing viability of the city centre relative to centres in other South African cities.

4   The informal sector has always been a part of Cape Town's economy, but there is strong evidence of recent rapid growth due to economic restructuring and growing unemployment, and a relaxation of controls in the post-apartheid era.

5   Only 20–30 per cent of this movement takes the form of home to work commuting.

6   Of course the potential 'depth' of this consensus must be treated with caution. The primary lesson of the Forum experience (Chapter 4) was that people may give formal approval to ideas which they do not thoroughly understand, or to which they may not have any intention of binding themselves in the longer term. Discourse coalitions are fragile and can easily be broken or reconstituted if it is in the interests of those involved to do so.

7   Although at a local level it may be possible to provide a 'one-stop shop' which handles development control issues and small business support.

References

Adler, G. and E. Webster, 1995. Challenging transition theory: The labour movement, radical reform, and transition to democracy in South Africa. *Politics and Society* 23, 1: 75–106.

Ashworth, G., 1973. *Encyclopaedia of planning*. London: Barrie and Jenkins.

Baum, H., 1996. Practising planning theory in a political world. In *Explorations in planning theory*. Edited by S. Mandelbaum, L. Mazza and R. Burchell. New Brunswick, NJ: Rutgers Centre for Urban Policy Research.

Beall, J., O. Crankshaw and S. Parnell, 1999. *Urban governance, partnership and poverty in Johannesburg*. Birmingham: University of Birmingham.

Beauregard, R., 1998. Subversive histories: Texts from South Africa. In *Making the invisible visible: A multicultural planning history*. Edited by L. Sandercock. Berkeley: University of California Press.

—— 1999. Writing the planner. *Journal of Planning Education and Research* 18: 93–101.

Bekker, S. and R. Humphries, 1993. Regional forums. *Indicator SA* 10, 4: 19–22.

Bickford- Smith V., E. Van Heyningen and N. Worden, 1999. *Cape Town in the twentieth century: An illustrated social history*. Cape Town: David Philip.

Blowers, A., 1982. *State intervention 1: Planning and the market processes*. Block 5, Urban Change and Conflict, The Open University. Milton Keynes: Open University Press.

Borja, J. and M. Castells, 1997. Local and global: Management of cities in the information age. *United Nations Centre for Human Settlements (Habitat)*. London: Earthscan.

Boyer, C., 1983. *Dreaming the rational city*. Cambridge: MIT Press.

Breheny, M. ed., 1992. *Sustainable development and urban form*. London: Pion.

Bridgman, D., I. Palmer and W. Thomas, 1992. *South Africa's leading edge: A guide to the Western Cape economy*. Cape Town: WESGRO.

Bruner, J., 1986. *Actual minds, possible worlds*. Cambridge, Mass: Harvard University Press.

Bruner, J., 1996. *The culture of education*. Cambridge, Mass: Harvard University Press.

Bryson, J. and B. Crosby, 1996. Planning and the design and use of forums, arenas, and courts. In *Explorations in planning theory*. Edited by S. Mandelbaum, L. Mazza and R. Burchell. New Brunswick, NJ: Rutgers Centre for Urban Policy Research.

Burnett, S., S. Andersen and J. Nel, 1999. Planning for activity corridors, spines, streets and nodes. Paper presented to the South African Transport Conference, transport planning and policy session, Pretoria, 19–22 July.

Calthorpe, P., 1994. The region. In *The new urbanism: Towards an architecture of community*. Edited by P. Katz. New York: McGraw-Hill.

Cameron, R., 1986. Cape Town City Council: Policy analysis. Paper presented at the Western Cape Roots and Realities Conference, University of Cape Town.

—— 1999. *Democratisation of South African local government: A tale of three cities*. Cape Town: Van Schaik.

Cape Metropolitan Council, 1997. Towards effective metropolitan governance for the Cape metropolitan area. Submission to the Local Government Parliamentary Portfolio Committee, on behalf of the Cape Metropolitan Council and six municipalities, 11 November.

Cape Town Municipality, 1998. *Commission of enquiry into the Crossroads and Philippi crisis*. Cape Town: Report of the Commission.

—— 1999. *Municipal spatial development framework*. Cape Town: Planning and Development Directorate.

Central Statistical Services, 1998. *Expenditure of the general government 1995/6*. Statistical release P 9119. Pretoria: Government Printers.

Chipkin, I., 1997. Democracy, cities and space: South African conceptions of local government. Masters dissertation submitted to the Faculty of Arts, University of Witwatersrand, Johannesburg.

Chittenden and Associates, 1990. *Activity corridors as an urban strategy: A review of preconditions and principles in the context of Cape Town's south-east*. Report prepared for the Division of Roads and Transport Technology. Pretoria: Council for Scientific and Industrial Research.

City Planner's Department, 1989. *Cape metropolitan area guideplan 1988 (vol. 1: Peninsula: Comment on the implications of the approved peninsula guide plan for the city council operation)*. Report to the Town Planning Committee. Cape Town: Cape Town City Council.

—— 1993. A vision for the future of metropolitan Cape Town. Internal report. Cape Town: Cape Town City Council.

—— 1994. Metropolitan spatial development framework. Discussion document presented at the Urban Development Commission Workshop. Cape Town. Cape Town City Council, 14 September.

Cole, J., 1986. Against the wind: Pass law struggles in Crossroads, 1974–1986. *South African Labour Bulletin* 11, 8: 91–105.

Dear, M., 2000. *The postmodern urban condition*. Oxford: Blackwell.

Deleuze, G., 1986. *Foucault*. Minneapolis: University of Minnesota Press.

Department of Constitutional Development, 1997. *Integrated development planning for local authorities: A user-friendly guide*. Pretoria.

Department of Development Planning, 1988. *Cape metropolitan area guide plan. Volume 1: Peninsula*. Pretoria.

Department of Housing, 1994. *White paper: A new housing policy and strategy for South Africa*. Government Gazette number 16178: Pretoria.

Development Action Group, 1993. *Well-located affordable housing: A feasible alternative?* Cape Town.

Dewar, D., T. Rosmarin and V. Watson, 1991. *Movement patterns of the African population in Cape Town: Some policy implications*. Urban Problems Research Unit Working Paper No. 44. Cape Town: University of Cape Town.

Dewar, D., A. Todes and V. Watson, 1984. *Industrial decentralisation policy as a mechanism for regional development in South Africa: Its premises and record*. Urban Problems Research Unit Working Paper No. 30. Cape Town: University of Cape Town.

Dewar, D. and R. Uytenbogaardt, 1991. *South African cities: A manifesto for change*.

Urban Problems Research Unit Project Report 9. Cape Town: University of Cape Town.

Dewar, D., R. Uytenbogaardt, M. Hutton-Squire, K. Levy and P. Manidis, 1976. *Housing: A comparative evaluation of urbanism in Cape Town*. Urban Problems Research Unit Project Report 1. Cape Town: University of Cape Town.

Dewar, D., V. Watson, A. Bassios and N. Dewar, 1990. *The structure and form of metropolitan Cape Town: Its origins, influences and performance*. Urban Problems Research Unit Working Paper No. 42. Cape Town: University of Cape Town.

Escobar, A., 1993. *Planning. The development dictionary: A guide to knowledge and power*. Johannesburg: Witwatersrand University Press.

—— 1995. *Encountering development: The making and unmaking of the Third World*. Princeton, NJ: Princeton University Press.

Filion, P., 1999. Rupture or continuity? Modern and postmodern planning in Toronto. *International Journal for Urban and Regional Research* 23, 3: 421–444.

Finnegan, R., 1998. *Tales of the city. A study of narrative and urban life*. Cambridge: Cambridge University Press.

Fischler, R., 1995. Strategy and history in professional practice: Planning as world making. In *Spatial practices*. Edited by H. Liggett and D. Perry. Thousand Oaks, Calif: Sage.

—— 1998. Communicative planning theory and genealogical inquiry. Paper presented at the Conference on Planning Theory, Oxford Brookes University, April.

Fitzgerald, P., 1995. Towards a developmental public administration paradigm. In *Managing sustainable development in South Africa*. Edited by P. Fitzgerald, A. McLennan and B. Munslow. Cape Town: Oxford University Press.

Flyvbjerg, B., 1996. The dark side of planning: Rationality and 'realrationalitat'. In *Explorations in planning theory*. Edited by S. Mandelbaum, L. Mazza and R. Burchell. New Brunswick, NJ: Rutgers Centre for Urban Policy Research.

—— 1998. *Rationality and power: Democracy in practice*. Chicago: University of Chicago Press.

Forester, J., 1989. *Planning in the face of power*. Berkeley: University of California Press.

—— 1997. *Learning from practice: Democratic deliberations and the promise of planning practice*. College Park: University of Maryland.

—— 1999. Reflections on the future understanding of planning practice. *International Planning Studies* 4, 2: 175–193.

Forsyth, A., 1999. *Constructing suburbs: Competing voices in a debate over urban growth*. Amsterdam: Gordon and Breach.

Fraser, N., 1995. From redistribution to recognition? Dilemmas of justice in a 'post-socialist' age. *New Left Review* 212: 68–93.

Friedmann, J., 1989. *Planning in the public domain: From knowledge to action*. Princeton, NJ: Princeton University Press.

Friedmann, J., 1998. Planning theory revisited. *European Planning Studies* 6, 3: 245–253.

Gapps Architects and Urban Designers, 1993. An interim strategic framework for the central Witwatersrand. Discussion document submitted to the Central Witwatersrand Metropolitan Chamber.

Giddens, A., 1984. *The constitution of society*. Cambridge: Polity Press.

Ginsburg, D., 1996. The democratisation of South Africa: Transition theory tested. *Transformation* 29: 74–101.

Graham, S. and P. Healey, 1999. Relational concepts of space and place: Issues for planning theory and practice. *European Planning Studies* 7, 5: 623–646.

Hajer, M., 1995. *The politics of environmental discourse: Ecological modernization and the policy process.* Oxford: Clarendon Press.

Hall, P., 1988. *Cities of tomorrow.* Oxford: Blackwell.

Harre, R., 1993. *Social being: A theory for social psychology.* Oxford: Blackwell.

Harrison, P., 1998. A genealogy of post-apartheid planning in South Africa: The origins of the integrated development plan (IDP). Paper presented at the Eighth International Planning Society Conference, University of New South Wales, Sydney, 15–18 July.

Healey, P., 1992. A planner's day: knowledge and action in communicative practice. *Journal of the American Planning Association* 58, 1: 9–20.

―― 1997. *Collaborative planning: Shaping places in fragmented societies.* Basingstoke: Macmillan Press.

―― 2000. Connected cities. *Town and Country Planning,* February: 55–57.

Healey, P., A. Khakee, A. Motte and B. Needham, 1997. *Making strategic spatial plans: Innovation in Europe.* London: UCL Press.

Heymans, C., 1993. Towards people's development: Civic associations and development in South Africa. *Urban Forum* 5, 1: 1–20.

Heymans, C. and G. Totemeyer, 1988. *Government by the people? The politics of local government in South Africa.* Cape Town: Juta.

Hoch, C., 1996. A pragmatic inquiry about planning and power. In *Explorations in planning theory.* Edited by S. Mandelbaum, L. Mazza and R. Burchell. New Brunswick, NJ: Rutgers Centre for Urban Policy Research.

Howarth, D. and A. Norval, 1998. *South Africa in transition: New theoretical perspectives.* Basingstoke: Macmillan.

Hoy, D., 1986. *Foucault – a critical reader.* Oxford: Blackwell.

Innes, J., 1995. Planning theory's emerging paradigm: Communicative action and interactive practice. *Journal of Planning Education and Research* 14, 3: 183–189.

James, W. and M. Simons eds, 1989. *The angry divide: Social and economic history of the Western Cape.* Cape Town: David Philip.

Kritzman, L. ed., 1988. *Politics, philosophy, culture: Interviews and other writings, 1977–1984.* New York: Routledge.

Kuhn, T., 1962. *The structure of scientific revolutions.* Chicago: University of Chicago Press.

Lefebvre, H., 1991. *The production of space.* Oxford: Blackwell.

Liggett, H., 1996. Examining the planning practice conscious(ness). In *Explorations in planning theory.* Edited by S. Mandelbaum, L. Mazza and R. Burchell. New Brunswick, NJ: Rutgers Centre for Urban Policy Research.

Linz, J. and A. Stepan, 1996. *Problems of democratic transition and consolidation.* Baltimore, Md: Johns Hopkins University Press.

LUPO, 1985. Land use planning ordinance number 15, 1985. Cape: Province of the Cape of Good Hope.

Mabin, A., 1995. On the problems and prospects of overcoming segregation and fragmentation in southern Africa's cities in the postmodern era. In *Postmodern cities and spaces.* Edited by S. Watson and K. Gibson. Oxford: Blackwell.

―― 1999. From hard top to soft serve: Demarcation of metropolitan government in Johannesburg. In *Democratisation of South African local government: A tale of three cities.* Edited by R. Cameron. Cape Town: Van Schaik.

Mabin, A. and D. Smit, 1997. Reconstructing South Africa's cities? The making of urban planning 1900–2000. *Planning Perspectives* 12: 193–223.

Madanipour, A., 1996. *Design of urban space*. Chichester: John Wiley.

Mandelbaum, S., 1990. Reading plans. *Journal of the American Planning Association*, summer: 350–356.

—— 1996. Introduction: The talk of the community. In *Explorations in planning theory*. Edited by S. Mandelbaum, L. Mazza and R. Burchell. New Brunswick, N.J.: Rutgers Centre for Urban Policy Research.

Marais, H., 1998. *South Africa limits to change: The political economy of transformation*. Cape Town: University of Cape Town Press.

Marcuse, P., 1989. 'Dual city': A muddy metaphor for a quartered city. *International Journal of Urban and Regional Research* 13, 4: 697–708.

Marris, P., 1996. *The politics of uncertainty*. London: Routledge.

Marshall, T., 2000. *Urban planning and governance – is there a Barcelona model?* Paper presented at the Planning Research 2000 Conference, London School of Economics, March.

Metropolitan Development Consortium, 1998. *Economic trends and spatial patterns in the Cape metropolitan area: Overview synthesis report*. Urbanisation and Planning Directorate, and Economic and Social Development Directorate. Cape Town: Cape Metropolitan Council.

Metropolitan Spatial Development Framework, 1995. Western Cape Economic Development Forum and the Urban Development Commission. Draft paper for discussion.

Ministry for Provincial Affairs and Constitutional Development, 1997. *Green paper on local government*. Pretoria.

—— 1998. *The white paper on local government*. Pretoria.

Ministry of the Office of the President, 1995. *Urban development strategy of the government of national unity*. Government Gazette number 16679, notice 1111. Pretoria.

Morris, A., 1999. *Bleakness and light: Inner-city transition in Hillbrow, Johannesburg*. Johannesburg: Witwatersrand University Press.

Moving Ahead, 1999. *Cape metropolitan transport plan*. Cape Town: Cape Metropolitan Council.

Moving South Africa, 1998. *Strategy recommendations: Urban customers*. Pretoria: Department of Transport.

Municipal Systems Bill, 1999. Republic of South Africa. Pretoria.

Munslow, B. and P. Fitzgerald, 1995. The Reconstruction and Development Programme. In *Managing sustainable development in South Africa*. Edited by P. Fitzgerald, A. McLennan and B. Munslow. Cape Town: Oxford University Press.

National Development and Planning Commission, 1999. *Green paper on development planning*. Pretoria: Department of Land Affairs.

Nattrass, N. and J. Seekings, 1997. Globalisation, unemployment and inequality in South Africa. Paper presented at the Canadian Association of African Studies Conference, Newfoundland, June.

Newman, P. and J. Kenworthy, 1989. *Cities and automobile dependence: A sourcebook*. Aldershot: Gower Technical.

Office of the President, 1995. *Development facilitation act number 67*. Pretoria: Government gazette number 16730.

Osborne, D. and T. Gaebler, 1992. *Reinventing government: How the entrepreneurial spirit is transforming the public sector*. Reading, Mass.: Addison-Wesley.

Pilger, J., 1998. The betrayal of South Africa's revolution, *Mail and Guardian*, Johannesburg, 17 April.

Provincial Administration, 1997. *Road access policy*. Cape Town: Chief Directorate Transport, Department of Transport and Public Works.

Przeworski, A., 1991. *Democracy and the market: Political and economic reforms in Eastern Europe and Latin America.* Cambridge: Cambridge University Press.

Ransom, J., 1997. *Foucault's discipline.* Durham and London: Duke University Press.

RDP, 1994. *The Reconstruction and Development Programme: A policy framework.* African National Congress.

Report to METPLAN, 1988. Investigation into land for future housing for the coloured and black population groups. Consultant report, Cape Town.

Republic of South Africa, 1986. *White paper on urbanisation.* Pretoria: Department of Constitutional Development and Planning.

—— 1996a. *Local government transition act number 97.* Second amendment (number 1896). Pretoria.

—— 1996b. *White paper on national transport policy.* Pretoria: Department of Transport.

—— 1997. *Housing act number 107 of 1997.* Pretoria: Office of the President.

Rhodes, R., 1997. *Understanding governance: Policy networks, governance, reflexivity and accountability.* Buckingham: Open University Press.

Robinson, J., 1996. *The power of apartheid: State, power and space in South African cities.* Oxford: Butterworth Heinemann.

—— 1999. Planning the post-apartheid city: Comments on the Metropolitan Spatial Development Framework – Cape Town. In *Cities in transition.* Proceedings of the Urban Development Symposium, Planact, Isandla Institute, and School of Public and Development Management, Johannesburg.

Sandercock, L., 1998. *Towards cosmopolis: Planning for multicultural cities.* Chichester: John Wiley.

Saul, J., 1991. South Africa between barbarism and structural reform. *New Left Review* 188, July–August: 3–44.

Savage, D., 1998. Centralism and the crisis of legitimacy in South African local government: A critique of the white paper on local government. M.Sc. dissertation submitted to the Department of Government, London School of Economics and Political Science.

Schneider, K., 1979. *On the nature of cities: Towards enduring and creative humane environments.* San Francisco: Jossey Bass.

Schon, D. and M. Rein, 1994. *Frame reflection.* New York: Basic Books.

Seekings, J., 1991. Township resistance in the 1980s. In *Apartheid city in transition.* Edited by M. Swilling, R. Humphries, and K. Shubane. Cape Town: Oxford University Press.

—— 1996. The decline of South Africa's civic organizations, 1990–1996. *Critical Sociology* 22, 3: 135–157.

—— 1998. No home for revolutionaries: The structures and activities of the South African national civic organization in metropolitan Cape Town, 1996–97. *Urban Forum* 9, 1: 1–35.

Shubane, K. and M. Shaw, 1993. Tomorrow's foundations? Forums as the second level of negotiated transition in South Africa. *Centre for Policy Studies*, 33. Johannesburg.

Smart, B., 1985. *Michel Foucault.* Key Sociologists series. Chichester: Ellis Horwood Ltd.

Soja, E., 1995. Postmodern urbanization: The six restructurings of Los Angeles. In *Postmodern cities and spaces.* Edited by S. Watson and K. Gibson. Oxford: Blackwell.

Stark, D., 1992. The great transformation? Social change in Eastern Europe. *Contemporary Sociology* 21, 3: 299–304.

Stepan, A., 1986. Paths towards redemocratization: Theoretical and comparative considerations. In *Transitions from authoritarian rule – comparative perspectives.* Edited by G. O'Donnell, P. Schmitter and L. Whitehead. Baltimore, Md: Johns Hopkins University Press.

Stren, R. and R. White, 1989. *African cities in crisis: Managing rapid urban growth.* Boulder, Colorado: Westview Press.

Sturgeon, K., 1999. MLH Planners, Cape Town. Consultants to the Regional Services Council and Cape Metropolitan Council on the MSDF. Telephonic discussion, 20 June.

Swilling, J., 1997. Building democratic local urban governance in Southern Africa. In *Governing Africa's cities.* Edited by M. Swilling. Johannesburg: Witwatersrand University Press.

Talen, E., 1997. Success, failure and conformance: An alternative approach to planning evaluation. *Environment and Planning B* 24: 573–587.

Technical Report, 1996. *Metropolitan spatial development framework: A guide for spatial development in the Cape metropolitan functional region.* Cape Town: Cape Metropolitan Council.

The Planning Partnership, 1998. An assessment of the relative advantages and disadvantages of making the metropolitan spatial development framework a structure plan in terms of the land use planning ordinance. Report to the Cape Metropolitan Council and the Cape Town Municipality, Cape Town.

Theunissen, F., 1987. Origin, purpose and impacts of the land use planning ordinance (number 15 of 1985). *Town and Regional Planning.* Stellenbosch.

Throgmorton, J., 1996. *Planning as persuasive storytelling: The rhetorical construction of Chicago's electric future.* Chicago: University of Chicago Press.

Todes, A., 1998. Reintegrating the apartheid city? Urban policy and urban restructuring. Paper presented at the Cities at the Millennium Conference, London, December.

Todes, A., V. Watson and P. Wilkinson, 1989. Local government restructuring in greater Cape Town. In *The angry divide: Social and economic history of the Western Cape.* Edited by W. James and M. Simons. Cape Town: David Philip.

Turok, I., 1994. Urban planning in the transition from apartheid, part 1. *Town Planning Review* 65, 4: 355–374.

Vigar, G. and P. Healey, 1999. Territorial integration and 'plan-led' planning. *Planning Practice and Research* 14, 2: 153–170.

Watson, V., 2000. Learning from planning practice? Paper presented at the Planning Research 2000 Conference, London School of Economics and Political Science, March.

Webster, E. and G. Adler, 1999. Towards a class compromise in South Africa's 'double transition': Bargained liberalization and the consolidation of democracy. *Politics and Society* 27, 3: 347–385.

WESGRO, 1992. *South Africa's leading edge? A guide to the Western Cape economy.* Edited by D. Bridgman, I. Palmer and W. Thomas. Cape Town.

Wilkinson, P., 1996. A discourse of modernity. The Social and Economic Planning Council's fifth report on regional and town planning, 1944. *African Studies* 2: 141–181.

World Bank, 1993. *South Africa urban economic mission: Aide mémoire.* Washington, DC.

Wrong, D., 1988. *Power: Its forms, bases and uses.* Chicago: University of Chicago Press.

Yiftachel, O., 1999. Planning theory at the crossroad: The third Oxford conference. *Journal of Planning Education and Research* 18: 267–270.

Official minutes and reports

CMC IDP files (1997): 30/15/9/30, item 6, Cape Metropolitan Council, Cape Town.

EDF (1992): Draft proposals for a Western Cape Economic Development Forum, September. Economic Development Forum Steering Committee, Cape Town.

EDF minutes (1993): Economic Development Forum Steering Committee, item 5 (20/9/93). Davidson archives.

MDF-CWG minutes (1993a): Metropolitan Development Framework – Co-ordinating Working Group meetings, item 10 (9/6/93). Davidson archives.

MDF-CWG minutes (1993b): Informal written communication from NGO representative to facilitator, item 28 (10/12/93). Davidson archives.

MDF-CWG minutes (1993c): Metropolitan Development Framework – Co-ordinating Working Group meetings, item 20 (23/9/93). Davidson archives.

MDF-CWG minutes (1994a): Metropolitan Development Framework – Co-ordinating Working Group meetings, item 34 (10/2/94a). Davidson archives.

MDF-CWG minutes (1994b): Metropolitan Development Framework – Co-ordinating Working Group meetings, item 56 (25/10/94b). Davidson archives.

MDF-CWG minutes (1995): Metropolitan Development Framework – Co-ordinating Working Group meetings, item 58 (10/1/95). Davidson archives.

MSDF-CWG minutes (1995a): Metropolitan Spatial Development Framework – Co-ordinating Working Group meetings, item 20 (31/10/95). Cape Metropolitan Council Archives, Cape Town.

MSDF-CWG minutes (1995b): Metropolitan Spatial Development Framework – Co-ordinating Working Group meetings, item 18 (31/10/95). Cape Metropolitan Council Archives, Cape Town.

MSDF-CWG minutes (1995c): Metropolitan Spatial Development Framework – Co-ordinating Working Group meetings, item 10 (31/10/95). Cape Metropolitan Council Archives, Cape Town.

MSDF-CWG minutes (1996a): Metropolitan Spatial Development Framework – Co-ordinating Working Group meetings, item 23 (5/3/96). Cape Metropolitan Council Archives, Cape Town.

MSDF-CWG minutes (1996b): Metropolitan Spatial Development Framework – Co-ordinating Working Group meetings, item 26 (5/3/96). Cape Metropolitan Council Archives, Cape Town.

MSDF-CWG minutes (1999): Metropolitan Spatial Development Framework – Co-ordinating Working Group meeting, (13/10/99). Cape Metropolitan Council, Cape Town.

MSDF-SWG minutes (1999): Metropolitan Spatial Development Framework – Statutory Working Group meeting (11/6/99). Cape Metropolitan Council, Cape Town.

Provincial Administration (1992): Letter to the Chief Executive Officer, Western Cape Regional Services Council 14/12/92, attached to the document Proposed Principles for Planning and Development in the Cape Metropolitan Area, second draft, MDF Co-ordinating Working Group, March 1993.

RSC files (1989a): 30/15/9/5(1), item 3, Cape Metropolitan Council archives, Cape Town.

RSC files (1989b): 30/15/9/5(1), item 11, annexe D, Cape Metropolitan Council archives, Cape Town.

RSC files (1989c): 30/15/9/5(1), item 6, Cape Metropolitan Council archives, Cape Town.

RSC files (1990a): 30/15/9/5(1), item 19, Cape Metropolitan Council archives, Cape Town.

RSC files (1990b): 30/15/9/5(1), item 23, Cape Metropolitan Council archives, Cape Town.

RSC files (1990c): 30/15/9/5(2), item 27, Cape Metropolitan Council archives, Cape Town.

RSC files (1990d): 30/15/9/5(2), item 12, Cape Metropolitan Council archives, Cape Town.

RSC files (1990e): 30/15/9/5(3), item 12, Cape Metropolitan Council archives, Cape Town.

RSC file (1991): 30/15/9/5(5), item 11, Cape Metropolitan Council archives, Cape Town.

RSC file (1992a): 30/15/9/5(6), item 49, Cape Metropolitan Council archives, Cape Town.

RSC files (1992b): 30/15/9/5(6), item 24, Cape Metropolitan Council archives, Cape Town.

RSC files (1992c): 30/15/9/19/1(1), item 4, Cape Metropolitan Council archives, Cape Town.

UDC minutes (1993): (29/6/93), item 14, Urban Development Commission. Davidson archives.

UDC minutes (1994): (28/6/94), item 36, Urban Development Commission. Davidson archives.

Interview sources

Interview 1 (1998): Francois Theunissen, Head: Regional Planning, Regional Services Council. Subsequently, Branch Head, Spatial Planning, Department of Planning, Environment and Housing, Cape Metropolitan. Now private planning consultant.

Interview 2 (1998): Peter de Tolly, Deputy City Planner, Cape Town City Council (1990–1995), now Director of Special Projects and Acting Director of Economic Development, Cape Town Municipality.

Interview 3 (1999): Cecil Madell, MLH planning consultancy, now MCA Planners, Cape Town.

Interview 4 (1999): Peter de Tolly.

Interview 5 (1999): David Shandler, facilitator, Zille Shandler Associates. Now partner in Common Ground Consulting, Cape Town.

Interview 6 (1998): Wolfgang Thomas, WESGRO economist, Cape Town.

Interview 7 (1998): Basil Davidson, then member of the ANC Western Cape executive, and employed as a planner by the NGO Development Action Group. Now head of the Housing Department, Directorate of Planning, Environment and Housing, Cape Metropolitan Council.

Interview 8 (1999): John Neels, then chair of SANCO (Western Cape), and one of the four chairpersons of the Western Cape Economic Development Forum. Now a businessman.

Interview 9 (1999): Peter Tomalin, planner, then Deputy Chief Director of Planning, Western Cape Regional Services Council. Now Executive Director, Directorate of Planning, Environment and Housing, Cape Metropolitan Council.

Interview 10 (1998): Peter Tomalin.

Interview 11 (1998): Kim Van Deventer, then employed as a planner by the NGO Development Action Group, Cape Town. Now Executive Director of the Directorate of Economic and Social Development, Cape Metropolitan Council.

Interview 12 (1999): Kim Van Deventer.

Interview 13 (1999): Nico McLachlan, Head of Organization Development Africa, Cape Town.

Interview 14 (1999): Francois Theunissen.

Interview 15 (1999): Peter Clarke, Manager, Strategic Planning, Directorate of Transport, Cape Metropolitan Council.

Index

Abercrombie's London Plan 112
Adler, G. 3, 157
African National Congress (ANC):
  centralist vision 74, 75; councilors 91,
  119, 135; flag 19; Interim Convener of
  31; majority in municipality 81, 87, 160;
  members at workshops 40, 50; in
  national level negotiations 43, 44, 54,
  56; as opposition movement 3, 18, 72;
  in Provincial Council 132; represented
  by 38, 47, 50, 51, 69, 80; role in Forum
  96; ruling majority party 1, 66, 71, 137;
  unbanned 30
agency 7
Agenda 21 124
AIDS 150
Ashworth, G. 161
automobile dependence 107

Barlow Commission Report 20
basic needs 44, 45, 98, 102, 103, 110, 159
Baum, H. 9
Beall, J. 148
Beauregard, B. 10
Bekker, S. 46
Bill of Rights 44
Blowers, A. 162
blueprint planning 1, 16, 62, 70, 114,
  121–2, 138, 141
Borja, J. 143, 150, 151
Boyer, C. 5
Breheny, M. 35
Bridgman, D. 160
Bryson, J. 46
Burnett, S. 162

Caledon Conference 38, 39, 47, 56, 100,
  110, 158, 159
Calthorpe, P. 112
Cameron, R. 22, 74, 75, 76, 78, 79, 80, 81,
  82
Cape Areas Housing Action Committee
  (CAHAC) 50, 91
case studies 7, 8, 9, 10, 11
Castells, M. 143, 150, 151
Central Witwatersrand Metropolitan
  Chamber 160
Century City 135, 163
Chipkin, I. 76
civic associations 47, 49, 50, 55, 69, 74,
  90–1, 96
civil society 4, 43, 90
Cole, J. 17
communicative action 8
compact city: alternative spatial model 32,
  41; applicable to Cape Town 23, 40, 52;
  basis of discourse coalition 55, 69, 115,
  140, 141, 142; in international
  literature 35; new idea 1; in
  Reconstruction and Development
  Programme 45; required by law 83
Comprehensive Anti-Apartheid Act 18
Congress of South African Trade Unions
  (COSATU) 3, 44, 47, 49, 53
Constitution 95, 160, 162
Convention for a Democratic South
  Africa (CODESA) 44
Copenhagen 'finger plan' 103, 112
corridors: applied to Cape Town 114, 120,
  125, 145; as component of grid 113; in
  Curitiba 108; depicted on maps 99, 121;
  earlier conceptions of 103, 112; as

corridors, *continued*
spatial element 64, 65, 92, 111;
supported by business 67; in transport
policy 124, 126–8, 162; ways of
promoting 134, 135
crime 114, 128, 145, 148, 150
Crosby, B. 46
Crossroads squatter camp 17, 80
Curitiba 107–10, 111, 112, 116

Dear, M. 143
deconcentration points 18, 20, 23, 31, 40
Democratic Party 94
design paradigms 112, 113
Development Action Group (DAG) 53,
59
development control 15, 132, 152, 163
Development Facilitation Act 81–3, 162
Developmental local government 122–8;
138
Dewar, D. 34, 35, 103, 158, 161
disciplines 5
discourse: of integrated development
planning 139; in context 10; in maps
and text 115–16; in national policy 55;
as persuasion 100; planning discourses
25, 26, 41, 140, 141, 142; and power 5;
as problem framing 40; role in change
and continuity 6; tactical polyvalence of
7; welfare-based 87
discourse coalition: broadening of 55,
69–70; around entrepreneurial local
government 11, 87, 116, 117, 139, 142;
fragility of 163; framing Cape Town's
problems 40–1; in Hajer, M. 6–7;
around urban integration 11, 87, 141,
153
discursive hegemony 139
dual city 105

entrepreneurial government 87
entrepreneurial local government 11, 124,
138, 139, 142
Environmental Impact Assessments 124
Escobar, A. 5, 152
exclusion 144–5, 148

Filion, P. 112
Finnegan, R. 157

Fischler, R. 9, 100
Fitzgerald, P. 71, 85, 160
Flyvbjerg, B. 5, 8, 153, 154
Forester, J. 7, 8
Forsyth, A. 8, 107, 153
forums: as arenas for debate and policy-
making 45–6; for national policy 55; for
negotiations 39, 75, 79, 91, 130; newly
formed 40; as phase of metropolitan
planning 43; for regional development
42; representatives from 67, 84; slide
presentations given to 89
Foucault 5–7, 9, 115, 153–4
Fraser, N. 152

Gaebler, T. 85
Ginsburg, D. 43, 90
global positioning 87, 128, 131, 138
Government of National Unity 44, 71, 72,
88, 159
governmentality 5
Graham, S. 107, 112, 143, 148–9
growth management 13, 28, 29, 32, 37
Growth, Employment and Redistribution
(GEAR) 72, 140
Guide Plan: as blueprint plans 121–2;
challenge to 20; as controlling
development 16, 88; multi-nodal
strategy in 30, 53; as national plans 92;
problem framing in 36; racial
designation of land in 23; uncommitted
land in 22

Hajer, M. 6–7, 116
Harre, R. 6
Harrison, P. 8, 34, 83, 84, 107, 112, 143,
148–9, 160
Heymans, C. 74
Howarth, D. 4
Hoy, D. 157
Humphries, R. 46

Institute for a Democratic Alternative in
South Africa (IDASA) 46, 79, 160
identity 10
income distribution 144
influx control 18, 19, 158
informal sector 144, 145, 148, 151, 163
Innes, J. 7, 8

integrated development plan (IDP):
attempted in local government 128–31;
basis for new discourse 139; as
encouraging development 135;
incompatibility with statutory planning
134; in new legislation 81, 140, 162;
related to new public management
83–6; role in local government 87;
spatial plan as element of 117

James, W. 78

Kenworthy, J. 107, 161
Khayelitsha 17, 80, 81, 114, 119
Kritzman, L. 6

Lefebvre, H. 115
Liggett, H. 7
Linz, J. 43
Local Government Negotiating Forum 74,
75, 79
local government transition 72–81, 93,
119, 138
Local Government Transition Act 75,
134, 162
Local Government Transition
Amendment Act 81, 83, 85
Los Angeles 107–9, 148, 161

Mabin, A. 25, 144, 160
Mandanipour, A. 112
Mandelbaum, S. 7
Marais, H. 19, 43, 71, 72
Marcuse, P. 105
Marris, P. 142, 149
Marshall, T. 153
mega-projects 125, 145, 163
modernist planning 1, 25–6, 34, 35, 41,
87, 98, 141
Mount Grace Conference 85
multi-culturalism 143, 152–3
multi-nodal city 19, 20, 23, 30, 36, 37, 53,
97
Multiplex city, urban region 107, 149
Munslow, B. 71

narratives 7, 10, 157
narratology 10

National Environmental Management
Act 124
National Housing Forum 83, 124
National Party: on Demarcation Board 80;
domination in Western Cape 66, 88;
influence in municipalities 79, 81, 94,
96, 119; influence in Regional Services
Council 16, 32, 56; performance in
election 71; in political reform process
37; in power-sharing 44, 54; role in
forums 45, 50, 74; as ruling party 3, 43
National Security Management System
(NSMS) 18
Nelson Mandela 30, 80
neo-liberal 4, 11, 44, 72, 84, 87, 98, 116,
139
New National Party 132, 135, 136
new urbanism 1, 112
Newman, P. 107, 161
Norval, A. 4

Osborne, D. 85
'one city–one tax base' 31, 74

pacting elites 26
physical development planning 34
plan implementation 115, 130, 138, 139,
140, 141, 150, 152
political transition: absence of progressive
political movement in 153; influence of
previous regime in 43; in literature 6,
90; local government prior to 78; at
national and local level 71; negotiations
phase of 37; process of 13, 45, 149;
stages of transition 2–4
power: balance of 38, 39, 59, 94; in Baum,
H. 9; and continuity 96–7, 142;
exercised by planning professionals 60,
117, 137, 141; exercised by shack-
dwellers 26; in Flyvbjerg, B. 8; in
Foucault 5–6, 153; persuasive 11, 100;
potential to exercise 41, 55, 154; tactics
of 70, 139; through statutorization 93,
121; within forums 45, 69
power-sharing: between National Party
and ANC 16, 44, 52, 56, 66, 159; in
forums 46, 51, 75; in local government
74, 76, 81
practice movement 7

Prague Spring 135, 136
Progressive Development Forum (PDF)
    38, 39, 40
project-based planning 150, 151
Przeworski, A. 3
public management 84–6, 130, 139
public participation: as 'selling' ideas 90;
    in forums 46, 154; in metropolitan
    planning 40, 43, 54, 55; in planning
    legislation 27; recognizing importance
    of 37, 42, 93; in Western Cape
    Economic Development Forum 66–8,
    154

racial capitalism 16
Ransom, J. 6, 157
rational choice 110, 115
rational arguments 139
rationality 10, 26, 116, 139, 154
Reconstruction and Development
    Programme (RDP): comment on local
    government 73, 76; comment on urban
    restructuring 1, 45, 102, 140; on
    development planning 81, 83, 84; on
    environmental management 124; as
    informant of programmes 65;
    philosophical stance 44–5, 54, 55, 71–2,
    87, 98, 160; production of 3, 72
reflective transfer 8
Reforma 2
Reforma-pactada 2, 3
regimes of rationality 116
regional development strategy 13, 23, 27,
    28, 37
Rein, M. 8
representations of space 115
Rhodes, R. 86, 161
Robinson, J. 74, 75, 105
Ruptura-pactada 2, 4

Sandercock, L. 152
Sao Paulo 107–9
Saul, J. 3
Savage, D. 77, 85
scenario-building 107–10, 111
Schneider, K. 161
Schon, D. 8
Seekings, J. 50, 90, 91
segregated development 141, 142

segregation 1, 12, 22, 25, 26, 41, 73, 97,
    103, 145, 148
Separate development 20, 22, 36, 41
Shapiro, J. 77
Shaw, M. 45
Shubane, K. 45
sieve method 22, 23, 25
Simons, M. 78
Smart, B.157
Smit, D. 25
Soja, E. 143, 144, 148
South African Communist Party (SACP)
    3, 30, 44
South African National Civics
    Organization (SANCO) 40, 47, 49, 50,
    51, 54, 65, 74, 90, 136
Soviet Union 3
space-economy 12, 115, 125, 143, 150
spatial models 19, 29
spheres of government 76, 95, 117, 118,
    133, 134
statutory plan, planning: experience of F.
    Theunissen 15; in integrated
    development plan 130; to legalize
    metropolitan plan 88–9, 92–6, 117, 161;
    municipal challenge to 118–22, 130–5,
    136; as stage of metropolitan planning
    101; as tactic 138–9, 141, 162
Stepan, A. 2, 43
story-line 6, 7, 25–6, 40, 41, 116
strategic planning 28, 40, 42, 62, 70, 115
structure plan 27, 28, 38, 42, 88, 117, 121
sunset clause 3, 4
SWOT 110

Talen, E. 161
Throgmorton, J. 8, 153
Todes, A. 78, 144, 148
Toronto 112
Totemeyer, G. 74
transport policy (national) 124
Tricameral Parliament 18, 159
Turok, I. 45, 159

unemployment 144
Unicity Commission 138
Urban Development Commission: to build
    discourse coalition 55; closing of 66, 68,
    88, 89; labour representative on 96;

limitations on Chair of 69; limited participation in 64–5, 142; placing metropolitan plan under 51–2, 56–7; plan produced by 98; setting up 53–4; tensions within 57–65; as way of gaining mandates 49; within Western Cape Economic Development Forum 48, 111; workshops within 67
urban transformation projects 150–2
urban underclass 144
Uytenbogaardt, R. 34, 35, 103, 161

Vigar, G. 84
vision: of compact city 36; economic 30, 42, 122; for integrated development plan 128, 130; for local government 73, 76; as part of plan 29, 59, 62, 110, 114, 137, 142; politically centralist 74; spatial 54, 98; of Witwatersrand Metropolitan Forum 31

Warwick Business School 84
Watson, V. 8, 154
Webster, E. 3, 157
WESGRO 30, 37, 40, 46–7, 49, 66, 102
Western Cape Economic Development Forum: after closure 66, 88; establishment of 46–8; 102, 159; exercise of power within 154, 163; limits on participation in 69; NGO representative on 124; participants in 49–51, 160; structure of 58; Urban Development Commission within 51–2; vision for 110
Wilkinson, P. 25, 158
Witwatersrand Metropolitan Forum 31
World Bank 72, 84, 102, 143
Wrong, D. 100

Yiftachel, O. 8